All children go through problem patches: times when they're difficult to understand, moody and miserable or when they're faced with situations with which they cannot cope.

Parents do need help. Sometimes, confronted with specific acute problems like bed-wetting or extreme eating fads, they may have to resort to the doctor or a child guidance officer for advice. This book provides parents with exactly the practical, down-to-earth advice they need to help them through the times of emotional crisis with their children that are part-and-parcel of modern family life. This is not a book of psychiatric theorizing, but aims to do three things: to reassure parents that, whatever their child's problem, they are not alone; to give advice on what to do with the child and, finally to tell them what help is available if the problem becomes too serious for the parents to cope with alone.

This is a reference book to keep in the bookcase beside the medical dictionary and the guide to first aid. There are over a hundred entries arranged alphabetically, and, from shyness to exam phobia, stealing to thumb-sucking, Tom Crabtree offers sensible, balanced advice for worried adults treading the tricky path of parenthood.

D1458303

By the same Author

TOM CRABTREE ON TEENAGERS

An A-Z of Children's Emotional Problems

TOM CRABTREE

London
UNWIN PAPERBACKS
Boston   Sydney

First published in Great Britain by Hamish Hamilton/Elm Tree Books Ltd
1981
First published in Unwin Paperbacks 1983. Reprinted 1984
This book is copyright under the Berne Convention. No reproduction
without permission. All rights reserved.

UNWIN® PAPERBACKS
40 Museum Street, London WC1A 1LU, UK

Unwin Paperbacks,
Park Lane, Hemel Hempstead, Herts HP2 4TE, UK

George Allen & Unwin Australia Pty Ltd,
8 Napier Street, North Sydney, NSW 2060, Australia

© Tom Crabtree 1981

British Library Cataloguing in Publication Data

Crabtree, Tom
   An A-Z of children's emotional problems.
1. Emotional problems of children—
Dictionaries
I. Title
155.4   BF723.E598
ISBN 0–04–649018–3

Condition of Sale. This book is sold subject to the condition that it shall
not, by way of trade or otherwise, be lent, re-sold, hired out or otherwise
circulated, without the Publishers' prior consent in any form of binding or
cover other than that in which it is published and without a similar
condition including this condition being imposed on the purchaser.

Typeset by Saildean Ltd
and printed in Great Britain
by Hazell Watson & Viney Ltd, Aylesbury, Bucks

Dedicated to Mary, Amanda, Tim and Sally
who grew up with me
and are still my good friends

Acknowledgements

My thanks are due to Connie Austen Smith for her skilful editing, and for her general cheerfulness and encouragement during those busy, hectic months that I spent writing this book.

Introduction

Although it seems a little immodest to say so, I think this book is unique. It isn't yet another mother and baby book – nor is it a medical book. It deals instead with the *emotional* difficulties which children of varying ages, *and* parents, have in coping with life, and with each other. It gives advice on *specific* problems which crop up within the family and aims to be a ready reference in dealing with these problems. It is concerned, not with the child's physical well-being, but with his happiness: with his heart and his emotions. My hope is that parents can and will enjoy bringing up their children rather than it being a constant battle against misunderstandings, conflict and a pervading sense of failure.

In my work as an educational psychologist the headmasters of the schools I visited had one recurrent request: 'Please,' was their cry, 'don't give us too much psychology. Just tell us what to *do* with him (or her).' I've tried to follow my rule of giving *practical* advice here: to allay the fears of parents and to draw upon my experience in dealing with the problems that they face. After all, none of the problems in this book are new. They have cropped up before, in many, many families, and they'll crop up again in the future.

Twenty sections of the book are devoted to general advice on how to be a good parent. These are specified as (For Parents).......
What I have tried to do here is to influence your *attitude* towards your children and try to provide something of a philosophy behind the day-to-day hard work of rearing young children or teenagers. In my section on **Dependency**, for example, I have pointed out that bringing up children can be extremely enjoyable; it can also be absolute hell. Youngsters, of any age, can be very demanding, some seem to need us constantly. In the middle of these demands it is vital to have interests, hobbies, friends, possibly a job, all of which are yours. *You* have to grow as a person, be an independent human being, as well as your children. Our outlook as parents, our attitude, determines to a large extent the success we have in dealing with the inevitable emotional crises which none of us escape.

In the sections on **Guilt, Hatred** and **Intense Dislike of a Child** I have dealt with some of the negative feelings, the destructive emotions, which afflict many parents from time to time. In other of these sections devoted to parental feelings and problems I have tried to say something useful about **Mother Love** and **Morality,** to discuss **Quarelling**, the **Generation Gap, Values, Over-permissiveness** and other issues which beset most parents. I also say something of **Working Mothers**, the **Parents' Relationship with Children** as well as the thorny topics of **Tidyness, Fathers** – and their role – together with the **Emotional Needs** (i.e. of the parents). These sections are meant to reassure parents, to allay their fears and to give them a chance to build up, and hold fast to, a positive, optimistic outlook while involved in the hard job of bringing up children in the ever-changing, kaleidoscopic world of today.

The remainder of the book, the major part, is, as I have indicated, directed towards giving practical, realistic advice on those emotional problems which – come they singly or in bunches, rarely or frequently, briefly or more persistently – form part and parcel of the development of a great many children. Sometimes, I have repeated advice which I have used in dealing with some other, quite different, problem and readers may find this repetition puzzling. The reason for it is that certain themes recur in dealing with children, certain ways of coping with problems can be applied to a variety of situations, certain truths about the parent-child relationship remain true despite the alteration in the child's way of behaving (or in his method of signalling his problem to the parents).

To find your way around the book you must, first of all, consult the alphabetical guide to the particular problem which is worrying you. Having done that you will come across some cross-referencing about which I hope you will be reasonably patient. If you persevere with it you will find that the information and help which you seek is there, contained in the section to which the alphabetical index guides you, or in an associated section. Thus, if your child is shy, a common affliction, it will be useful for you to read besides **Shyness**, the sections on **Daydreaming** and the **Walter Mitty Complex.** (Don't worry, this is clearly cross-referenced and you are told where to find it.) If, say, your child is aggressive you may find what you want in the section on **Aggression.** If you don't I very much hope you will find the information that you require by reading the closely-linked sections on **Destructiveness, Disagreements** or **Frustration**. It sounds confusing but isn't and you'll soon get used to finding your way around the book and will, I sincerely hope, receive the practical help you need to solve, or alleviate, your child's difficulty.

I haven't tried to make this a book about tending young infants, nor have I included medical topics. For example, I have something to say about **Eating Fads** in youngsters since this is something that both annoys, and worries, many parents. I have not, though, given any comprehensive advice on anorexia. This, in my view, is a *medical* problem which should be tackled under the supervision of the family doctor or some other medical specialist. What I have tried to do, whilst reassuring parents on children's difficulties is, at the same time, to alert them to those signs which suggest that the child is in need of expert help. In other words, where I think that a parent should seek further professional advice – from the family doctor or from a child guidance clinic – I say so. There are *some* (and, I believe, a minority of) problems which become so acute that the parent cannot deal with them alone and the advice of a specialist is needed to solve the problem. This caveat, in no way, detracts (I trust) in the usefulness of the book as a practical manual which tells parents how to deal with their children's problems in a sensible, down-to-earth way.

One of the aims in having children is to enjoy their company, have fun together. Often, I hear descriptions of what children do at home and am reminded of the Battle of Britain, with mum and dad in a domestic dug-out being blitzed from all sides by rampaging, demanding youngsters. It doesn't have to be like that. We can negotiate with children, learn to give them space to lead their own lives, teach them to give us sufficient space to lead ours. We can, I believe, gain the respect of, and become firm friends with, our own children.

Of one thing I am sure. There is no greater, more rewarding, aim in life than to give a child a happier childhood than the one you had yourself.

TOM CRABTREE, 1981

Adopted Children

If you're an adoptive parent you'll probably feel that you have taken on just that little bit extra responsibility. You may try to do just that little bit more. Sometimes, if things go wrong – and things go wrong whether the child is with the natural parents or not – you'll feel just a little bit more guilty. Friends may not help. They may say daft things like, 'Your child is adopted so there must have been something awfully wrong in his background.' That kind of remark will worry you, even though you know in your heart that what matters is the quality of love and affection you can give to the child now. A few adoptive parents may believe in the 'Myth of The Perfect Child' and try to bring up a child with no faults at all. That's a mistake. Few children, like parents, are perfect.

What do adopted children want from you? They want things, including where they came from, explained fairly and squarely. They want the truth, from the moment that they are old enough to understand. You should tell them how you desperately wanted a child, how long you had to wait, how overjoyed you were when you were eventually given one. Explain that all those interviews, all that waiting, all that anxiety, were more than worthwhile when you knew that the child was to be yours. Explain that when things don't come easy you tend to enjoy them more and say how much you have enjoyed your child. (How sad that parents can have children and, having made that decision, not enjoy them.) Accept in your own mind that you *have* made sacrifices, financial and social, to bring up the child and that the enjoyment of the child is part of your reward. Accept, too, that if you have problems with the child you'll worry (who doesn't?) but realize that everybody has problems, at some stage of development, with their children. Your adopted child wants to be the same as other children. He doesn't want a psychoanalyst for a mother (or a psychologist for a father). He wants you.

Your adopted child's long-term aim is to grow up to believe in himself. He may know who his 'real' parents are. (What does 'real'

1

mean? You could say, with a lot of truth, that you are the real mother since it's your love that fuels his journey through life.) He may not know who his 'real' father is. He may, or may not, want to know. He may worry about his roots; he may, later on, want to search for his real mother. Then, again, he may not. That is for him to decide. Support him in his decisions. If he wants, as a teenager, to make contact with his 'real' mother, advise him, help him. If he accepts that it is you who is his 'real' mother – the person that brought him up, loved him – then so be it, leave it at that. The main thing is that he should grow up with a healthy self-respect, with integrity and a sense of identity. Please don't believe all that stuff about inherited character defects. The way in which your child behaves, what he believes in, result not from some obscure, in-built original sin but from *the way you handle him and the ideas that you pass on to him.*

These days, of course, because of economic circumstances and the advent of the pill, there are fewer babies being born and, consequently, far fewer babies available for adoption. The pattern has changed; in the sixties we had a glut of babies; now, many of the children who are available for adoption are older and may fall with the 'Hard to Place' categories, e.g. ethnic minority children, handicapped children or youngsters who are part of a sibling group and require to be adopted alongside their brothers and/or sisters. It's clear that, if you have adopted – or intend to adopt – a child, say, over the age of five this is different from adopting a baby. The child may have been in care; he may have been in a foster home which he didn't like; he may have been in a children's home, or a number of children's homes, which he didn't particularly take to. If a child has this sort of unsettled background then he is going to have *some* problems and it is vital for you to know what you're taking on and have a tremendous determination to give the child the love and the security which he so badly needs.

Fortunately, adoption is worked towards sensibly these days. A social worker who specializes in adoption will tell you all about the procedure for adopting a child with special needs (call in at your local social services department and ask for information). It is rather like an arranged marriage but with infinitely more care taken over the matching. First, there is a period of *familiarization* in which you have a number of meetings with the child and get to know him. Next, you *foster* the child to see if you like living together (during this time the ultimate responsibility for the child rests with the social worker – the local authority – or the adoption agency). If that works out then you may decide to adopt the child and, if an adoption order is granted (the social worker will help you with all the legal side of it), then the child becomes, in law, and from that moment, one of your own children. This is right and proper since adoptive parents, having been through the preparation for adoption, often feel that now is the time that they would like to be left alone to get on with the job of bringing up the child as one of their own children, and under their own steam, without too much fuss.

With adopted children the main things to remember are timing – don't rush things – honesty and, of course, caring. Those parents who have successfully raised adopted children will tell you what a marvellous sense of achievement, not to mention the enjoyment, they have gained from the experience. It's a compassionate thing to do; it's an act that brings many rewards not least of which is to see an adopted youngster with self esteem, optimism about the future and, despite all the vicissitudes and disappointments in his life, with a firm and unshakeable sense of his own being.

Parents who are interested in adopting a child should contact The Association of British Adoption and Fostering Agencies, 11 Southwark Street, London SE1 1RQ (Tel: 01-407 8800). Ask for further information and for the booklet entitled *Adopting a Child*, which lists voluntary societies and local authorities throughout the country which belong to the Association. This booklet also contains a very useful list of inexpensive books and pamphlets with titles like *Talking about Origins* and *Adopting a Black Child* which can be obtained from them.

If you are interested in adoption you may like to meet adoptive parents to chat about how things have worked out for them. You should write to: Parent to Parent Information on Adoption Services (PPIAS), 26 Belsize Grove, London NW3 and they can tell you of the group closest to where you live.

Aggression
See also: **Destructiveness** *Page* 53, **Disagreements** *Page* 58, **Frustration** *Page* 88

While putting up some shelves you hit your thumb with a hammer; then the shelves fall down. You'll know what I mean when I say that aggression can be caused by frustration! The trouble is that we're bound to experience a certain amount of frustration in life but some adults and children seem to be able to cope better with it than others.

Besides frustration, what else causes aggression? If we are surrounded by people who fight and quarrel, the chances are that we'll fight and quarrel too. If we live with aggression we learn to be aggressive. I'm not denying that there's instinctive aggression deep down in all of us (a mother will fight off a dog if it goes to bite her child); I'm simply stressing that aggression, like measles, is caught from others (or taught by them).

The whole question of aggression hinges on how good you are at *diversionary tactics*. Do you want destruction or construction? Often, especially if we watch the child carefully, we can see frustrating situations looming up. One play-group leader I know, observing a fight over a tricycle just about to break out, said to one of the protagonists: 'John, I've got some big cardboard boxes that want stamping on to make them really flat. Could you do that for me?' It's clever but it shouldn't be necessary to divert the child into aggressive, destructive activities. For younger children, finger-painting, water play, playing with sand, or play-dough (or Plasticine or papier-mâché) are all marvellously soothing activities and, psychologically, well suited to calm the savage beast.

This diversion technique was known, when I was a young teacher as 'tidying the stock cupboard'. Young teachers soon learn that the devil finds mischief for idle hands to do. I applied the same idea to a boy who was hitting other boys on the way home from school. I gave him an old bike which we kept in a shed at home. 'Any more aggro?' I asked him a few weeks later. 'No,' he said, 'too much trouble to get off the bike.' In other words he had something more interesting to do than go about causing trouble.

Please, when your child is aggressive towards you try to stay calm (difficult, I know). Avoid escalation. You know the sort of thing:

Mother: (Shouts) You'll break it.
Child: (Yells) I won't. (The cup, or Ming vase, breaks.)
Mother: (Screams) I told you so. Go to your bedroom, you awful, terrible child.
Child: I won't. I'm staying here. (They fight. Eventually, they both burst into tears and start hurling abuse at each other.)

Wouldn't it have been better to say, 'I'll take that cup, darling. You come over here and whisk these eggs for me'? Similarly, an aggressive child wants to go for a walk immediately. Don't turn it

4

into an argument, or a fight. You could say something like: 'When we do go for a walk, when I've finished this job, remind me to buy some cake-mix and, later, you can help me with the tea.' *Try to be positive, not argumentitive,* and avoid confrontations. If you do have a shoot-out make sure you win. Aggressive children will concede to an imaginative (cunning?) adult; after all, they want to be protected from their own aggression. They will, sadly, terrorize any adult who they see is frightened of them.

Here are ten tips for dealing with aggressive children:

Don't provoke crises. Try to see them looming up and divert the child.

Avoid boredom. A child with nothing to do will quickly find some mischief to fill his idle hours.

Ensure that your child has adequate outlets for constructive play. If he's in a mood give him some newspapers to tear up to make papier-mâché: it is (I've tried it myself) very calming!

Don't reward aggressive behaviour. If you can, ignore it. If you can't, deal with it sharply and firmly. *And remember to praise the child when he is being cooperative and helpful.* Reward, in other words, when he's good; don't save up all your attention for when he's bad.

In group situations, have some rules of sharing. Who's turn is it for the tricycle? Which programme do we watch on TV? Take turns to choose. A dash of law and order in the home avoids an avalanche of arguments.

Be brisk and snappy in dealing with childish aggression. Don't answer aggression with aggression, or get caught up in the child's anger.

Give the child some success, even if it's only that his scrambled eggs are better than anybody else's you know. A child with a healthy self-respect, and plenty of confidence, doesn't need to be aggressive.

Make it plain that using aggression to get their own way doesn't work. Courteous behaviour does, and brings more attention (and praise) from you. Most children will soon get the picture.

Set a good example. Don't go about the place shouting and raving yourself. Children are great mimics.

Keep calm, and remember the word NO. It's a very handy little word but bear in mind that, when you have to use it, you must mean what you say.

I think that children, deep down, like a sense of order and fair-play. They want to live their lives within a safe framework in which they (and others) can get on with the task of learning new skills. With a bit of commonsense I'm sure that we parents, you and me, can give them that framework.

ANGER
(For Parents)

Very few of us enjoy being angry: it's a disruptive emotion that leaves us feeling drained and irritable. Some of us are afraid of our own anger knowing how powerful it can be. I have a friend who is a 'berserker'. Most of the time he is the nicest chap you could wish to meet; then, he goes berserk, and all hell is let loose. Fortunately, his wife and children can see his anger coming; and they make sure they go elsewhere until he gets over it.

There *is* such a thing as righteous anger; we *are* entitled to become angry from time to time. 'Bottled up' anger can poison relationships and take the joy out of living. There is nothing good nor bad about anger, when you've been hurt or slighted. It is just one of the many emotional reactions we show to the people around us and we have to accept that we are all capable of it.

Why do we have such difficulty in expressing anger when and where it's appropriate? Consider your own childhood. Probably, when you were a child, you were taught to repress your anger: to be angry is to be bad. With your children you try to be patient, not to be angry and, suddenly, it bursts out of you in a flood.

When you lose your temper you may, like me, act as though you had gone completely mad. All your 'gripes' and resentments pour out of you and you say things that you later regret. You may scream, insult people and rush about the place yelling your head off. Afterwards, you feel quite guilty and resolve never to have a repeat performance – until the next time your frustrations build up and you totally lose control of yourself.

It's no use saying that you resolve never to be angry again. That only makes it worse when you are. Anger is like a storm at sea: it's always a possibility and it has to be prepared for. What you can do (having shown your children that you are quite capable of being very, very angry) is to warn them when a storm is brewing up. Most children have sensitive antennae about this sort of thing; they can sense when you're annoyed and they'll know all right, when you announce a storm warning, that you're not joking.

There *is* a place for anger within the family. If you fail to get angry at certain moments of mischief or catastrophe you may convey to the child the feeling that you just don't care. If you care, you get angry, sometimes. The thing to do is to make it clear to the children what it is you want them to do, or not do. Tell them what makes you particularly angry. Demonstrate your wrath, if you must. Don't have little bursts of anger, flurries of violence and abuse, which are not related to what they're doing at the time. If your children are 'playing up' say to them: 'You are about to find that there are limits to my good nature. Stop that, or I'll become angry.' If you threaten that you will, then do. (Never issue warnings to children that you don't intend to carry out.)

Anger has a use. It gives you some relief from your frustrations; it indicates to your children that there are limits beyond which they mustn't go (not if they want to avoid an angry scene). There should be some justice about it all: the child has done something wrong (and he knows it) and you're really mad at him. *Don't* tell him off in front of his friends (or yours); don't bear grudges so that waves of anger issue forth from you for the next few days/weeks/months. Be angry and get it over with. Get your point across and try to recapture, in your heart, that calm, sunny outlook for which you are known and loved by your nearest and dearest.

Here are some tips to handle your anger:

Express your anger, when you must. Love, and anger, are two sides of the same coin.

Accept the fact that, from time to time, your children are going to make you angry.

Give your children a 'storm warning' if you can.

If you do go berserk don't feel too guilty about it: it happens to us all.

During the storm be angry at the child for what he's done (or not done). Don't attack his character and say things like: 'You're a horrible, nasty little sneak and I'll never like you again.' Such words, uttered in the heat of the moment, can be taken seriously by children.

When the storm's over (e.g. the next day, or later the same day) say: 'I was really, truly angry wasn't I?' This identifies what has happened, and implies that it isn't going to be a daily event. Talk about it (even laugh about it) and this gives the child an important truth: that anger is not catastrophic, and doesn't mean the end of your love for him.

At some time or other, make it clear to the child what makes you furious. It could be an untidy bedroom, being rude to visitors, or eating in a sloppy way. Whatever it is, it's only fair to let the child know.

'Institutionalize' any bursts of cosmic, irrational anger that are about to sweep over you. When my berserker friend is about to experience a Force 9 gale everybody goes to their bedroom to batten down the hatches, or goes out to find a (temporary) safe harbour elsewhere in the street. 'Mummy's getting annoyed,' is quite enough, or, 'I feel furious' (if you do). Alternatively, just start counting to ten. They'll get the picture.

One last and very important point. Children get angry too and they can become very frightened at their own anger. It's helpful if you can tell your child: 'You're very angry. Everybody gets angry at times. You may annoy me when you get angry but you can't destroy me.' Children, can, with reassurance from you, learn to accept and master the unruly emotions within them. There is a marvellous picture-book for children called *Where the Wild Things Are* by Maurice Sendak (Bodley Head) in which Max, the child hero, learns to overcome the Wild Things by looking at them straight in the eye. That's what we must all do with our emotions, however monstrous they may appear.

ANOREXIA
See section on: **Eating Fads** *Page* 65

ANXIETY
See also **Fears** *Page* 81, **Insecurity** *Page* 115, **Nervous Children** *Page* 154

I don't know anybody who isn't anxious about something: money not going far enough, pressures at work, whether they'll be able to afford a holiday/new clothes/new shoes for the children. Young people worry about exams. Wives, many of them, worry about bringing up a family (a hard enough task in itself) and holding down a part-time, or full-time, job. Adults are worried and so are children. Some years ago I surveyed over one thousand ordinary, normal youngsters in school. Very few of them had no anxieties. In fact, the odd ones out were those who weren't worried! Anxiety is the most common symptom of our age: witness the numbers of pills taken by adults to 'soothe their nerves'.

What *is* anxiety? Physiologically speaking, it's preparation for action. When we're under stress the brain stimulates the adrenal glands (two small glands near the top of each kidney) and adrenalin pours into the bloodstream. This is the fight or flight hormone which gives us the energy to fight, or to run away. Large quantities of sugar are pumped from the blood into the liver (to provide more energy), muscles become primed as blood is diverted from such places as the skin – that's why we go pale – to places which need it most. The heart beats faster, breathing becomes more rapid, blood pressure increases. The idea of these changes is to get us ready for immediate action. *If we don't act and do something, we still feel anxious.* It's as though something awful were about to happen but it never does. We worry that it might. Sometimes, the worry is worse than the catastrophe that we think, rightly or wrongly, is just about to land in our laps.

What can we do to help children who are anxious? The first thing is *not* to say, 'Don't worry.' This particular piece of advice isn't very helpful to youngsters (and adults) who *do* worry. It's better to point out that everybody worries some of the time. Don't continually express your fears in front of the child: if *you* see danger in all of life's situations – a tiger behind every hedge – then you can be quite sure your child will. Take precautions against real dangers (e.g. traffic, a child falling into a pond, electrical apparatus, keeping dangerous medicines out of reach of children) but don't suggest that, day-in, day-out, life is made up of terrible catastrophes. We meet enough troubles in life without worrying about what might happen beforehand.

If you do discuss problems with your child (i.e. financial difficulties, family quarrels, your own worries) be reasonably cheerful about it. Say, 'We'll manage', or, 'Never mind, worse things happen at sea.' Don't overburden children with all the pessimism and insecurity of adult life. They don't mind difficulties as much as your despondency or your depression. Say what the problem is and try and do something about it. Whether you succeed or not you live to fight another day. If you're courageous, honest, in there battling with the rest of us, children will pick up something of your optimism and your refusal to be beaten by day-to-day worries. It's your *attitude* towards it, rather than the problem, that counts.

Never aim for perfection with children. Life isn't perfect; neither are our offspring. Nothing makes a child more anxious and depressed than a mother who keeps telling him that he could do better, that he must try harder. If you set standards that are impossible for your child to reach he may refuse to try at all. What we have to do is to give the child some chance of success and so build up his self-esteem. *Don't* make him anxious by asking more from him than he can cope with.

Anxiety sometimes results from children having too much freedom to do exactly as they want. Children like some limits; they like to know how far they can go, what is allowed and what isn't. If you lay down some limits, some rules, then the child can cope better with the outside world, where he'll sooner or later meet restrictions on his actions. So lay down a few laws (the fewer the better) and stick to them so that everybody in the family knows where they are. Don't try to solve an anxious child's problems by spoiling him and don't make the mistake of being vague and uncertain about what you expect of your children. Doubt breeds anxiety. As far as your own moods are concerned it's a good idea to say to your child: 'Don't rub me up the wrong way today. I'm irritable' (or sad, or worried). Children can cope with anything so long as they know where they are. Nothing is more likely to make a child more anxious than the mum (or dad) whose moods change like the weather, and for no apparent reason. Don't try to be perfect; do try to be open and honest.

Remember that whether your child is taking exams, starting a new school, going for interviews or going in for competitions, it's your calmness and reassurance that's most helpful. None of us can avoid competitive situations in life; what we should relay to our children is that we fail in something sooner or later and failure *is* hard to take but we get over it. We can't succeed all the time: the main thing is that the child does his best and that we show interest and support him in what he does whether he wins or loses. *That* takes a lot of the sting out of failure.

Here are a few suggestions which will help your family from becoming too anxiety prone, from getting into the habit of worrying about day-to-day, inevitable, stress:

Don't sit there being anxious, do something. It's always better to act.

Smile and be cheerful. It may never happen or, more probably, it already has. In a family, courage and optimism, like fear and anxiety, are contagious.

Don't continually find fault with your child. We all have our faults and shortcomings: it doesn't build up our confidence to be perpetually reminded of them.

Do be honest about your feelings but don't indulge in threats to your child, or prophecies of doom, or sarcastic comments. Life's bad enough for most of us without those we love making it worse.

Give your child some responsibility in the home, some jobs to do. One of the best answers to anxiety is a feeling of competence, a sense of self-esteem.

Provide adequate outlets and interests for your child. Social contacts (through sport, joining a club or, for example, going ice-skating or bowling once a week) are essential to 'take us out of ourselves'. Friendship is a good antidote to loneliness and fears.

ATTITUDES
(For Parents)
See also **Parents – Children's Relationship with** *Page* 170

One thing I've learned in life is that it's not only our problems and difficulties that count but our attitude towards them. It's strange how some people make a mountain out of every molehill, seem to look for problems (if you look for difficulties you'll find them). Others seem to cope marvellously: with children, with life. I knew a mother with four young children who was the original 'Super Mum'. She never flapped, never shouted, always looked smart. In cases of woe, strife or accident she'd give the child involved a cream cracker (she had a huge tin of them!). That wasn't her secret, though. Her real secret was, as she told me herself: 'I never look for trouble.' This outlook is vital, especially with children.

We can't all be 'Super Mums' or 'Super Dads'. We *all* worry about a first child and get up in the middle of the night to make sure he's still breathing. We all have our own styles of bringing up children, and our own attitudes to problems. 'I'm not happy unless I've got something to worry about,' one mother told me. I told her that I knew the feeling; she wasn't alone; there are lots of people like that. I said: 'Then you should worry about the electricity or gas-bill, the curtains or what's for tea. Don't worry about your children. *They'll* be fine. They'll get by.' Your children *will* run into difficulties; if you can react sensibly and calmly towards them you're already half-way home to solving them.

To be fair, your attitude towards your children is very much tied up with self-confidence and with the way that you've been brought up. My wife had an easy-going attitude towards our own young children making a mess and being untidy. Her mother had been (and is) a very tidy person; my wife had reacted against that and made sure that she, when she grew up, wasn't going to make a fuss over mess. Other mums will take after their own mothers: they will be keen on tidiness, or politeness or 'eating properly' at table. *Each of us will have our own strengths and weaknesses: childish behaviour that we can tolerate, other childish behaviour that we can't abide and brings out the worst in us.* As we go on we learn to be more

11

easy-going about it all. You *can't* live in a palace with children about. Children do make a mess and we shouldn't impose too high a standard on them. As we grow in confidence we realize that being dirty (for children) could mean having 'great fun' rather than being naughty. We accept that they will come in from time to time looking like red indians and *we slowly learn to make less fuss.*

To bring up children, especially through the bad patches, you need faith and love. There was a time when I despaired of my eldest daughter. She was very shy and had very few friends. She didn't seem very happy at school. When she came home I'd scan her face, trying to hide my anxiety, say something like: 'Had a nice day?' I lived through that awful patch and my daughter is now a happy, extrovert girl with loads of friends, and marvellous at making new friends. Something happened, she coped, she won through. Most children do. Whilst they're doing it, we should show that *we* believe in them, show them lots of affection. Faith and love conquers mountains, as well as molehills.

I think attitudes are extremely important. In order to have the right attitude towards bringing up your children I think you should remember that:

Children are not the enemy. Tiredness may be, or the mortgage repayments, but not children. Children are supposed to be our friends.

Don't lean on experts too much. Stick to your own style and use your own common sense. If you find you can't cope, *that's* the time to have a word with another mum whom you respect or consult your family doctor.

Don't exaggerate 'problems'. With children, you'll get *some* problems but they come and go like the tides. Try to enjoy your children, at every stage, and remember they'll be grown up and be gone very soon.

Bringing up children is a hard job and, often, there seems to be little in the way of rewards for all that hard slog. Yet, there are rewards. Bringing up a happy child is, in itself, a reward and if you're doing a good job reward yourself occasionally? You deserve it.

No family is normal. Each family has it's own style.

AWKWARD QUESTIONS CHILDREN ASK

Before I give you an idea of the kind of awkward questions that children ask let me give you a simple piece of advice: *always*

12

give a straight answer to a straight question. If you're anxious about a child's query, or evasive, your child will guess that it's a subject that worries you, or makes you feel guilty and ashamed. Don't pass on your guilt, or shame, to your offspring. Answer him honestly, and he'll be happy enough; until such time as he wants to find out more about it. Try to answer according to the age and stage of your child. If your infant asks you a question about sex, he doesn't want all the details. He simply wants to know about what's puzzling him. You can elaborate, fill in the bits, later, when he's old enough to understand. Don't hide things from your child. It's what they don't know that hurts children, so pass on your hard won experience so that they don't have to make the same mistakes as you, or cope with the lies and evasions that you had to put up with.

Here are some of the questions that children, of varying ages, might ask. I also suggest the way in which the queries should be answered:

Q. *Why has that lady got such a great big tummy?*
A. She's having a baby. Daddy plants the seed in the mummy's tummy and the seed grows into a baby. The tummy has to be big to give the baby enough room. When the baby's born the tummy goes down again to its ordinary size.

Q. *How does daddy put the seed into the mummy's tummy?*
A. His penis gets stiff and he pushes it into the mummy's baby hole and a seed comes out of his penis and makes friends with an egg inside mummy's tummy. Together, the seed and the egg make a baby.

Q. *How does the baby get out of mummy's tummy?*
A. It comes out through mummy's vagina. That's her baby-hole. She has a wee hole and a baby-hole. The vagina stretches, the baby comes out, and the vagina goes back to it's ordinary size; like you can stretch an elastic band. It will stretch a lot but it always goes back to it's usual shape.

Q. *Have you hurt yourself, mummy? (she has noticed a blood stain on your underclothes).*
A. *No. The blood is from mummy's tummy. It comes out through her vagina. Mummy's egg is ripe every month but, if it doesn't meet a seed, it passes out of mummy, with some blood, through the vagina. It's called having a period. When you're a big girl, you'll have periods just like mummy.*

Q. *What's a queer?*
A. A queer is a word you shouldn't use. There are men who like

each other, love each other, and may have sexual relationships together. Some people call them homosexuals which means that they are attracted to persons of the same sex. The word they use to describe themselves is 'gays'. That's the word you should use if you want to talk about them. Queers is very insulting. Most young people are attracted to other people of the same sex for a time. With gays, they wish to spend their time mostly with people of the same sex, and two gays may decide to live together. When women are sexually attracted towards each other they are called lesbians.

Q. *Do you believe in God?*
A. I'm not sure. There seems to be something that is very powerful in the world, and very beautiful. I'd like to believe but I don't, really. Not in the way that people who go to church every Sunday believe. You must listen to what they tell you at school about God, and what other people say, and make up your own mind. I'm willing to talk about God, and how the world came to be here, but it would only be what I think. I don't really know the answers. That's something you may have to find out yourself.

Q. *What's an abortion? Does that mean that they kill a baby?*
A. Yes, it does. It may be harmful for the woman to have a baby or the baby may be so badly damaged before he's born that the mother and doctor decide between them that it would be wrong to bring the baby into the world. Most of the time, women want their babies. Sometimes, they don't. It's something that the woman must decide with the doctor. It doesn't hurt to have an abortion if doctors do it and it may be better for a woman to live her life without that baby though she may be sad at having to take the decision.

Q. *Mum, what is love?*
A. Love is being very fond of a person, or people, in a very unselfish way. When you love someone you want to help him, be with him, and make him feel that he's great. There's romantic love – like in story books – and love for things like dogs, and cats, or collecting postage stamps. It just means being fond of something, or someone, and wanting to show it.

Q. *What does 'fuck' mean?*
A. It means when two people have sexual intercourse. Usually,

two people care about each other before they fuck. Fucking is best when the two people love each other. I don't like you using that word, though, and neither do a lot of other grown-ups. It's better to say sexual intercourse or say: 'They made love to each other.' Although, you should know that there are other ways, besides sexual intercourse, that people can make love to each other and show that they love and care for one another.

Don't misunderstand me. I'm not saying that you will answer these questions in the same way I have answered them: particularly the ones about abortion, or the existence of God. What you must do is speak from your own heart, be open, honest and direct. The child may not accept everything that you tell him (especially as he gets older and wants your opinion about various tricky subjects) but at least he'll respect you for respecting him: by telling him the truth, as you see it, without flannel.

BEDWETTING

Bedwetting is a very common problem but it causes the parent, and the child, concerned a lot of anxiety. Most bedwetting problems clear up with good management and a bit of common sense. *Punishment rarely works.* Reassurance and extra affection may cure the situation without further ado. What happens if it doesn't? As well as being calm and matter-of-fact about the wetting here are some practical steps you can take:

Make sure your child's room is warm and leave the landing light on (or give the child a torch) so that he can go to the bathroom when he needs to without having to cope in the dark.

Your child *may* prefer a potty under the bed. This means that he can, if necessary, empty his bladder without having to leave the bedroom; a useful advantage, especially with younger children.

Make sure that your child avoids last-minute drinks, and ensure that he goes to the toilet, before dropping off to sleep.

Protect your child's mattress with rubber sheeting and ensure that the sheets (and his pyjamas) are made from easily-washable, drip-dry material.

Encourage the child to go to the toilet during the day and avoid frantic, last-minute dashes to the lavatory. Many young children, involved in their play, wait 'until they're bursting' to go to the toilet. This is not a habit to encourage, particularly with the bedwetter.

With younger children, find out from your child's teacher whether he goes to the toilet at school. Some children find school lavatories inaccessible or frightening or generally unpleasant. If he does, perhaps an older child can be given the job of going with him if and when he needs to go.

If you have an older child who still wets the bed you might like to try a system of *small* rewards which may help the child to build up his confidence by 'scoring' a succession of dry nights. Reward your child when he doesn't wet his bed but keep your rewards on a reasonable level (a Penguin biscuit, or 2p, or perhaps a coloured star in a note book which can be exchanged for a larger prize when the child has gained five – and, later, ten – stars.) Blatant bribes such as, 'If you stop wetting the bed I'll buy you a bike,' *don't* work. They may make the child more anxious and the situation worse. If you try this reward system do remember that *a calm and understanding attitude towards the child acts as a powerful additional reward for your child to stop wetting the bed.*

You could keep a calendar on your child's bedroom wall and put a ring around those dates when your child has a dry night. Again, when the child has had a run of three, or five (or, later, ten) dry nights he can be rewarded with some special treat. *Don't* lose patience if the method doesn't work at first but *do* congratulate the child on his successes. Your patience may be sufficient encouragement in itself for your child to stop wetting.

Another method of helping bedwetters is the 'buzzer'. This is a pad which goes under the bottom sheet of the bed and which contains a (perfectly safe) electrical alarm. When the child starts to wet the bed the alarm goes off, the child goes to the toilet (or potty) and completes his urination. Eventually, the child learns to anticipate the bell; he gets up when his bladder is swollen. It may seem to you that where a child sleeps very deeply, the buzzer wakes up everybody else in the house except him! Even so, in my experience, the buzzer has helped a great many children and (when you get used to it) is very simple to use. Moreover, your local children's clinic will advise you as to how to use it to the best advantage with your particular age of child.

Another way of gaining bladder control is called 'day clock training'. Here, an alarm clock is used to remind the child to go to the toilet at set intervals during the day: every two hours to start with, and increasing the time to every four hours. Since an alarm clock is not (unless the child is in the house) always convenient, it may be necessary for some adult or older child to remind him that it is now time to go to the toilet. In school, the cooperation of the teachers and the head is essential; and a gentle reminder is better than making the situation too embarrassing for the child (by too obvious remarks such as, 'Have you been to the toilet yet?'). After some time the child should be able to get into the habit of going to the toilet at regular intervals.

Should bedwetting, with your child, persist do seek professional advice. However, bear in mind that many infants of school age still wet the bed, as do plenty of older children. Bedwetting is, as I've said, a very common problem but, where parents are calm and sensible about it, it very often clears up of its own accord.

Sources of Help

1 The local child welfare clinic.
2 The family doctor who may recommend which approach will be best for your child.
3 The educational psychologist (an appointment may be made via the head of your child's school, or through your GP).
4 The paediatrician at the children's department of the local hospital. (A referral note from the family doctor will be necessary to get an appointment.)

Bereavement

Eighty years ago people discussed death fairly openly but sex was a taboo subject; nowadays, we hear about sex *ad nauseam* but most of us fear death and we pass on that fear to our children. Children, let's be frank, have no innate fear of, or anxiety about death: they learn that fear and anxiety from you and me, their parents. It is for us to explain to them that death, as it were, is a fact of life.

The young child tends not to understand that death is permanent: that neither he, nor you (the parents) can bring back the deceased. Once the child is old enough to respond to loss (and children of infant age are quite capable of feeling sorrow, and loss) *the child, like the adult, has a right to mourn*. The child also has a right to express unhappiness and to talk about it. The conspiracy of silence which surrounds death is not much use to the person (adult or child) who needs to mourn.

It's thought that a child goes through four stages of mourning: first there is an initial numbness with occasional bouts of distress or anger; this is followed by yearning for the lost person, and then by a feeling of despair and sorrow; finally there comes re-organization, and an adjustment to the loss. What can we do, as parents, to help in this process of adjustment? If a child's pet tortoise dies, that's easy enough: we can buy him a new one. What do we do if his grandmother, or somebody he loved, and loves, very dearly dies? We can say: 'You loved granny. You miss her a lot. I miss her too.' Such simple statements are helpful to your child in coming to terms with his grief. We can put an arm around him and say: 'You're sad because granny has died.' Nothing too elaborate is necessary providing we give the child an opportunity to talk about his loss rather than bottle up his real feelings. We shouldn't bottle up our real feelings: we shouldn't be afraid to show our sorrow, or to talk about our sadness.

If you can act naturally, and express (and explain) your own sorrow to the child then the child will accept the sadness, and the inevitability, of death without lasting emotional harm. *You* have to accept that there is a pattern to life, and death is part of that pattern. Nobody would deny that to lose a loved one may be a bitter experience; we can only console ourselves that the pain of grief is the price we pay for the joy of love.

When children are bereaved we must let them cry, if they wish to, without feeling embarrassed and let them talk openly and honestly about their feelings. If you, as a parent, have been bereaved you may have to learn to cope: to go out more (rather than less) following the death of your spouse. The widower, and the widow, does not want to be treated as an outsider, a freak. You will need to discuss your feelings with, perhaps, your family doctor, your friends and neighbours; and to admit, yourself, that you suffer from a feeling of loss. Time is, itself, a great healer: a holiday, a job, a new circle of friends, new commitments can all help you to a renewed life, setting you free from too much sorrow, giving you a chance of a new life, and giving your child(ren) an opportunity to see that you are overcoming your own grief.

There are several sources of help available to those who may be, or have been, bereaved.

Begin Again: A Book for Women Alone. (J. M. Dent & Sons) written by Mrs M. Torrie, the Director of *Cruse* – the name is taken from 1 Kings, Ch. 17, verse 14, where Elijah speaks of the cruse, or pot, of oil which will not run out – offers a great deal of practical advice to widows and their children. The headquarters of *Cruse* is 6 Lion Gate Gardens, Richmond, Surrey and the

organization provides postal counselling plus a wide range
pamphlets on various topics. *Cruse* also has affiliated clubs i̇
different parts of the country.

Bereavement: Studies of Grief in Adult Life by Dr Colin Murray
Parkes (Penguin) deals with the emotional aspects of the loss of
a loved one and lists organizations offering help to the bereaved.

The local Citizens' Advice Bureau should have copies of its
pamphlet *Practical Problems following the Death of a Relative or
Friend.*

All local libraries should have a copy of *What to do When
Someone Dies* (Consumer Publications). A short, easy-to-read
book which deals with practicalities.

Boisterous Children
See also **Hyperactive Children** *Page* 110

Some children are placid and easy-going. Others are cheeky,
boisterous, a little bit unruly and blessed with a considerable
amount of energy. When a boisterous child plays with other
children he may be rather rough, inadvertently, hurting other
children, or 'messing up the game' because he plays it too
vigorously. Boisterous children show a strong desire for freedom
and independence: they want to do their own thing, do it their way
and, sometimes, they show scant regard for the feelings of other
children, or their parents.

What to do about them? If your child is very lively and
boisterous I don't think it's a good idea to knock the spirit out of
him by continually criticizing his behaviour or nagging at him. All
you'll get is defiance and a constant battle of his will against yours.
Don't be too strict but don't let your child behave in a way that
ignores the needs and feelings of others. Explain that if he plays
with other children and hurts them they simply won't let him play
with them any more. Have your rules – about coming in for meals,
about 'giving cheek', about hitting other children. Talk these over
with him, explain why you have those rules, and, as far as possible,
make *him* responsible for disciplining himself. Let him say what he
thinks and explain his side of things; otherwise, he'll rightly think
that talking to adults is a waste of time because (and this is a
constant complaint of teenagers and young children) *his parents
never listen to what he says.*

One of the age-old tricks in dealing with a too-boisterous child is to *give him some responsibility*. Teachers know this. They give the over-lively child jobs to do, especially first thing in the morning when their nerves can't take the strain. It may be a job like counting and giving out pencils, feeding the gerbils, taking the register to the school secretary. At home, let your child help with laying the breakfast table, getting a younger sibling off to school, or making sure that the kitchen is tidy. Put him in charge of the washing; let him, if he's old enough, do the ironing. It's surprising how boisterous children calm down when they see that adults trust them with doing important jobs and leave them to get on and do them.

Look out for trouble and forestall it. If your lively, bossy child is having a friend in to play who is another boisterous 'natural leader', make sure you give instructions as to who's in charge of what, who takes turns on what. If there's to be no arguments, say what they should do (i.e. come and ask you) if there's any difference of opinion between them. Get them out in the open air if you can: a boisterous child is less trouble in the local park than he is playing by the (expensive) record player, or coming in and out of the kitchen whilst you're trying to work. Don't set too high standards but make it clear what you want and that you expect him to be able to play, without disasters, whilst you get on with what you've got to do.

Be available to talk to the child sometimes. Don't always say: 'Off you go. Mummy's busy,' but make it clear when you're not available. Similarly, respect his right to play without constant nagging and interference. Say where he can play: what areas of the house he can go in and what areas he can't. If you don't want him in the kitchen, say so. If he comes in, extend your right arm and say one word: 'Out'. He'll get the message. The quicker he learns to play without annoying you the sooner everybody can get on with their lives with the minimum of fuss.

Give him plenty to do and get the child 'out of your hair'. A playgroup joined or – for older children a scout/guide/rangers troop – saves an awful lot of squabbling; it also ensures that you have a much-welcomed break from each other. Groups have rules, they insist that children fit in with other children. This is valuable social training so don't try to do it all by yourself. An outside club joined (whether it's a sports club, a museum club or a train-spotters' club) is worth a thousand words of discussion and criticism.

Keep your own interests, and be reasonably lively yourself. Get out and mix with other people, join an evening class, get away for a morning to have coffee or a drink with a friend. If you're isolated and depressed the boisterous child – even when that boisterousness is quite normal and just a genuine expression of childish energy – will strike you as quite unbearable and really get on your nerves. Get your child out of the house, doing things, but don't forget to get out of the house yourself. If you're outgoing, reasonably sociable and enjoying *some* of your week, the boisterous child should hold no terrors for you.

Boredom
See also **Destructiveness** *Page* 53

Boredom is Public Enemy No 1 as far as children and parents are concerned. The devil, they say, finds work for idle hands to do and, with children, if you let them get bored, you'll find that you're working twice as hard shouting at them than if you found them something to do in the first place! Just a moment (I hear you say) whose job is it to find something? Surely children ought to be able to entertain themselves? Perhaps so. All I'm saying is that one good idea to keep them occupied, one suggestion to keep them out of your hair, is going to save a lot of complaints, aggression and weariness on your part. It's the mum or dad who comes up with ideas when they're needed who has the easiest time of looking after children.

The thing to remember is that there's a natural rhythm to children's activities. It's like an orchestra playing a symphony: there are noisy bits, quiet bits, lively bits and (you hope) restful bits. If you're conducting children's play you shouldn't burst in with lots of exciting ideas just when they're busy anyway. Judge the mood. If the mood is 'We've got nothing to do,' or, 'What can we do next, we're bored', then that's the time for mum, or dad, to suggest something.

As far as young children are concerned there are plenty of books on the market crammed full with good ideas for play activities. *What to do when 'There's nothing to do'* by Boston Children's Medical Centre and Elizabeth M. Gregg (Arrow) lists various ideas, under various age groups. For example, two- and three-year-olds might like water (or clay) paint, pasting, painting and music and dancing; three- to five-year-olds might find interest in building, printing, using leaves, potatoes and other items – sewing, dressing up, making a 'house' from boxes, cooking, animals, working with tools, or outings (even if it's only to the High Street shops, since everything's interesting to youngsters). The local library has a selection of books on the under-fives; better, you could go and talk to your local playgroup leader and have a discussion about play ideas for children.

It's important to provide materials, to provide a setting, but not give your child the notion that you are responsible for thinking up each and every idea for play, or that you will programme his day for him. He has to learn to entertain himself. What you should do is provide materials – whether it's paper and pens, or wood hammer and nails, or some old clothes and whatever. Don't take it upon yourself to be responsible for the games they play; just provide the materials or an opportunity to run around in an open space with other children, and they'll do the rest. If you live in a city, or crowded town, make good use of your local park: it's better to sit on a park bench, talking to other mums or dads watching your children play than to be cooped up at home all day with them. If you live in a tower block of flats it will be tricky but, instead of getting depressed, get together with other mums of young children and work out a roster and some play activities for them. Joint action, instead of individual helplessness, is the best way to drive away those feelings of anger and annoyance at your own young children's constant demands to 'do something'.

With older children do keep an eye on whether your child is bored in school. Many children, from good homes and with lively, enquiring minds do badly in the classroom simply because they are bored stiff. If you think that your child is bored in school, if he seems to tail off in his school work and become unanimated and unhappy do go up to the school and have a word with the class teacher. I've seen quite a few outgoing, bright children who fared badly because the teacher made them feel inadequate, bored and resentful. The reason why they were resentful was that the teacher wasn't giving the children anything interesting to do. A chat with your child's teacher will do no harm and may lead to the youngster being given more appropriate, and more interesting, school work. Boredom in school can lead to apathy, day-dreaming and wasteful failure so, if you think it's happening, do something about it.

The school holidays can be a problem with older children. The local education office will be able to tell you of any holiday play schemes or the address of any adventure playgrounds in your area. Although you may, if your children are bored, suggest that they build a trolley from old planks and old pram wheels, or do a project on space, or learn to sew or go out and collect materials to make up a collage, and various other ideas, I think that the best solution for bored children is to be in groups with other children of varying ages. So, if you have a chance to *build* an adventure playground, or to *start up* a holiday play scheme – perhaps with some help from your social services office – you are doing more to help the children in your neighbourhood than trying to cope with your own children in your own back garden or, worse, in your house. Get together with neighbours, do something *together*. Perhaps ask some of the unemployed teenagers (many of whom, very tragically, won't have enough to do) in your area to help. A neighbourhood scheme for young children, providing facilities in a local church hall, or anywhere else, for youngsters is much better than mums or dads trying to cope alone.

Teenagers are, as we all know, notorious for the frequent use of that ominous statement, 'I'm bored'. Young people, these days, are used to being spoon-fed, having pleasure laid on for them. Many of them can't get out into the country and explore, or kick a ball about on a field, or go for a country walk and talk. Some equate pleasure with transistor radios, discos, or the cinema – all passive activities in which all you have to do is listen, or watch. Thousands more youngsters watch football on a Saturday afternoon than play it. Again, the answer lies in the community and in doing something active in the community – whether it's joining a youth club, helping in a playgroup or perhaps visiting elderly people. It seems strange that young people should be able to say 'I'm bored' when, looking around us, we can see so much that needs doing, and so many people that would be glad of some help or some extra company.

Do – and I know many youngsters are very reticent about this – get your youngster to *join*, rather than just be a watcher. He could join a karate club, or the scouts, or a boxing club, or the YHA. Once he gets used to mixing with others, and contributing something to the group, he'll be less tempted to lie about feeling sorry for himself. Leisure, he'll find, is pleasure when it's filled with activity. As those unfortunate young people on the dole have discovered, few human beings can cope with too much leisure. Most of us prefer something to do. It's only when we all learn to help each other, when we realize that different age groups needn't be segregated from each other, that we'll conquer the problem of boredom by setting up facilities for children and young people in our own neighbourhoods. *That's* the way to beat delinquency and the way to beat boredom.

Breath-holding

The very first thing that should be said about breath-holding is that it can't really do much damage to your child – though it may very well frighten the life out of you. If your child holds his breath long enough and faints, and that is the worst that can happen, what happens next? Nature ensures that your child, once he has fainted, resumes normal breathing again. It's the same with those strong-willed babies who get so angry when they cry, and pause so long for breath in between sobs, that they actually turn blue. It *is* alarming, I know, but the truth is that when the baby needs to breathe, he'll breathe. Panicky action on your part makes the baby feel frightened. If you keep calm, he'll get over his fury or frustration. If you are in any doubt about this go and see your family doctor and he will be able to reassure you.

With older children – and breath-holding is most common amongst children between one- and four-years old – more than a little bit of manipulation may creep in. If you do panic then your child has a tremendous weapon if he wants to annoy or scare you. The child may hold his breath for a few seconds, for ten seconds – or even longer. He may turn blue, faint, or even have a slight convulsion. This *is* alarming because it looks like an epileptic fit. Again, there is no need to panic since these sudden movements have nothing to do with epilepsy and the child is merely raising the stakes in his bids to get his own way and to frighten, or blackmail, you. The best approach is to nip the whole thing in the bud, stop it before it starts. Don't let it get to the stage of breath-holding – panic – longer breath-holding – more panic. If your child does try it on say something like, 'You can cut that out, my lad, and get on with your ordinary business. Young children are very shrewd and they're shrewd enough to realize that there's no point in carrying on breath-holding if it simply isn't having any effect on you. Once more, if you're in doubt – and if your child's tactics really do put the fear of God into you – then you must go and have a word with your GP about it.

You ought to know that breath-holding is quite common amongst two-year-olds. It's part of their urge to control you, part of their struggle for independence, part of their confusion about how separate they are from you, part of their probing to learn more about you and your reactions to certain behaviour. In this way, it's similar to defiance, little trials of strength (see section on **Tantrums**). Please, don't let it get to the stage where you become anxious, alarmed and he becomes over-excited or even more manipulating because he knows he's got you just where he wants you. Live through your fears, don't respond to breath-holding and your child's attempts to terrify you will stop quite spontaneously. Have a sense of humour about it. He *is* trying it on. He *is* testing you out. If you panic, over-react, you won't stop him breath-holding. If you play it cool you will. What point is there in playing the central role in a little drama called 'Time to Frighten Mother' (or Father) if nobody's appreciating his performance?

Bullying

How do you spot if your child's being bullied at school? The warning signs are that a child, previously happy, suddenly becomes unhappy and withdraws into himself. Perhaps your child will be apprehensive about going to school in the morning or ask to stay away 'because he isn't feeling well'. You may find that your child comes home without his cap, or some books, or some other belongings which have been taken from him. Or, it may be that your child's work, previously good, deteriorates. Again, the child may show a lack of interest in school, and an unwillingness to talk about it. There are three kinds of bullying: physical brutality, psychological bullying (teasing, mocking, taunting) and bullying for gain (where your child may have to pay up – whether in money, sweets or other belongings – in order to buy peace and quiet). *Strangely enough, many children who are the victims of bullies neither complain nor tell their parents. They keep it a secret and the inevitable loneliness and sense of isolation is even worse than the bullying itself.* Make no mistake, being bullied in school can make a child's life absolute hell. With bullying, whether it's of the sporadic variety or the persistent, cruel, sadistic sort, it is vital that parents and teachers are aware of what's taking place and put a stop to it.

You (like me) will be deeply shocked by bullying and by the fact that it still goes on in *some* schools. What can you do about it?

If you do suspect your child is being bullied have a word with him about it but keep any discussion of the problem calm and matter-of-fact. It is of no help to the child if you become upset and over-emotional. *He* has quite enough troubles as it is. Don't rush off to the school (or to a neighbour's house) swearing vengeance on the bully. (This kind of behaviour may help you but it won't stop your child being bullied when you're not around.) Take a deep breath. Let your child talk about it, if he wants to. Keep things in the home as normal as possible and try to steer a middle course between over-reacting, making a huge fuss, and appearing not to care. Give it a week. It may be that your child, having told you – with all the relief that brings – may now be able to sort the problem out by himself. If, after a week, your child is still unhappy and there is no improvement in the situation then you *must* intervene.

It is often a good idea for mum (and/or dad) to visit the school, have a word with the teacher and make themselves known to the classmates, simply by having a quick word with the teacher in the classroom. The fact that the parents are there (although they may not know the bullies, or care to know them) is sufficient to indicate to the children that something is going on and that the adults around them are doing something about the bullies. This, in itself, may be sufficient to deter them. Similarly, a parent of a teenage child may stand outside the school gate. (Don't say anything. Just stand there. One dad I know who tried this 'send a gun-boat' approach just gave the bullies a look for three consecutive evenings. It was enough.) A mother of an infant child may – since a great deal of bullying takes place just before, or just after, school time – escort her child to the school gates and be around when he goes into, or comes out of, the playground. It is the physical presence of the adult (rather than the adult 'telling off' the bullies, or making a scene) which acts as a deterrent. Make it clear that you are around *and* aware of what's happening.

If it is one particular child who is making your child's life a misery, and if your appearances up at the school have failed to frighten him off, the next step is to have a discreet word with his or her parents. (Though most bullying goes on with boys, girls bully too. At one time girls mostly resorted to psychological bullying; these days, the victim is more and more subjected to physical abuse and attack.) Keep it, again, as calm as possible. Don't arrive on their doorstep breathing fire and brimstone, looking for vengeance. The idea is merely to indicate to the bully that you know exactly what's going on and that you are determined to stop it. In most cases, nothing more is needed.

If these 'warning shots' fail to put a stop to the bullying then your next step is to seek an appointment with the headmaster and gain the cooperation of the school. Tell the head that what concerns you is not revenge (it's *his* business to decide how to stop the bullying and whether the bully should be punished). Just say that you are deeply concerned about what is happening to your child and would like to feel that this kind of thing won't happen in the future. Most head teachers will handle the situation with tact and ensure that your child is not labelled 'a sneak' by the other children (and subjected to further less overt, more subtle, forms of torment). Bullying *can* do so much damage, cause so much pain, that you must work together, very closely, with the school to put an *early* stop to it.

To prevent your child becoming a victim, you should:

Be on the lookout for the signs I've mentioned.
Point out to your child (if you think he's a victim of bullying) that it's not being a 'tell tale' or a 'cissy' to say what's going on.
Intervene at an early stage so that nobody gets really hurt.
Give your child a few days to see if he can sort it out himself. If he cannot, then you try. If this doesn't work, call in the help of the headmaster of the school.
Build up your child's social confidence by teaching him to swim, to play a new game, learn a new skill. Children who have plenty of self-respect, and confidence, are more able to defend themselves against bullies and less likely to become victims.
If in doubt, find out. Go to the school and ensure that no bullying is taking place.

Now, a nasty one. What should you do if you find out that your child is a bully? What I think you have to do first is to look at yourself. Are you adopting a bullying manner at home? Are you using a hectoring or sarcastic tone when the child does something wrong? (Remember, words *can* hurt, and very deeply. Girls, as well as boys, will use verbal taunts and nasty comments to hurt others if they are set a bad example at home.) Marital problems and arguments in the home, conflicts which cause parents to quarrel, to avoid each other or even come to blows can make a child become a bully, make him vent his frustration and aggression on to some quite innocent victim.

If you are inconsistent in your discipline at home, i.e., very strict one minute, very easy-going the next, the child doesn't get a chance to model himself on sensible, caring behaviour. He may think that anything goes and his anything may include bullying – despite the unhappiness it causes to the recipient of his actions. The moral is to set a good example and to make sure that you have a *consistent* way of handling the child within the family.

It may be, of course, that your child's bullying has nothing whatsoever to do with the home situation. He, or she, may have fallen in with 'the wrong crowd' and may bully to imitate others or to 'keep in with the gang'. If so, you must make it clear that you are not going to put up with that kind of behaviour, whether it happens in school or elsewhere. Explain to your youngster the real pain and acute stress of being bullied. (Explain, too, if you wish, that some victims of bullying have committed suicide, so great has been their agony at being the victim of bullying.)

You must make it clear that if the bullying continues your child will forfeit his pocket money or forego some other privilege. Make sure that you or your child (preferably the latter) makes a full apology to the victim. If you make it clear that you aren't going to accept bullying at any price the chances are that your youngster will get the message, and stop.

Sometimes – and I have to admit this, though it makes me sad and angry to do so – *schools* are at fault when it comes to bullying. A bullying teacher, poor, and especially inconsistent, discipline within the school or lack of any clear standards, can all lead to bullying on or off the school premises. What you must do, if your child has got himself or herself caught up in this kind of situation is to go to the school, tell the teacher that your child has been bullying, say that you find the whole thing unacceptable, shocking and ask what the school proposes to do about it. The school – either by clamping down on its running of the place or by making sure that the bullies concerned are actually doing something useful and achieving something in the classroom – *can* stop bullying if the headmaster and staff feel strongly enough about it.

As a rule of thumb, if you wish your child not to be a bully, you must remember three things:

Don't be a bully yourself.
Do praise your child, build up his morale, rather than criticize him the whole time.
Do tell him you won't accept bullying under any circumstances. Say it in a quiet voice, and mean it.

Cheating

I remember one less-than-illustrious occasion when my son was playing a game called 'Risk' with my brother (the aim of the game is to conquer the world). Both of them were cheating like mad. The game ended when both of them, at the very same time, kicked the board, and the pieces, all over the living room floor. Each wanted to win; neither could bear to lose; so they both cheated and nobody won. I've played golf with somebody who wanted to win so badly that he altered his score card every time we played; I've been in shops where the shop assistant has, deliberately, tried to give me change for £1 instead of £5; I've known friends who cheated in examinations, at chess, and cheated their wives and husbands. *Why* do people cheat? The desire to succeed, sheer dishonesty, lack of respect for others (or dislike of them); the notion that because 'everybody does it' it's all right – these are the kind of things that make us cheat. Many adults would never cheat a close friend but would have no scruples about cheating the government, the railway or the tax man. 'I need the money more than they do,' an acquaintance told me after a large store had given him too much change. Maybe he does. It's still cheating.

With children, there are stages of moral development. At first a child obeys rules to avoid being punished: he doesn't want to be shouted at, or smacked. Then, he conforms to adult values in order to obtain approval – a nod, a smile, a word of praise. Later he conforms to authority outside of the home because there, too, he wishes to gain approval and avoid censure. This is a kind of conscience, but it depends on other people, mostly adults, keeping an eye on him and making him feel guilty if he doesn't behave. The next, and most important stage, of the child's morality is when he gains a sense of *duty*. He does things because he knows, inside himself, that they ought to be done. He censures his own behaviour. He knows, very well, what is right and wrong and when he doesn't do right he pays the price (not of adults frowning at him, since he may never be found out, but of guilt). The moral pressure should come, as the child grows older, from inside rather than outside. You don't do things, in other words, because somebody tells you to; you do them because they are right.

Children have to be given a set of values (see **Morality**). Also, they mustn't be cheated by their own parents. If you cheat, and tell your child not to cheat, you're cheating. If you cheat the tax man, boast about it, and then tell your child he must be honest you are confusing him. It's a confusing enough world as it is and few of us abide by a ready-made set of rules, such as the Ten Commandments, any more. Many people believe in a rough-and-ready, common-sense morality ('Don't hurt people'; 'Do as you would be done by'). Others don't have any code of morality which they could put into words but they still have a sense of values. Human beings can't live without *some* values, some guide-lines as to behaviour.

The main thing is to tell your child the truth, as you see it. Discuss things with him, make a point of talking about honesty, cheating, relationships with others. Say what you think and tell your child that most people feel guilty if they do something that they know, inside of themselves, is wrong. If your child cheats in a game, if you find that he's been cheating in an examination in school, or cheating a friend out of something then say, 'That's wrong.' Don't punish him severely, don't harp on the fact of how honest you are, and don't accept his plea that 'everybody else does it'. Say it's dishonest and that you don't like that kind of behaviour. Some cheats prosper; most of them, sooner or later, are found out. There's no easy way in life; the vast majority of people who 'get on' do so by dint of hard work and overcoming disappointments. Tell your child how *you* think it is, what *you* think the best way is, and leave him to make up his mind for himself. When you're talking to him you can be open and honest; or you can cheat.

I think it's cheating when parents give their children the idea that school and examinations and working hard aren't important. They are important. Those 'bits of paper' give the youngster a chance of finding a job, choice in a career. I think it's cheating when the record companies and the media suggest that pop music is an answer to life. It isn't, nor does it pay the rent (except for the promotors and disc jockeys). When the music stops some of these youngsters face a very bleak future indeed; simply because few adults tell them the truth.

To encourage honesty in your child you should try to give him lots of affection and reasonable control. Build up his self-esteem by praise, and by discussing things with him. Then, he will, because he respects himself, have his own system of inner controls, or conscience. Not to do things because we fear punishment, or because we're afraid of being found out, is a second-rate kind of morality. If you're warm and loving towards your child, and reasonably democratic, you'll encourage his innate sense of justice. If you're too critical and over-punitive, you'll merely encourage him to cheat when you, and other authoritarian people, aren't around and when he thinks he can get away with it.

You can't give your child too much affection. You can give him too stern a morality to cope with, and you can over-do punishment. Let him make some choices for himself, let him take some responsibility. In one experiment where children were asked to look after a hamster (and not to touch the toys left on a table) some children – despite the instructions and because of the fact that the adult had gone out of the room – left the hamster to play with the toys. (If they did so, rather cruelly, a trap-door opened and the hamster disappeared.) One little girl did her duty marvellously; she wasn't tempted by the toys; she carefully tended to the hamster despite the lack of adults. After the experiment the mothers were interviewed. The mother of this last little girl was sensible, a warm and loving person. I suspect her daughter had a conscience because she would never like to let her mother down; she loved her too much for that.

That's the point about cheating to get across to your children. It's not a good idea to cheat because it lets other people down, it lets yourself down and (last but not least) it's wrong. Only you can make your child honest – since children gain a great many of their values from parents – and the best way to ensure honesty in a child is to be open and honest yourself.

Child Guidance Clinics

In most towns of a reasonable size there is a child guidance clinic. The 'clinic team' consists of a child psychiatrist, a psychologist, a psychiatric social worker plus a secretary. The last-named is very important to the success of the clinic since she frequently is the first one to meet worried parents (and worried children) and to try to make them feel less threatened by all these grandiose-sounding titles. Many parents find the word 'clinic' rather off-putting since they associate it with out-patients clinics, eye clinics and other clinics found within a hospital setting. In fact, a child guidance clinic may be situated in a purpose-built general clinic, or it may be part of the local hospital facilities or it may be located (as have several of the clinics I have worked in) in some old building with a reasonably friendly and welcoming atmosphere.

Parents very often get very confused as to the difference between a child psychiatrist and a child psychologist. The child psychiatrist is a doctor; he has qualified in medicine and gone on to specialize in child psychiatry (i.e. in helping children with emotional problems). Most child psychiatrists work closely with the paediatrician (a specialist in children's physical problems) and with the child neurologist since, these days, we know that physical and emotional problems may be linked together. Although there are Freudian child psychiatrists (who subscribe to the theories of Freud) and other child psychiatrists who may belong to particular 'schools' of psychiatry, most child psychiatrists these days are eclectic— i.e. they use any theory that seems to them to be useful in helping the child with his problem.

The psychologist working at your local clinic will either be an educational psychologist (who spends a great deal of time going around schools advising teachers and parents on behaviour and/or learning difficulties) or a clinical psychologist, i.e. a professional person but not medically trained (i.e., *not* a doctor) who has had experience of dealing with the emotional and nervous difficulties of both adults and children. The psychologist may give your child an intelligence test to see whether he is working up to his potential and to find out in which areas of his school work there are weaknesses. If your child, for example, is doing very badly in reading it is quite possible that the educational psychologist will arrange remedial help in this, very important, skill.

The psychiatric social worker is a professionally qualified social worker who has gone on to specialize in hospital, or clinic, work. He or she is the clinic's link with the home. The social worker may visit a home and discuss the child's difficulties with the parents so that the 'clinic team' can help the child more effectively.

The methods used at most child guidance clinics are very similar. Play therapy may be used with young children (i.e. the child playing with toys in the playroom and the child psychiatrist, and the mother, observing). The main approach to both older children and parents is *discussion*. In talking about the problem in complete confidence to professional people with a great experience of such problems it is usually possible for parents to gain reassurance and practical help with regard to dealing with the child. A child guidance clinic is really the 'long-stop' of the child advisory services. Since the team members are highly qualified and experienced they should be able to deal with most problems of child behaviour, however harrowing to the parents.

It is a great pity that the word 'psychiatrist' is associated in the minds of many with Sigmund Freud and leather couches. Many modern child psychiatrists take what is useful from the ideas that Freud put forward but they don't follow him blindly, nor do they put parents, or child, on a leather couch to talk to them. The discussions in a child guidance clinic have one aim in mind – to help the child. If you have a problem with your child that neither the school, nor the family doctor, has been able to help with, you should seriously consider getting an appointment for your child at the child guidance clinic (the address can be obtained from your local health clinic, from your GP or from the local library). You will need a note of referral, usually, from your family doctor, with whom you should discuss the problem first. It's better to be sure than sorry and, during my years in the child guidance clinic, I met many mothers and fathers who said to me: 'We've had a lot of help. My only regret is I didn't bring him/her along a few years earlier. It would have saved such a lot of worry.' Certainly, child guidance clinics are there to guide the child and, more important, to help parents to know the best direction in which to guide the child. If you're terribly, terribly worried about your child my advice is: don't hesitate to seek an appointment at the child guidance clinic.

Clumsiness
See also **Crossed Laterality** *Page* 37, **Dyslexia** *Page* 62, **Left-Handed Children** *Page* 132

What makes your child clumsy? The causes may be physical (see sections on **Crossed Laterality** and **Left-Handed Children**). They may be emotional. Perhaps, he lacks confidence in himself, or is never allowed to do anything for himself or (when he is) he is told: 'You'll make a mess of it.' Remarks such as, 'Don't drop it' and, 'Here, let me do that for you', especially when said in an anxious, or impatient, way are *not* going to build up your child's feelings of competence, nor improve his general motor coordination. Clumsy children need a lot of patience if they are going to have faith in themselves. When you're in a hurry (and with young children you usually are) and the child offers to help in the kitchen, or when he is trying to fasten his own shoe-laces, the temptation is to say, 'Let me do that. I'll be quicker.' You may be, but you're taking away a chance for the child to learn vital skills and to enhance his hand-eye coordination and manual dexterity.

Some children are naturally graceful (I have one of them). Other children are all fingers and thumbs, hopeless at games, butter-fingered (I have one of those too). It's no good your nagging at clumsy children; they need encouragement and plenty of opportunity to learn for themselves by trial and error. Practice is important. It's useful for a young child to undress (and, later) dress himself – even though he puts a vest on inside out or a shoe on the wrong foot. He gets a tremendous sense of achievement from bringing his potty to you, turning the pages of a book, eating with a fork and spoon, washing himself and helping you with the cooking and cleaning. So, let him. It may be quicker if you do it, but what's the point of saving time if your child never learns to do anything for himself?

From the point of view of your child's motor coordination you should think of two main areas of development: *large motor movements* (walking, running, hopping, skipping, and even painting with a large paint brush help to develop these); *finger*

33

movements and eye-hand coordination (sewing, knitting, cutting out, playing with Plasticine, cutting and sticking, mosaics, jig-saw puzzles, playing with blocks and drawing are all useful here). I think that children like to do 'real things' (such as make some cakes, or help to polish a table) as well as play with toys. Let your child help you when he's young, and he'll have more chance of being coordinated when he's older.

Your young child should be encouraged to do up (or undo) his own buttons, knot his tie, help you to lay the table. Older children should learn to swim, to ride a bike, to play a musical instrument such as the piano or recorder, to crochet, to use the sewing machine, to prepare (and serve) a meal. These skills help the clumsy child's coordination as well as building up his self-esteem. With clumsy children, too, a golden rule is: *make the most of the great outdoors.* The local park, the swings, a nearby field – these are the places where children can learn, by their own efforts, to balance, to control their bodies, or to throw and catch a ball. All skills which are vital to a growing child.

Your child may be one of those tall angular children who are for ever falling over (simply because their centre of gravity is so high and they find it difficult to keep their base and stay on their feet). Curiously, once these children have passed through their awkward stage, they can be extremely graceful. Perhaps you could encourage your child to join a gymnastics club (there are over two million youngsters who partake in gymnastics in this country and enjoy it at every level, from rudimentary to highly skilled). Or, you could see if your child would like to go to a dancing class (ballet lessons are very popular with some youngsters) or join a local sports club. There are many 'clumsy' children who, with a bit of encouragement, have gained a great deal of pleasure (and, sometimes, have excelled) in activities such as these.

Remember, though, the simple things. Speak to your child in a warm, unhurried way. Show confidence in him. Show him plenty of affection. Clumsy children will exasperate us from time to time but nobody should be able to say that we don't care about them, or that we won't do everything within our power to help them to overcome their disability.

Two useful games to play with clumsy children are 'Simon Says' and (if you have the energy) the 'Hokey-Cokey'. For older children Scottish dancing (and ballroom dancing, which is making a come-back with the young) help children to gain control of their own bodies and to take a pride in the mastery of fairly intricate movements. It's a question of attitude. If *you* have confidence in your child's abilities, he will quickly gain confidence in himself. If you say things like, 'Oh, for goodness sake, let me do it', he'll just as quickly lose confidence in himself.

Remember, to help a clumsy child, you must:

Avoid calling him 'ham-fisted'. If you call him names, he'll live up to them.

Encourage him to do things for himself and to have a go at new manual skills. Don't put him off, or do the job for him or he'll never learn to cope.

Avoid scoffing at him (or punishing him). It's not his fault he's clumsy. You're there to help, not make things worse.

Avoid making the child an outsider. Encourage him to take up as many social pursuits as he can.

Give your child lots of affection. He'll feel, sometimes, just as annoyed and frustrated as you. That's when he'll want, not criticism, but your love and reassurance.

If your child is extremely clumsy and the clumsiness persists despite everything you do, have a word with your family doctor about it.

Corporal Punishment

In my view it does no harm to smack a young child occasionally when the child is very naughty, or has done something dangerous, or persists in bad behaviour. It's better to chastise, and forget, rather than store chronic resentment or have a prolonged shouting match. A quick smack may be the answer to a particular piece of bad behaviour. The young child may learn not to do that kind of thing again and, equally important, the parent may feel better for having given expression to his or her righteous anger (see section on **Anger**). A child who persists in touching electric light fittings may need (if verbal warnings fail) a short, sharp physical rebuke. Children will accept punishment if it's fair.

Having said that, let me stress that smacking as a way of life or as a means of chastising older children is doomed to failure. I haven't smacked any of my own children for years. This isn't because, in order to reach them, I'd have to stand on a chair. It's mainly because older children are capable of reason; to hit them (especially teenagers) is very undignified. It's also because, if you overdo smacking, smack too much and too often, it simply loses its effectiveness and makes children despise you.

Years ago, my five-year-old son broke a fret-saw that I was doing a job with (he'd followed me up a ladder, stepped on the saw, and it had snapped). I was extremely angry, smacked the boy and sent him upstairs. When I told a group of Health Visitors about this incident they were very shocked. Yet, he came back downstairs after ten minutes (he could time, even at that age, how long it would take me to calm down), he said, 'Sorry, dad,' and the whole incident was forgotten. Three things emerge: first, the smacking incident has not scarred him, psychologically, for life; second, I wouldn't hit my boy now – he is four inches taller than me for a start; and third, at seventeen, any form of physical punishment would be bizarrely inappropriate. He is, I hope, now my friend and we don't hit friends.

My advice, therefore, is very straightforward: smack if you must, but don't overdo it. It's to be kept as a last resort: for when you are very angry or for when you're child is very naughty. When you have smacked your child, forgive and forget. *What counts is that the child feels that you've smacked him out of love, and because you care about him.* Children would rather be smacked (providing that the smacking is justified) than have lasting resentment, or rejection. They would rather have a parent who is capable of smacking them (but as a last resort) than have a parent who will, however far they go, let them do exactly as they like. I stopped smacking my own children when they had reached the age of about seven; after this, I felt, an appeal to reason (or some other form of punishment such as loss of pocket money or doing 'extra duty' in the house) was more appropriate. I can't say too strongly that if you want (as I want) children to grow up as reasonable human beings, and good friends, the less you resort to physical punishment the better.

You may agree with me that parents have a right to smack (within reason) their own children but what about corporal punishment in schools? Do teachers have the right to act *in loco parentis* (i.e. in place of the parents) and smack, or cane, children for misdemeanours in the classroom? Let me be honest. I would be most annoyed if any of my children were caned in school without my prior approval. I'd want to know exactly *why* it was necessary to resort to physical punishment. I would prefer that some other sort of punishment were used (such as lines, detention, telling off, foregoing of privileges) rather than caning. Britain and Eire are, at the time of writing, the only countries in Europe which permit the caning of children in schools. Currently, *no* Education Authority in England and Wales has banned the use of the cane in schools: only the Inner London Education Authority has banned its use in *primary* schools. Teachers, for the most part, favour the use of the cane, especially in secondary schools, and mostly as a last resort. There are some teachers (e.g. members of STOPP, the Society of Teachers Opposed to Physical Punishment) who don't see the use of the cane in schools as serving any useful purpose.

What are you, as a parent, to make of all this? If you wish to be more aware of the arguments for and against the use of the cane in schools you should read *Corporal Punishment, a discussion paper written by Peter Wilby for the UK Association for the International Year of the Child (obtainable from 85 Whitehall, London SW1, or from your local library)*. Also, *Where* – the education magazine for parents – discusses this topic frequently and back copies are available from the Advisory Centre for Education (ACE), 18 Victoria Park Square, Bethnal Green, London E1 9PB.

My advice to parents on corporal punishment can be brief. It is that you:

Limit smacking to those occasions when *you* are very frustrated or *your child* has annoyed you intensely.

Have a 'count-down' system ('Mummy's going to count to ten. If you don't stop, you'll be smacked.') If you threaten, do it, but do give them some early warning of your wrath.

Don't hit too hard. A short, sharp smack is sufficient to let them know you're really angry.

With schools, make sure you know what's going on. Ask the school what their policy on corporal punishment is.

Talk to children about why you were (or are) angry *and* about what you will allow and won't allow. It's no use smacking them if you haven't made clear what the rules are.

As children grow older treat them with dignity as you would a reliable friend. They'll respond. If children live with aggression, they learn to be aggressive. If children live with reason, they learn to be reasonable.

Crossed-Laterality
See also **Clumsiness** *Page* 33, **Dyslexia** *Page* 62, **Left-Handed Children** *Page* 132

A 'crossed-lateral' is somebody who is left-handed and right-eyed, or right-handed and left-eyed. I'm crossed lateral myself: I use my right hand but look through a telescope with my left eye.

It is very easy to find out whether your child is crossed-lateral. Simply ask him to peep through a hole in a piece of paper (or look through the 'funnel' of a rolled up newspaper). For predominance of handedness, ask your child to do the following ten tasks: *write, throw a ball, catch a ball, screw in a screw, hammer in a nail, brush his hair, clean his teeth, thread a needle, cut with scissors and pretend to saw a log.* Count up the number of jobs your child does with his right and left hand and multiply both by ten. This gives you the percentage handedness. I am one hundred per cent right-handed. My wife, who is ambidextrous (i.e. uses both hands) is forty per cent left-handed.

A few words of warning, though. Most children are not sure which hand to use, up to the age of about four years. About the time they go to school, left- or right-handedness should be much more obvious. It would be silly to worry about a young infant using both the right and left hand. *Crossed-laterality is very common.* I estimate that (as with left-handedness) crossed-laterality is present in about ten per cent of the general population. It does not necessarily mean that your child will have reading difficulties: I was a good reader when I was five and my son (who is crossed-lateral) learned to read at the age of four.

What you may find is that your child is clumsy, or he may find (if he has a handicap such as poor hearing or imperfect vision) that crossed-laterality is an extra burden. He may get his directions wrong, or he may tend to read from right to left instead of the other way around. The thing you should do is try to build up your child's confidence in himself. It is best to talk to him in a calm, unhurried manner and make sure that he knows that you, at least, have faith in his ability. If he's clumsy *don't* say, 'You'll drop it,' or, 'Here, let me do that.' Otherwise, you'll lower, rather than boost, his self-esteem.

What else can you do, in a practical way, to help the child? The activities I suggest are equally useful for young children who are clumsy, awkward, or accident-prone. What we have to teach them is left-right orientation and hand-eye coordination. To do this, you can tie a coloured ribbon to the child's left wrist, or a piece of wool to a left hand finger. 'That,' you emphasize, 'is your left. We look at the page from that side.' The child can learn, 'My heart is on the left,' or, 'I write with my right hand' (if he does!). Numbers from one to ten, the days of the week, months of the year (in fact, any sequences) may have to be taught rather than left to chance. The concepts of 'before' and 'after', 'above' and 'below' should be carefully explained.

Playing dominoes, learning to knit, sew and crochet are very useful and doing jig-saw puzzles (to develop spatial awareness) is helpful. The kind of puzzle books sold in Woolworths contain plenty of ideas to help hand-eye coordination. A series of pictures, representing a time sequence, can be given to the child: such as a house being built, a child getting up in the morning, a dog stealing some sausages from a butcher's shop. Your child has to put the pictures in order, from left to right.

Children can be asked to continue a pattern of letters or dots and dashes, or to repeat sentences (or number sequences) from memory. This helps them, again, to remember sequences of letters, words and numbers. When reading, a coloured piece of wool down the left hand side of the page will remind the child where to start and a reading card is useful since this presents the child with one line at a time, rather than the whole page. For general coordination any activity that uses *both* sides of the body at the same time such as riding a bicycle or learning to swim is extremely helpful and provide skills which, when mastered, help to build up your child's confidence.

For young children climbing stairs, hopping, kicking a ball, skipping and climbing build up a feeling in the child that he is in control of his body. Finer hand movements can be developed through painting, cutting with scissors, drawing around templates, playing any games which involve running about and throwing, kicking or catching a ball.

If you find out that your child is cross-lateral, *don't* worry about it. If you want to help your child, don't shout at him for his clumsiness. Take him to the swings in the local park, play football with him (or her) and do some of the exercises I have suggested (remember, don't over-do it: twenty minutes at a time is quite enough). That's much better than criticizing him, or suggesting by negative comments that he is destined to be a life-long member of the awkward squad. Crossed-laterality presents no difficulty where it is treated with sympathy and common sense.

Cruel Children

When young children pull the legs off a daddy-longlegs, or the wings off a fly, are they being cruel? Or just curious? There is a difference between curiosity, and aggression, and cruelty. With cruelty there is an element of premeditation or of sheer delight in seeing somebody suffering. Children, as all parents know, can be cruel. They can be thoughtless, too outspoken, hurt others by being spiteful or malevolent. These outbursts of cruelty may be sparked off by a strong-willed and rather vindictive child in the group or by sheer and utter dislike of somebody (usually a weak and vulnerable member of the group). Yet for a child to be consistently, habitually cruel to others weaker than himself suggests to me that the child is unhappy. I do not feel that a happy child, brought up in a loving home, would get a great deal of fun or delight in being cruel to another child, or children, day-in, day-out.

Fear, hatred and jealousy are three emotions aroused by neglect and harsh treatment. The cruel child – or the cruel adult – projects his hatred and his resentment at those who have harmed him on to some innocent person. He may attack, either verbally or physically, somebody who has done him no harm at all. Or he may harm animals or insects; *not* because he is curious about their reactions but because he simply wants to see them hurt and suffer. Cruel children may have been given little chance to express their quite natural aggression as infants. Or their desire to hurt living things may spring from a very strong hatred of 'authority' (i.e. anybody who is in charge or who gives orders). Sometimes, if parents punish a child for playing with his sex organs or are themselves disgusted by sex, the child learns to value destruction rather than creation, death rather than life, hatred rather than love. The child has a real capacity for hatred because what he hates is other people who remind him of his own weaknesses: the things he has been taught to repress. His own nasty side is projected on to an innocent stranger (there is nothing unusual about this since we are all quite capable of taking an instant dislike to somebody or having an irrational dislike of certain people. What we do is to project the nasty side of ourselves on to them and claim that, 'there's something about them I can't abide.').

The solution to cruelty in children is, simply, love. With sympathetic handling by the parents, and by building up the child's self-confidence (through words of praise and guiding the child's energy into interesting and productive hobbies and leisure pursuits) the child is guided back to self-love. No child who loves himself – as no adult who loves himself – would wish to be cruel to another human being. Why should he be? If you want your child to avoid being cruel to others you must remember that love – the antidote to hatred and cruelty – has to be learned. It is parents, in this matter, who are the child's first teachers.

Dark – Fear of the

It is not surprising that fear of the dark is quite common amongst young children – it's not unknown amongst adults. I wouldn't like to spend an hour in a pitch-black cellar, or alone in a wood at night. It's not only the dark that frightens us but the shadows, strange noises, and the association of darkness with mystery, danger, the unknown, the sinister and the downright nasty. In films, many of the more gory incidents happen in the dark. Is it any wonder that, with our fantasies fed on horror films, vampires and murder stories, many of us are scared stiff of the dark? Actually, the dark is neutral and no more sinister than the light. There is no reason why children should be afraid of the dark if we handle their worries with sympathy and understanding, plus a certain amount of commonsense.

What happens if your child does develop a fear of the dark? Is there anything you can do to help him overcome this fear? What you mustn't do is say things like: 'There, darling, you're not really afraid.' The fact is he is afraid (even terrified) and he'll need more practical help than that. Do try to reassure him by saying something along the lines of: 'Yes, you are afraid but we'll soon put things right.' Your calm and matter-of-fact manner is more important than your words. Don't argue with him, or tell him not to be so silly or say that his older brother or sister isn't afraid of the dark. That's nothing to do with it. He has learned to be afraid and what has been learned can be unlearned – providing you go about it the right way. The main thing, at the beginning, is to appreciate the reality (and the depth) of the child's fears; having said that, the best way to deal with them is to be sensible and brisk.

Down to practicalities. If your child cries in the night one parent should, of course, go to comfort him. Don't, however, make a long, loving, cuddling or chatting session out of it: if you do this you're simply rewarding the child (very handsomely) for crying. Just a few words of reassurance, and tuck the child in. Even more important than not cuddling the child too long is that *you mustn't turn on the light. Don't* go into his bedroom, switch on the light, then give him a cuddle. If you do this he'll associate the light with your presence (and lovely cuddles) and the dark with your absence (and, perhaps, feeling lonely). When you've comforted him (fairly briskly, remember) say: 'I'm going back to bed now,' or, 'I'm going downstairs.' If you are still up, let the child hear you moving about, or leave the television set on (but not too loudly!) so that, in the dark, he'll hear lots of familiar, comforting noises and know that although he's in the dark, all's well with the world.

If you wish you can leave a very dim electric light on in his bedroom. Alternatively, you can leave the landing light on (and his bedroom door slightly ajar) or – with older children – give them a bedside lamp which they can switch on if they wish. You can switch it off when the child is asleep but (and this is the important point) the child can switch it back on if he wishes. *Because the situation is under the child's control there is no cause for panic reactions if he wakes up in the dark* and after a while, especially if you leave the lamp a couple of feet away from the bed so that he has to sit up to switch it off or even a yard or more away so that he has to climb out of bed to switch it off, he'll soon become fed up of getting up and will probably sleep, reassured by the fact that he can switch the light on if he wants to.

The main things to remember about fear of the dark are:

Cut out Late Night Horror Movies, scary stories and frightening TV shows. Obviously, a child who has learned to be afraid of the dark isn't going to be helped by this kind of thing.

Give your child the Good Treatment in the day. Let her do some jobs for you, be a little bit extra sympathetic and make sure she plays with other children and, in her social life generally, lives as normal a life as possible.

Never shout, bully, threaten or bluster. This won't cure your child's fear of the dark.

Be brisk and sensible but let the child talk about his fears. The best antidote is some sympathy plus a practical, down-to-earth attitude.

Daydreaming
See also **Shyness** *Page* 206, **Walter Mitty Complex** *Page* 261

We can daydream for the sheer pleasure of it. Adults think of marvellous things that might happen to them: they dream of winning the pools, of gaining promotion at work, of meeting the perfect lover. Children dream of owning a lemonade factory, adolescents dream of love (and sex). Daydreaming is a useful method of escaping from harsh reality and refashioning the world nearer to our hearts' desire. 'Sometimes I just sits and thinks,' my old granny used to say. 'Sometimes I just sits.' Our fantasies offer some compensation for a demanding world and a refuge into which we may retreat when things go against us.

Adults use fantasy to deal with stressful, unpleasant, unfamiliar circumstances; they also use it when things have gone wrong. Say you have been for an interview for a job you badly wanted; you make a mess of it all, giving the wrong answers and wearing the wrong clothes. Probably, after the event, you'll think of what you might have done, of what you might have said. The French call this mental post-mortem *pensées d'escalier* which means 'thoughts on the staircase' – what you think about when you're coming downstairs, too late, after the event. We can fantasize before an event too: often, for example, the thought of going to the dentist is worse than the reality. There are times when our thoughts about an event to come simply outmatch the reality and we're terribly disappointed. Daydreaming seems to be almost universal: a natural accompaniment to the world of deeds. One young woman told me that she never enjoyed her annual holiday very much; what she did like was thinking about it for months and months beforehand, and thinking of what might have been when she got back!

It's worth pointing out that many outstanding writers, painters and scientists have been daydreamers. Archimedes, Galileo and Einstein would never have made their great discoveries if they hadn't been prone to reveries. Newton, we're told, was sitting under a tree (no doubt, daydreaming) when the apple fell on his head. It is at this level, just below the level of awareness, that much creative thought takes place. After all, eminent novelists do no more than put their daydreams into words and sell them.

The snag with daydreaming in both children and adults is that it may become too much of an escape from the world of reality (see **Walter Mitty Complex**). A child may fantasize too much, become the 'misunderstood hero' (or heroine) who cannot cope with reality and who uses the escape-route of daydreams to get away from the demands of the real world. Fantasy, here, compensates for lack of achievement and bolsters the child's self-esteem by giving him in his mind the central role in the play, rather than a walk-on part in which he makes a mess of his lines which is nearer the facts. The border between fantasy and reality can become blurred and the child may seek less and less contact with peers and adults, preferring his own make-believe world to the demands of everyday life.

Teenagers, in particular, are prone to daydreaming. Many girls daydream of romance, of becoming famous, or rich, or visiting some exotic country. Teenage boys daydream about adventure, being madly attractive to the opposite sex, fame, wealth, passing their exams at school with flying colours. It is when daydreams interfere with work (including school), with friendships and with relationships within the family, or prevent the child from making real contact with members of the opposite sex that they become cause for concern. Can the child cope with life and achieve results roughly in line with his ability level? If the answer is yes, I don't think we should fret too much about his daydreaming. If the answer is no, we may have to think of ways of making him less morose, thoughtful, withdrawn and reluctant to make contact with others.

It's exactly the same with reading. A lot of mothers say to me, of their child: 'He's always got his head stuck in a book, reads one after the other. Is it normal?' I would say that if the child uses reading as an excuse for not making contact with other children, or adults, then perhaps we ought to do something about it. As with daydreaming, it's normal, but it depends what else the child does. If the answer is 'very little' then we should try to bring the child back a little more into the real world.

What can you do, as a parent, if you think that your child does daydream too much? I suggest that you:

Praise your child for his achievements and tell him that you love him for who he is, not what he achieves. If you love him in the real world, and show it, he won't have to seek love, attention and praise in some fantasy world.

Do something with the child, some shared activity. It could be anything from going on a walk together, collecting stamps to doing jobs around the house, providing that it gives you an opportunity to chat, to get to know each other, and where you can tell the child something of your own dreams and ambitions. This sharing with the parents is the first step towards sharing with other adults and peers: it helps the child to learn that all of us have our dreams, hopes and disappointments. It also helps to bring him out of his shell by giving him somebody to talk to see **Shy Children**). And don't forget to listen to the child. Many children become dreamers because *nobody* ever listens to them.

Encourage him to join a club, a society at school, or the scouts, or guides or some other youth movement. Get him out of the habit of staying in the house (whether to read, or just sit and think).

Encourage him to 'have a go'. Getting to know people is painful for many of us. Tell him that everybody has hopes, fears, dreams and disappointments. The idea is to bounce back when you've been disappointed, live to fight another day; not to take flight to a world of dreams where you can opt out of the battle.

If your child persistently daydreams do have his hearing checked. This can be done at the local health clinic via the family doctor. A few children, in my experience, simply can't hear what is going on around them.

Just one more point about daydreaming. I'm sometimes asked how a parent can tell the difference between a daydream (a reverie) and petit-mal (especially as all the children have a 'miles away' look). The child who is merely daydreaming can be 'snapped out' of his reverie at once; the petit-mal child cannot be 'brought back' immediately to his surroundings. If your child loses consciousness, goes off into a different world, and then carries on as though nothing had happened (and this kind of thing happens several times a day) you should ask the family doctor for advice.

Death in the Family
See section on **Bereavement** *Page* 17

Defiance
See also **Tantrums** *Page* 228, **Uncooperativeness** *Page* 245

I met a very old lady at a party who told me about the very first time that she defied her mother. They were in a shop buying knickers and the mother selected two or three pairs and said to her daughter: 'Go to the counter and pay for these.' The daughter shouted: 'No, I won't. I want to choose my own knickers.' (Which she did.) I asked the senior citizen how old she was when all this happened. 'Thirty-three,' she replied.

These days, defiance usually sets in earlier. Most parents have had to deal with a defiant toddler, or a stroppy eleven-year-old; many parents despair over recalcitrant, sullen teenagers. It's an unusual mother (or father) who hasn't had to deal with a defiant child at some time or other. Like most things, there's a right way of doing it and a wrong way.

The first thing to remember if you're faced by a defiant child is not to become too emotional about the whole thing – it doesn't help. If you go to see your doctor (or dentist, or bank manager) you don't expect him to move about the room, slap his forehead in dismay and weep copious tears as you tell him your problem. What you want is for him to do something about it or suggest something sensible in the way of a solution.

It's exactly the same with your child, confronting you as a parent. He's trying it on, waiting to see what sort of reaction his defiance is going to evoke. Keep calm, be brisk, avoid doing an impromptu Indian war dance or reacting to the child's anger with even greater anger on your part or (worse) total loss of control.

What options are open to you when your child *is* going through a defiant stage? Let's take a particular instance – a toddler who, wearing new shoes and clean socks, decides to walk in some mud and stands there, filthy, refusing to come out of it. Your possible strategies are as follows:

> *Sweet Reasonableness.* 'Not in your new shoes, darling. Tomorrow you can wear your Wellies and play in the mud.' (This was the approach taken by the mother I observed. However, since the child's shoes and socks were already muddy it may not strike the child as reasonable.)
>
> *Diversion.* 'What a lovely time you're having but come over here on the grass now and let's look for worms/flowers/tiny creatures together.'
>
> *A Direct Order.* 'Get out of that mud AT ONCE.'
>
> *Physical Punishment.* The child is smacked and told not to play in the mud again.
>
> *Ignoring him*, either through exhaustion, or because you've decided that you just can't put up with the hassle of arguing with the child.

Whichever approach you use I think you should be consistent: it's no good being reasonable and then shouting at the child. It's even less useful to ignore him, then smack him afterwards, and then try to be reasonable. Decide what you aim to do about it and make sure your child knows what you want. If he knows you're expecting to be obeyed, he'll probably obey you. If you're frightened of his defiance (or just too tired to deal with it) he'll cotton on that he can boss you about and make your life a misery *and* get his own way whenever he wants to (see section on **Obedience**).

With a toddler or young child it's a good idea to be brisk ('Put your blue coat on, darling. We're going to the shops,' and not, 'Do you want to come to the shops? Which coat would you like to put on?'). Don't be surprised if your two- or three-year-old goes through a stage of defiance (most of them do) but, certainly, don't be daunted by it, and don't over-react when he does try it on. (*Child:* 'I'm *not* going to the shops.' *Mother:* 'You're strong. You can carry the bag. Remind me to get some flour so we can make a cake together this afternoon.' She puts the child's coat on and whisks him away cutting out any further discussion.) As in so many things, it's your manner and attitude (business-like, no-nonsense) that's going to avoid a confrontation.

46

Older children should be given plenty of opportunity to choose for themselves: if you give your child freedom of choice you show that you respect his individuality, and you avoid making too many demands on the child (if these are unreasonable your child will, sooner or later, defy you). Let him make the choices, as much as possible: 'Do you want to stay in or come to Aunt Freda's with me?'. When you come around to those situations where he has to do something you can still give him the illusion of choice: 'Do you want to wash to dishes, dry them, or vacuum the carpet?'. The more reasonable you are at this stage, the less you have to resort to bribes or punishment in the face of defiance, the less likely you are to run into trouble at the awkward teenage stage. Just a word about punishment. No 'over-kill'. If you are defied, give your child a 'dirty job' to do (and see that he does it), cut his pocket money for a couple of weeks but *don't* stop him going to the boys' club or playing football on Saturday. To a child, a punishment like this (besides breaking his heart) can appear totally unfair and make him more defiant since, as far as he's concerned, the worst that can happen has already happened.

With teenagers, rebellion is to be expected now and again. They'll want more than you ever had as a teenager – new clothes, all-night parties, going out instead of doing homework – and, often, they'll appear to you as unreasonable and defiant in insisting on their 'rights' (i.e. what they say all their friends have, or do). Teenagers are obsessed with fairness, any real (or imaginary) injustice, slight or sarcasm hurts them deeply. What they complain of most, in disputes with parents, is not being listened to and nobody understanding their point of view. This is the inevitable generation gap but it has to be crossed somehow.

I must be honest and say that, as far as teenagers are concerned, sanctions and punishment don't work very well. You *can* say in the face of defiance: 'OK no new shoes for you,' or, 'Stay in the rest of the week.' However, what this does in most cases is build up resentment. A much better approach is to express your anger, make your point, and (when things have cooled down) resort to reason. If you do something, insist on something, you should explain your reasons. Tell them to use the telephone less and keep calls brief. You can put a lock on the phone but you should say why. ('I can't afford all those expensive calls. So this is to remind you that I'm the one that's paying.') Don't forget to reward your teenager (with a smile, or a word of praise) when he's cooperative, and don't forget that you should treat him as a *good* person: he'll probably respond

47

to that more than treating him as a villain or as a mentally-retarded human being. Let them choose, push the responsibility for choice on to them, discuss issues, respect their opinions, bring them into your family councils (about money, the cost of living, who mows the lawn). If you treat them as adults they'll respond as adults; if you treat them like two-year-olds they'll react like two-year-olds with all the tantrums and defiance of the immature and frustrated. I wish I could tell you, in the face of a defiant teenager, that punishment works. It doesn't. Calmness, reason and a sense of humour works better. What we call 'greater experience' is really our own track record of failure, and glosses over the fact that we defied our parents, too, only we were much more sneaky about it. Nobody, with teenagers, should expect defiance in a situation where everybody is working together, and they've all made up the rules, over the tea-table, together. We defy tyrants. None of us defy our friends – there isn't any point.

Dependency
(For Parents)

Bringing up a young child can be bliss; it can also be hell. You may have had, before the baby came along, an interesting job, plenty of outside interests: independence, freedom. Suddenly, you find that there's a small, helpless human being who needs you constantly. You may find being a mother excruciatingly hard work – and with less thanks than a woman would get for working fewer hours in an office or factory. Motherhood *is* exhausting. Children are totally dependent upon the mother (or mother-substitute) for the first six months of their lives; they need constant contact with mother during the first five years; even as teenagers, they can be demanding. Motherhood, or fatherhood, is not something to be entered into lightly! Your tiny baby is dependent on you so what is the best way of coping?

Talking with other mothers and fathers about how parenthood affects you is a good first step. Don't use your baby as an excuse to cut yourself off from the world; use your relationship with the baby as a means of making new friends. Meet at the clinic, in the park, at the shops. Don't keep your problems to yourself but talk and share them whenever and wherever you can. You'll find it very reassuring to discover that lots of people have exactly the same worries about the baby – and doubts about themselves – as you do.

If there isn't one in your neighbourhood why not organize a

Mother and Baby (or Mother and Toddler) group? Call it a Cuppa Club: get together, bring the children along and talk. It's better, believe me, to chat in this way than take valium for your shattered nerves. You could join the National Housewives Register (write to National Organizer, South Hill, Cross Lanes, Chalfont St Peter, Bucks. SL9 0LU or find out the telephone number of your local branch secretary from the library). *Whatever you do get out of the house and meet other people.* The way to encourage independence is to be outgoing and independent yourself. Don't let you and the infant lean on each other like two broken pillars. It is tough, it is hard work, but it's the same (or similar) for everybody and that has to be some sort of consolation!

The long-term aim with your child is simply to encourage him to be a real person and to enable him, when the time comes, to fly away from the family nest and to make his way in the world. You must give him lots of love in the first year, and continue to show him lots of affection until he goes to school. Love is like petrol to the young child: it fuels his journey through life and there's no substitute for a 'full tank' as he sets off.

When your child reaches the peak age for clinging behaviour (during his second year) expect it but don't do everything for him. He'll cling, wanting to be near you and be given approval and attention. Give him as much attention as you can but encourage him to have a go and do things for himself, experiment with this and that, so that he has a chance to learn more skills. Toddlers *are* demanding and some mothers have been known to iron in the play pen so that the baby can't get at them. He'll need you a lot but he won't need you, I hope, every second of the day.

Do get a babysitter and go out occasionally. If you have the same babysitter regularly the child will know and accept him or her. Motherhood shouldn't be matyrdom: you are allowed to go off occasionally and enjoy yourself. What the child wants is a safe base. He'll accept the pattern you lay down. If you are there most of the time and he senses that you are happy, he'll be happy. If you do have to go away for any length of time, tell your child. If you go into hospital, make sure your child visits – each day if possible. (The same applies if *he* goes into hospital. A day is a long time in the life of a child. A week can be an eternity.) Luckily, most hospitals these days encourage visiting; some have facilities for the mother to stay overnight with the child. (If your child does have to have a spell in hospital you may think it worthwhile to contact the National Association for the Welfare of Children in Hospital (NAWCH), 7 Exeter Street, London SE1; telephone: 01-261 1738.)

As your child reaches the age of three make arrangements for him to attend a playgroup (see section on the **Under-Fives).** You'll love him more if you aren't always with him, and if he isn't always clinging to your skirt or asking, 'What are we going to do next?' Besides, playgroups are a good preparation for the trauma of going to school when he – at last – reaches the age of five. (I'm told that one little boy, on his first day at infants' school asked, his mother outside the gates: 'How long do I have to stay here?' His mother told him two years. 'Don't forget to collect me,' said the boy, forlornly.)

Encourage your child to be adventurous, and to explore. Don't get into the habit of saying, 'Don't do that', 'Not on the swings, darling.' Children are tough and a few bumps and scratches won't hurt them. Remember that the romantic idea of love ('I can't live without you') is both destructive and stultifying. Your child may be dependent upon you – both financially and, to some extent, emotionally – until his late teens. You simply won't have the energy to cope with being everything he wants – and pandering to his every need. You'll need a little bit of space to do your own thing. So do it, right from the word go. Get a carry cot, take the baby with you, live your life and he'll live his quite happily alongside you. You have lots of things to give to each other so don't make the child an excuse for you becoming frowsy, uninteresting and a cabbage.

If you want a clingy child the thing to do is stand around by yourself, being depressed. If you want an outgoing, independent child, you should make friends and be out-going (literally) yourself. It's much better than that two-pillar arrangement. Who wants somebody leaning on them the whole time? Your child can be the gateway to the world, or he can be a prison. It's up to you.

Depression
(For Parents)
See also **Zap – How Not to Lose it in the Presence of Children** *Page* 274

Depression (whether long-term or short-term) is not a very pleasant experience. Various mothers have described it to me as: 'like walking through a dark tunnel with no light at the end'; 'having Monday morning blues every day of the week'; 'like having rising damp of the soul'. If you're depressed, you probably feel helpless, inadequate and (worst of all) that you're a person of little

50

worth, with very little going for you. Women suffer from depression twice as much as men but it's worth remembering that men *do* suffer from depression and, when we consider solutions, we have to bear them in mind too.

The sort of things that *can* make a woman feel 'down' are: *the birth of her baby* (post-natal depression can consist of a brief attack shortly after the baby is born or longer spells during the baby's first year); *being cooped up all day with young children* (the incidence of depression is highest amongst women with children under the age of six); *having a husband she cannot talk to or confide her troubles to* and *having little opportunity for contact with the outside world* – unlike those mothers who have part-time or full-time jobs.

If you're a woman, and depressed, you're likely to find difficulty in running your home and you may become erratic in your handling of the children, veering between being over-strict and over-indulgent. The children (or child) will get on your nerves; you won't feel like doing the housework; you'll have a desperate need for social contact and a break from the children but you probably won't have the energy to go out and make new friends, or find a childminder. If you live in a small house, a flat, where space is very limited you'll probably feel that the children are on top of you the whole time. Sometimes, you may feel angry, hostile and rejecting of your children or child. It's as though you've lost all your confidence in yourself as a mother (or father) and this is, believe me, a nasty feeling. Although it's an awful thing to say, we are, all of us, quite capable of battering our own children when we feel really hopeless and helpless.

What to do? Let me say, right away, that I believe that the answer to depression lies in *friendship* rather than in tranquillizers or in any kind of pills. *It is important, if you're depressed, to go and see your family doctor; he may give you pills and these may be of help to you.* This, however, is a short-term solution. The real answer to your problem lies in having the courage to make contact with other people in the community who can offer you practical help, a chance to have a chat about your problems (and you're *not* alone: thousands of young mothers do get depressed and feel terribly lonely and isolated) and a chance to bring back your feelings of self-esteem.

Down to practicalities. What steps can you take to contact other parents, other organizations, in the community who may be able to help you? I suggest that you get in touch with one of the following:

Your local *Mother and Toddler Group* You can find out where the group meets by asking the health visitor, or ringing the department of social services. Alternatively, get in touch with your local church, or pre-school playgroup or your local library, citizen's advice bureau, or health clinic: any one of these should be able to help you.

A registered child-minder Social service departments have a list of these. Remember, though, that child-minders charge to look after your child (at the time of writing the going rate, on average, is about 40p an hour).

A local Woman's Group/Women's Switchboard where women can meet or talk to each other is helpful to a great many young mums. If you only make *one* friend at a group like this, you're a hundred per cent better off. If there isn't a group like this in your area why not get out a duplicated letter, push them through letter-boxes, and find out if there is anybody else interested in starting one up.

The National Childbirth Trust are building up a network of support for mums suffering from 'baby-blues' or that cooped-up feeling. Counsellors can be contacted by telephone, by day or night, and will provide practical advice as well as a listening ear. The headquarters of the NCT is 9 Queensborough Terrace, London W2 3TB, from where further information can be obtained.

The local Pre-School Playgroup Started in the early sixties the PPA has given help and support to thousands of mothers; not to mention re-instilling in them a feeling of confidence and competence. Your library (or department of social services) will have a list of local playgroups.

The National Housewives Register If you once saw yourself as an active 'career woman' and now find yourself housebound (and want to meet women in a similar situation to talk to) you should contact your local library for the address of the secretary of the National Housewives Register in your area.

State nurseries Unfortunately, there is a great shortage of nursery places. Nevertheless, if you are a single parent, or have some other special reason (whether in terms of finance or family situation or health) why your child should be given a place in a nursery class, you should go along to the health clinic (or to the local DSS) and give your reasons why you think your child should be given priority.

Gingerbread Groups These provide support to single parents (whether mothers or fathers, divorced, separated or bereaved).

The address of your local Gingerbread Group can be obtained from the library.

If you are depressed you *must* summon up the courage to contact others in the local community: you'll be quite surprised at how many people suffer the same feelings of despair as yourself! It's up to you to go out (I know this is hard) and find people to talk to. You will, believe me, find that listening ear, the understanding that you need. You *aren't* alone.

Men, too, can contribute towards the local playgroup; they can (if they're single parents) join Gingerbread; they can offer to help at the local youth club, join an evening class or (if the children are older) offer to help at the child's school. We have to learn to help each other more. It is community spirit, doing things together to help our children (and ourselves) rather than tablets and pills, which is the real solution to those ghastly, debilitating feelings of depression.

Destructiveness
See also **Aggression** *Page* 3, **Boredom** *Page* 21, **Frustration** *Page* 88

I remember seeing a little boy in the clinic many years ago. He came into the playroom, took hold of a wooden hammer, searched for some dolls, then proceeded to hit the dolls with the hammer. I told him: 'We have some rules here. You can't do that. You'll spoil the dolls and other children won't be able to play with them.' His next move was to take two large cans of powder paint and spill the contents on to the floor. 'We'll go to my room,' I said, where I sat him at my side and gave him some paper and crayons, whilst I chatted with him. If I'd left him to his own devices, in the playroom, he would, no doubt, have reduced the place to a total shambles. That wasn't on. I *wasn't* prepared to accept that level of destructiveness.

Some destructiveness, especially in pre-school children, is to be expected. Children are naturally curious: they want to see how things are made, take them apart, see what's inside. Also, we have to concede that knocking down a sand-castle, or a wooden-brick building, or flattening a tin with a hammer or tearing up paper to make papier-mâché *can* be great fun. There's sensual pleasure in taking a clay animal and rolling it back into a ball; there's muscular pleasure in jumping up and down on a sand-castle;

there's excitement in banging walls with a hammer. For young children, often frustrated in making things, there's an obvious attraction when the child is frustrated, bored or angry in breaking them.

When a child is particularly aggrieved with his parents, or siblings, when he has some hidden resentment, he may turn his spite on to some quite neutral object: he will tear his clothes, deliberately 'scuff' his shoes, break his toys, or spoil his books. Another way of the child dealing with his own, often unconscious, aggressive feelings is to turn the aggression against himself and resort to head-banging, picking his skin, or biting his nails (see **Nail-Biting**). The solution is to give the child a chance to express some of his aggression in a constructive, controlled way: by playing with water, or with finger-paints, or large brush poster-paintings, or clay or Plasticine (see **Messy Play**). *You* set the limits; *you* give your child the materials and tell him what he can and can't do. It is possible to accept that the child has some aggression within him and to give him materials, such as a hammer and nails and some old pieces of wood, to let him express some of those feelings. Your child shouldn't however be allowed to destroy things that you don't want destroyed. That doesn't help him: he merely becomes overwhelmed, and frightened, at the powers of destructiveness within himself.

Conflict within the home – particularly parents who squabble and argue a great deal – can lead to a child being destructive. So can lack of discipline where the child simply doesn't know the limits of acceptable behaviour because he has never been told. A very worn-out and depressed mother (or father) may have a destructive child because mum or dad is too tired or miserable to respond to the child's needs. The youngster, in order to gain a response from the parent, resorts to anti-social behaviour and/or destructiveness merely to gain some attention from the parent. A poor diet, lack of sleep, general ill-health and, last but not least, buying children toys which are unsuitable to their age or just downright boring can all lead to destructiveness. Where you are puzzled about toys for your child do get in touch with the *Toy Libraries* in your area (address at your local public library) who will advise you on suitable toys, taking into account the age and interests of your child.

Most of us have suffered from feelings of destructiveness and most of us know the feeling of satisfaction, relief and inner peace when we turn that potential destructiveness into constructiveness by making something instead of knocking or tearing it down. At any age, children need to be given something constructive and interesting to do. With teenagers we hear a lot, these days, about violence and vandalism. Yet, in our cities we don't provide enough facilities for young people. Can we really be surprised when out of anger and boredom those youngsters turn to vandalism, bizarre dress and hostility towards adults to express their, quite justified, feelings that they, the youngsters, are being ignored and don't really count in our scheme of things?

The main things to remember about destructiveness as it concerns your own child are:

Normal children – especially between the ages of three and four – sometimes behave destructively. Some of it is due to curiosity or an excess of energy; some of it is due to boredom, resentment or frustration.

Set your own limits, and stick to them.

Talk to your child about his anger (see section on **Tantrums**). Say something like: 'You feel very angry. We all feel angry sometimes – even mummy (or daddy).'

Allow the child to be angry with you. Don't allow him to kick you or to smash up the furniture in his anger. If he's furious and destructive put him in the corner until he calms down.

Give your child something constructive to do. Children have a lot of natural energy; it's better that we control the way in which that energy is expressed than let it run riot and turn into destructiveness.

With teenagers, get them to contribute to something. Start up a sports club, a football team, a motor-bike club, a volleyball team or some other activity in your neighbourhood. Self-help is better than complaining. Have a Cuppa Club for parents of teenagers where you can discuss your problems and, more important, how you can help your youngsters.

It is the children, and adults, who feel unloved and ineffective who destroy. The answer to destructiveness in your child is to tell him, often, that you love him and take him to places where he can find a variety of things to do. The child who is interested in creating something, or proud of what he has created, is less likely to have to resort to destruction to make an impact on the world around him.

Differences Between Children in the Same Family
See also **Jealousy** *Page* 125, **Scapegoat Children** *Page* 192, **Sibling Rivalry** *Page* 209

I have three children and they're all different: in looks,

temperament and behaviour. But, then, when you come to think of it, why shouldn't they be? Each person in this world is different, and should be treated as a unique individual. Each of your children was born into a different family; the first is special; the second comes into a family of three; by the time the third comes along the family is very different from the one you started off with! It's a mistake to treat children as though they were the same: they (like you, I hope) grow and develop into people with minds, and qualities, of their own.

'Ah, but,' you say, 'I'd like to love all my children equally.' I'm not sure that you can. There are times when you 'go off' a certain child; we go through awkward patches when nothing we (or they) say or do is right. A case in point is teenage boys: mothers are always complaining to me that they love their teenage sons but they find them difficult to like merely because the lads seem unable to string more than four words together. It's harder to like somebody you can't talk to.

You, like a lot of mothers (or fathers), may worry a great deal over this question of loving children equally. I think the answer is that we love them in different ways. Take babies. Our first, and second, were very cuddly, affectionate babies. Our third was a 'wriggler' who refused to be cuddled. What she wanted (and still does) was *action:* she wasn't, and isn't, into all that sloppy, sentimental stuff. She wants our love but she wants it expressed in a different way from the other two. No good telling *her* you love her; she knows that. She wants you to take her along to the local bowling alley or the gymnasium without any chat. I sometimes think her ideal parent would be a taciturn taxi-driver!

Some children are self-contained and don't seem to need a lot of love. I think these children *do* need love but they may not like it when it is too overtly expressed, either through words, or hugs. Other children are terribly affectionate and like, even when they're older, to be cuddled by parents. One mother told me that she was worried because her twelve-year-old son hugged and kissed her before going to (and coming back from) school. I told her how lucky she was. With our own son, what we get is a grunt and, on good days, the immortal words, 'What's for tea?'

Where we ought to treat children *the same* is in buying them shoes, bicycles or clothes (*and* in taking them to see the dentist or insisting that they have their hair cut). Most children have very acute antennae when it comes to fair play: if we go to a nativity play, or concert, at one child's school then justice decrees that we should attend some functions at our other child's (or children's) school (s). Justice must not only be done but seen to be done.

Love is different. We can show love to one child by cuddling him; the best way to show love to another child would be to have a game of football in the local park. There are myriad ways of showing love: one child we kiss, the other child (a kiss is the last thing *he* wants) will be more likely to love us back if we bake him a chocolate cake. Take teenage boys, again. I took my son (aged sixteen) to school where he and his friends were boarding a coach to take them on the first stage of a school cruise. Only one boy (out of thirty) kissed his mother goodbye. Like that mother of the twelve-year-old I though she was lucky to have a son who wasn't afraid of expressing affection nor of the opinions of his own pals. It takes confidence to kiss your mother in that sort of situation.

Imagine three children at breakfast. Each wants his egg cooked differently: one boiled, one scrambled, one poached. They are (life is hard!) duly served. It's the same with love. The ingredients are the same (care and affection) but they're served up in different ways. I don't believe that treating children alike is the same thing as doing the best possible for each child in the family.

Consider the handicapped (or very sensitive, or physically delicate) child within the family. The handicapped child and the less fortunate child may need an extra ration of love and attention. The other children in the family usually understand this, especially if the child's difficulties are explained to them. 'What do you think of Emma, then?' one five-year-old asked me of his handicapped older sister 'I think she's great,' I told him. 'Good,' he said. 'I was going to kick you if you said you didn't like her.' That's loyalty. He was very protective towards his sister because he understood (however vaguely) something of her problems.

Problems *do* arise. For example, if an older child is not as clever (or attractive) as a younger one a certain amount of unfairness, and resentment, can creep in. You may find that, without wishing to do so, you are paying more attention to one child than another, or that you find it easier to love one child more than another. Don't worry. This happens. Don't compare, but try to treat each child for what he has to offer.

Sometimes, justice is beyond your control. A child goes to a school which an older sibling has attended. 'Why aren't you more like your sister?' the teachers ask, making ridiculous comparisons. Don't you make the same mistake as these professionals who ought to know better. Treat each child as unique and you can't go wrong. Each child has his own gifts; build up his personality upon them.

Here are six musts:

1 *Give each child a special place in your heart.*
2 *Accept that relationships alter as children (and ourselves) grow older.* Some children we despair of as infants grow into delightful young people, and adults.
3 *Encourage children to be themselves,* not pale imitations of somebody else. The best way to do this is to love them for who they are, not what they do, or don't, achieve.
4 *Avoid trying to feel the same for each child.* No child likes to be compared too much; each wants to be loved in his own way, for himself.
5 *Try to have a 'together time' with each child.* I know this is difficult but a regular, small, dose of uninterrupted attention from mum (or dad) works wonders.
6 *Have faith when you 'go off' a child.* It happens to us all. One of my best friends is my eldest daughter. As a child, she reduced me to despair on many occasions.

Disagreements
See also **Aggression** *Page* 3, **Frustration** *Page* 88

Here, I want to talk about squabbles and rows between children (for squabbles between parents see section on **Quarrels**). As with adults, disagreements between children are inevitable. The thing to do is to find some way of resolving them (or avoiding them) before they flare up into nasty, recriminatory scenes and a situation in which your children are constantly arguing and fighting.

Frequent quarrelling amongst your children may mean that they all feel a sense of injustice; each one feels that you favour another child rather than him. Again, it might mean that you don't have any rules for *sharing:* that the children grab at what they can (in the way of toys, food and anything else that's going) simply because they don't trust (rightly or wrongly) that they will get their fair portion of what's going. Children have a very acute sense of justice – what's fair and what isn't – and they look to us parents to see that justice rules. (See section on **Differences Between Children in the Same Family**.) If you buy, for example, new socks for one child you shouldn't be surprised that another wants new socks, too. This may not be possible but, if you explain why (e.g. that you don't have the money that week) the child will understand and lose any lasting resentment, until it's his turn for the 'good treatment'.

Try to set aside half-an-hour, or an hour, each week when one child has your sole attention. This is his time with mum (or dad). Don't let the others muscle in on it, and do talk about that particular child's interests (or worries). Remember, and this is very important, listen to the child. If you can give the child a regular (daily? weekly?) session with you it will save *all* the children fighting for all your attention *all* the time. Also remember to treat your children as individuals and don't compare them. Don't say: 'Mark has made a beautiful job of tidying his room. Why don't you tidy yours?' Just say: 'Your room's untidy. I expect better from you than that.' Each child has different needs but each has an innate sense of fair play. So, appeal to it.

It is possible to learn how to spot what quarrels and disagreements are likely to arise and nip them in the bud. This may be laying down firmly who is going to ride the bike first, and for how long. It may involve who is going to get new clothes (and why). Discuss such matters as pocket money and birthday treats. Make certain that the children are given a chance to say that *they* think that what you are doing is fair. If in doubt ask them: 'What would you do in my place?' It's surprising how scrupulously fair children are when they are given a chance to take decisions themselves. Remember, though, you are the referee in squabbles and, if you have to intervene, make sure your word is final. Don't resort to, 'If you let John push the shopping trolley I'll buy you an ice-cream later.' This is the road to ruin. If you have to pretend to be angry then do so but ensure that what you say goes and your judgement is fair in so far as you can weigh up the situation.

When children are infants there are bound to be disagreements, especially over the sharing of toys. This is all very normal (most of us like our own way and young children are still learning to play with, and share with, other children). Older children, especially adolescents, have arguments so you shouldn't worry too much if your family has arguments from time to time over who has what and when. This is all part of learning to live together in a group, to take into account the needs of others and be less selfish.

The trap you *mustn't* fall into is to have two parents with two different standards of discipline: one strict, and one lax. Don't say, when your children are arguing: 'You wait until your father comes home. He'll sort you out.' This is ducking the responsibility of facing up to the children yourself. Talk to your husband, or wife. Work out *between you* what you should do when various little squabbles arise amongst the children. Stick to your decisions, having taken those decisions together. If your children find out that you, as parents, disagree over discipline and justice they will, as sure as God made little apples, take advantage of you and play one parent off against the other.

Children are much more sensible than we give them credit for. Intervene in their squabbles; try to come to a fair decision, and *tell them* why you made that decision. This is good social training. It gives them an example: a model for resolving, fairly, the disagreements that crop up in their young lives.

Disturbing Dreams
See also **Sleeplessness** *Page* 213

Children, like adults, can have disturbing dreams as a result of a frightening incident the day before the dream or some time previously. Some children have disturbing dreams at the beginning of an infection or when they are running a high temperature. A feeling of suffocation – perhaps caused by a stuffy nose – can cause bad dreams. So can relatively simple things like shadows on the bedroom wall, being too hot in bed, or having a very heavy meal, and perhaps indigestion, before going to bed. Children who have been separated from their mothers – perhaps in hospital, or in some other unfamiliar place – sometimes have disturbing dreams, especially if their absence from home has been prolonged.

If your child has had a bad dream he may wake up, tell you about it, and, realizing that he was only dreaming, immediately feel better about it. With a nightmare your child may wake up quite panicky and very frightened. All you can do is to try to comfort and reassure him. Remember, it may take him a minute or two to 'come back to reality' so don't say too much at first, just sit with him and, when he's fully awake, say that he's had a bad dream, tuck him up, leave his bedroom light on and go back to your own room. It is your calm and soothing attitude which is of most use to the child following his somewhat alarming experience. Don't fuss or over-react. We all have bad dreams at some time or other.

If your child's sleep is disturbed by fidgetty, restless movements/alking in his sleep/calling out/nightmares it is worth considering the possibility that he is being over-pressurized at school (see section on **Sleeplessness**) or is being bullied or is in some other way unhappy. If your child has nightmares for more than two or three nights you should go to your family doctor and ask his advice. Before you do this have a chat with your child about the sort of dreams he is having: often the content of the dream gives some clue as to what the child is anxious, or frightened, about.

60

It may be that you won't be able to work out what is going on in your child's mind and you may need help (either from the child guidance clinic or from the school psychologist: an appointment can be made via your GP and your child's headmaster, respectively). It could be that the child is being told in his dreams, in pictures, what he fears to express to you (or to himself) in words. An eleven-year-old girl I saw some years ago dreamed that she was working in the kitchen of a large hotel. The head cook, a woman, kept producing babies out of the larder, cutting them up, and giving the remains to the girl with the words: 'Fry these.' In the clinic, the child told me of other, equally nasty, dreams she was having. The mother had recently had a new baby and, in my view, the girl, an extremely likeable and charming young lady, hadn't worked through her real feelings of intense jealousy, about this new arrival in the family. Tina (not her real name) was allowed to play in the playroom with various toys and with various figures representing a family. She felt, after a few weeks, safe enough to express her hostility towards her baby brother in play. (The 'baby' in play always had something nasty happen to him.) After that, we chatted about mother, the baby, the family, and feelings of jealousy, which, I pointed out, all children felt at sometime or other. The nightmares stopped. Once Tina could put her feelings into words, face up to her real feelings, she didn't need the nightly picture show to express how she really felt. It may be that you will not be able, in the case of bad dreams which go on for some time and of a disturbing intensity, be able to find out the reason for the dreams yourself so you should seek advice and help so that the child's anxiety and distress can be alleviated.

Children of infant school age are still not at the stage when they're quite sure about waking and dreaming experiences. Dreams are often as vivid as daytime events. A child may dream that he's at a birthday party and wake up and look under the bed for his piece of birthday cake! Many quite young children these days watch programmes like *Doctor Who* or *Star Wars* (or even frightening horror movies or detective films) on television. It isn't surprising, knowing how still unsure they are about reality and fantasy, that they have disturbing dreams when they go to bed. Here, the answer is to exercise a bit of commonsense and don't let your child watch television movies which frighten him and which are aimed at a much older, more mature audience. A consistent bed-time routine (see **Sleeplessness**) and calm, unanxious reassurance if the child does wake up as the result of a bad dream are the best pro-phylactics I know. Don't, of course, read your child gory fairy tales just before he goes to sleep and do remind him that giants and witches (and the people in *Doctor Who*) are only make-believe. He has plenty of fantasy so it's useful to remind him, from time to time, that some things are only a story.

You can't protect your child completely from disturbing dreams. We all have them, even adults. What you can do is to provide a calm, sensible atmosphere (and a down-to-earth reassurance when they happen) so that the child isn't too frightened by his fantasy. He knows, if you're sympathetic and sensible, that his world of reality is safe.

Dyslexia
See also **Clumsiness** *Page* 33, **Crossed Laterality** *Page* 37, **Left-Handed Children** *Page* 132

Mention dyslexia and you're almost bound to start an argument: there is great controversy about what it is, and even about whether it exists! Some eminent people consider dyslexia to be a serious handicap that leads to many young people going through life illiterate, or failing to achieve their full potential. Other people (equally eminent) say that there is no such thing. They argue that dyslexia (which comes from the Greek words *dis* – disorder and *lexia* – reading) is simply another name for bad reading and for children who are poor at dealing with the written word. So, they argue, why not just call them 'bad readers' and get on with the job of teaching them?

Whether dyslexia exists as a specific handicap or not there is no doubt that, if your child has severe reading difficulties, you will be suffering anguish and your child may be facing all sorts of emotional problems. At the very least, you will be very worried about whether the child will be able to cope in school. And what you need is not argument or debate but practical help.

First of all you must talk to the head or your child's teacher. Make an appointment so you can talk quietly and privately. If the head or teacher says that dyslexia doesn't exist, don't bother arguing. Instead, try to find out exactly what it is that your child can and cannot do. Explain your own experience and observations of what your child can cope with and what tasks seem to baffle him or her. Ask what special help is available from your Local Education Authority but, before you seek out more specialist help, you and the school will want to check out some of the more common causes of reading failure.

Physical You may think your child is perfectly healthy but often it is not until the child starts to read that his eyesight turns out to need attention. He may, for example, have no trouble in seeing the book that you hold in front of him but may be quite unable to see what the teacher writes on the blackboard some yards away – so check this with an optician. You should also have his hearing checked: children who have suffered from frequent colds or catarrh often lose their hearing from time to time. This, again, may mean that they accidentally miss important parts of the lesson, and without anyone being aware of it.

Emotional This is a question that only you, the parent, can really answer. Is your child worried and pre-occupied about failure in reading, or failure to do well at written work? Is he unhappy or depressed because he isn't as good at lessons as his brother or sister or his friends? Have there been, apart from his learning problems, any emotional upheavals at home which may have loomed large in his or her young life?

Intellectual What is your child's all-round ability? Is there a gap between his achievements in school and his ability as you see it at home? Do you get the impression, when talking to the child, that he is vastly more intelligent than his written work would indicate?

Teaching No child can learn to read without lots of help from a good teacher. Has your child had a fair chance in the classroom? Has he, perhaps, been off school a lot and missed too many lessons to catch up with the other children without special help? Has he been taught regularly by the same teacher, who knows how far your child has got and what help he needs?

What have you been doing, on your side, for the child? Are there any books and comics at home for the child to look at? Do you and his father talk to him a lot so as to teach him new words and how to use them? Do you really *listen* when he tries to talk to you?

Developmental Perhaps your child is physically, socially or emotionally, immature? You can judge his development by seeing whether he plays with other children easily. Or ask yourself if his speech is so well developed it suggests that he is ready to learn to read. If not, all that may be needed is time: to wait until he is a little older and ready for reading rather than put too much pressure on him at too early an age.

But if you've checked down this list, and none of these common causes of reading failure apply to your child, then it is time to look for symptoms of dyslexia. Some of these can only be discovered by an expert but you can look out for: confusion of letters (*u* for *n*, *d* for *b*); poor retention and recall of the written word even for a child whose memory is otherwise excellent; confusion of words (*saw* for *was*, *god* for *dog*); illegible writing and mirror writing (when the child may write from right to left); and difficulty in remembering sequences, including days of the week and months of the year.

Other signs of reading difficulty include what doctors call 'unestablished cerebral dominance' – which is another way of saying the child is neither predominantly right- or left-handed. (This often clears up while the child is at primary school, and the reading and speech difficulties may clear up with it.) Other signs are poor spelling, lack of concentration, a low tolerance of frustration, and clumsiness – which doesn't mean that your child keeps dropping his toast butter side down but that he has difficulty doing jig-saws, throwing and catching a ball, reading a map.

If your child has three or more of the symptoms listed here then he or she is probably dyslexic. However, many children with some of these symptoms *can* read. And some children with only one or two symptoms cannot. So, you see, dyslexia is far harder to diagnose than, say, mumps. And to complicate matters further, some older dyslexic children can read but have problems with writing, or spelling.

In the midst of this confusion, the important thing is that regardless of whether or not your child is labelled dyslexic, *if he has reading difficulties he needs appropriate remedial help from skilled teachers* and your local education authority is bound to provide this. The earlier your child is helped the better. So don't wait for the problem to get better, and don't wait for the school to contact you. If you're worried go to the teacher or head at once. With proper help (see section on **Reading**) a great deal can be done. And note that older children taking O-levels can be issued with a certificate explaining that they are dyslexic. The child's headmaster can obtain this from an educational psychologist or neurologist and the certificate is sent to the examining board so that due allowance is made for the child's disability.

Many people, including the actress Susan Hampshire, have overcome severe reading (and/or writing) problems to achieve adjusted and successful lives. Reading is a vital skill in our society: these children need all the *practical* help we can give them.

Further advice may be obtained from: The Dyslexia Institute, 133 Gresham Road, Staines, Middlesex, and The British Dyslexia

Association, 18 The Circus, Bath. There are, in many areas, local dyslexia associations. A useful booklet, containing plenty of practical suggestions, is *Dyslexia: Introduction. A Dyslexic's Eye View* by Helen Arkell obtainable from The Helen Arkell Dyslexia Centre, 16 Crondace Road, London SW6 4BB.

Eating Fads

Nothing is more irritating than a child who uses mealtimes to throw a tantrum, to 'get at' mother, or simply have the satisfaction of provoking her. Toddlers sometimes do it – given them a bowl of cereal and they'll whine they don't want it and/or play around with it or even sweep it onto the floor. In this kind of situation it's better to play it cool, let your baby get down from the table and tell him he can play until he *does* feel hungry. After all, if your baby has some meat or egg, a little orange juice and plenty of milk each day little harm will come to him. A few multi-vitamin drops or tablets, a carrot (vitamin A), an orange (vitamin C) can all be given to him without any fuss. Some mothers are terrified that their child will starve, or that he'll become unwell as a result of a lop-sided, picky diet. Eating becomes a duty not a pleasure. What should be a happy occasion with parent(s) and child sitting down for a meal together, becomes a battle. When the mother becomes angry or, more likely, distressed and upset it's her Waterloo, not the child's. He knows that everytime he wants to provoke a reaction from mother all he has to do is to make a fuss over food.

Your child won't starve. He'll estimate the amount of food he needs and he'll eat, if you offer him a variety of food, the things he needs for his health. Don't over-estimate his appetite: some children do very well on two meals a day. Give him a balanced diet but accept that, one day, he'll eat nothing but cheese, the next day, nothing but bananas. Adults do the same. If your baby is losing weight, and you're worried about it, have a word with the family doctor who should be able to reassure you that the sort of food you are giving your child is a balanced diet. With younger children don't worry too much about table manners (within reason – don't let him throw the cereal bowl at you) just so long as he eats. Don't worry about the order of eating and don't force food on him that he doesn't want. Make mealtimes a relaxed, happy occasion and he'll pick up his cue from you. Play it brisk, and play it without fuss.

With older children similar tactics apply. Don't say: 'You can only have pudding if you finish up your cabbage.' That's unfair. He

65

may not feel like the cabbage. He may hate cabbage. There's nothing special about cabbage: try some other greens with him. Don't heap his plate up with food and sit there, glaring at him, waiting for him to finish the lot. If he doesn't want to there is no way you can force him to. Why not give him smaller amounts and let him come back for 'a second-helping' if he wants them? At breakfast, don't come out with such platitudes as: 'You need a good breakfast inside you.' Who says he does? Many children – just like adults – *can't* eat a large breakfast so why make an issue out of it? After his tea let him have a piece of cake, some biscuits (or fruit and/or cheese). Put some of his favourite things on the table. Don't let him get all the things he likes from the shops during the day. Meals should be enjoyable and the main aim is to create a pleasant atmosphere at the table in which everybody can eat what *they* want to eat.

You may go through patches, as most parents do, when your growing child seems to want to eat nothing else but cakes, or biscuits, or chips, or packets of sweets. I don't think any of these represent a threat to a child's health and, again, providing you don't make too much fuss the child will usually eat other things as well. With sweets, you may be worried, rightly, about your child's teeth. Rather than giving him money to stuff himself with sweets and perhaps spoil his appetite why not let him have one or two after tea (or a couple of chocolate biscuits or whatever his passion is) and then make sure he cleans his teeth? At home, we have chips as a treat; most people like chips and your child will be pleased if you do include them in your meals, say, twice a week. Why not? He may even be less inclined to go off to a chip shop and spend his precious pocket money on food if he gets, from time to time, some of the things he likes at home.

A last word on sweets. If you bring up your toddler to have a piece of cheese, or a few peanuts, as a treat he won't look upon sweets as something bound up with special occasions, love, and lots of other good things. I noticed that, at an infant's school sports day, the children were given sticks of celery and peanuts (rather than chocolates or sweets) as prizes. I thought that was a nice idea. Look upon eating sweets not as a ritual associated with days out, or having visitors or going to the cinema. Have sweets, occasionally, after a meal; that's the right way to get them into perspective – as a treat, not a day-after-day diet, or a reward.

With teenagers, once more, it simply isn't worth turning meal-times into a battleground. Lots of mums say to me: 'He/she won't eat this and won't eat that.' I know the problem. All three of my teenagers, but especially my son, have a complete range of fads about food. My son won't eat fish; my daughter doesn't like cauliflower; my other daughter won't eat mushrooms. Does it matter? Why not give them some choice in what they eat. In our house they have choice simply because, once a week, they each cook the evening meal. If your teenager won't eat meat or fish but likes sausages and is crazy about hamburgers and other modern foods, the likelihood is that he is getting all the vitamins he needs so why make an issue out of it? He'll eat junk foods, or what you'd call junk foods, quite a lot but it's worth remembering that hot-dogs, pizzas and lots of other snacks have plenty of vitamins in them. It's exactly the same with ice-cream and crisps. As long as your child has enough adequate meals as well, leave his strange culinary tastes well alone.

There is one, important, exception to my philosophy of 'the least fuss the better' over eating fads. There is a condition known as *anorexia* in which adolescent girls – it's usually girls, but not always – refuse to eat for a variety of reasons. The girl will *say* that she wants to be thin to look attractive but anorexia is an illness: a symptom of some conflict within the youngster. An anorexic teenager may refuse to eat at all, or eat minute amounts, or eat her meal and then make herself vomit in the bathroom. She won't realize how painfully thin she is and will say things like: 'Do you think my arms are fat?' (when, in fact, her arms and the rest of her body are emaciated). Many anorexics are unable to cope with the pressures of adolescence; all of them need help. It is difficult these days, with the emphasis on slimness as being attractive, to distinguish between a girl who is slimming and one who has started to become morbid about eating food. In this kind of situation it's much better to be safe than sorry so, if you think your daughter is too thin for her own good, don't make a scene, or 'keep going on at her' about it. Take her to see the family doctor for a check on her weight and on her general health. This can't do any harm. It will save you from a great deal of worry (and you can tell your daughter, quite genuinely, but without too much panic) that you *are* worried about her. In my experience the sooner that anorexia is spotted and dealt with the better so please don't hesitate if your daughter *is* painfully thin. If your daughter's weight dramatically decreases over a period of weeks, or if she seems to be repelled by the idea of eating anything at all, do seek professional advice from your GP.

Eccentric Children
See also **Maladjustment** *Page* 140, **'Normal' Behaviour** *Page* 159

First of all, what's the difference between being eccentric and being maladjusted? If you're maladjusted, you may be unhappy and/or not able to cope with your life and/or create difficulties for other people around you. (See section on **Maladjustment**.) If you're eccentric you *are* different from other people, slightly odd, but you're not unhappy, you can cope and you don't make problems for those with whom you come into contact. Many of the adults I have liked most in my life have been eccentric. There was, for example, the man I worked with who used to wear smart suits, beautiful shirts and a pair of old, much-worn boots ('They're comfortable,' he'd point out). For lunch, wherever he was, he'd eat six olives, no more or less, which he carried around with him in a little bottle, plus a glass of water. He wasn't at all concerned about what other people thought of him; he was just getting on with his life and – this is the important thing – he was happy and he never harmed anybody else. With eccentric adults, and I'm sure you know or have known some, we can afford to stick by the old maxim 'Live and let live'.

With eccentric children exactly the same thing applies: if they're happy leave them alone; don't try to make them like all the other children you see around you; they're not the same and they don't have to be. Obviously, if a child is isolated and alone, finds it difficult to mix with others (see **Shy Children**) then you may have to do something about it. But if he's getting on with his life and ploughing his own furrow quite happily, then the best advice I can give you is: 'Leave him be.' Why should a child's behaviour, or dress, or mannerisms, conform exactly with those of other children?

What about social isolation? Won't the child who is 'different' be shunned by other children? Won't he – since children can be extremely observant and rather cruel – be rejected from the group unless he conforms to the behaviour and values of that particular set of youngsters? This hasn't been my experience with eccentric children. They *may* be given nicknames: 'Doctor Who' for a child who is clever, 'The Incredible Hulk' for the gentle giant, 'Hay' for a girl who loves ponies, but they are still accepted into the group despite – and, in some cases, because of – their differences. One girl, I knew, always wore her mother's hats; one boy had a collection of spiders and knew an encyclopaedic amount about insects; another boy was always reading – he even read as we sat about at the top of the road just talking – and he's now a film producer in Hollywood. Then, he was the group expert in anything you'd care to name and was known as 'The Prof'. One girl in the group used to eat tar from the cracks in between the pavement. I think it would be a grey world indeed if everybody was 'normal'. Signs of individuality should be encouraged, not feared or scoffed at by the rest of us. Those children, and adults, who insist on their own individuality give us the freedom and the example to be ourselves.

I remember one mother who brought her four-year-old son to see me in the clinic. I took mother and child into the playroom where the boy started to play with a doll, putting it to sleep, tucking it up, in a cot. 'There,' said mum, 'I told you he wasn't normal.' A strange thing to say: not only because it *isn't* abnormal for infant boys to play with dolls (lots of boys these days play with Action Man, which is a very popular doll) but because mother had had a baby recently and her four-year-old was obviously identifying with her and copying some of the things he saw happening at home. Mother eventually came to believe – after several sessions with us both observing her son play – that he was a perfectly normal boy. He *was* a bit eccentric (he had, I remember, a very grave, serious manner, a deep voice, sticky-out ears and a tendency to stand very close and look at you very solemnly straight in the eye) but he *wasn't* abnormal.

The best way that I can illustrate my point is by reference to my own three children, now teenagers. They are, I would claim, reasonably normal but have, and always have had, their own eccentricities. My eldest daughter is very vague about train times, and about where the train is going. She'll set off for Ipswich and end up in Crewe. It doesn't seem to worry her. Last month she went to France. I was expecting a phone call: 'Do they yodel in Paris?' She seems to lead a charmed life, despite her little foibles, and everything seemed to turn up all right in the end. My son, after saving up for a car for more than a year, announced last night that he was going to buy a music centre instead. No reason given. Just a, 'Well, cars are expensive, ain't they?' I said nothing; I'm used to odd decisions. My youngest daughter will spend hours making little hats out of odd pieces of material. 'D'you know a shop where I can sell these?' she asks me. 'No, not until they make smaller dolls,' I tell her. A friend of mine claims that whilst you *can* have eccentric adults there is no such thing as an eccentric child. The child is maladjusted or normal. I can't agree with that. I seem to be surrounded with eccentric children. If you are then I can only repeat my advice: accept their oddities, do not try to make them normal, like yourself. Actually, if you look at yourself a little more closely, or ask your friends, you may find that you're slightly odd if not positively eccentric. If you are, I'm glad. At least it shows that you are an individual, a one-off, and that you don't feel the need to hide yourself in the herd. Respect your child's individuality, just as you expect your friends to respect yours. It is, after all, our little foibles and oddities – perhaps even our little weaknesses – that enable other people to like us.

Emotional Needs
See also **Motivation** *Page* 149

Before you read any further it might be a good idea to take a piece of paper and just jot down your own list of children's needs. (It's funny, but when you ask *children* what they need they usually say things like 'a new bike' or 'more pocket money'. *Parents* usually start off their list with 'love' closely followed by 'discipline'.) Done your list? Right, I'll plunge in and list ten things which I think are as vital to children's emotional development as are air, water, food and shelter to their physical development. My list of emotional needs is: *to be loved; to love somebody; new experiences (i.e. some kind of stimulation); a feeling of belongingness; praise; some responsibility; an idea of right and wrong (i.e. some code of values); self-discipline (so that they have some control over their own emotions); self-respect* and *some security.*

This is a formidable list I know but I want to qualify it straight away by saying that few of us (if any) have each and every one of our emotional needs satisfied. Even if we did, even if we had a terrific amount of security in childhood, and a vast amount of love, that is no guarantee that we won't meet crises and stress later on. Also, on an optimistic note, I have seen a great many children deprived of love and affection as youngsters who grew up to be loving, caring (and happy) adults. Don't worry if you are not satisfying every single need of your growing child. It would be a miracle if you were. Life is a hectic, tough business and none of us get exactly what we want: some degree of frustration is part and parcel of growing up. All I ask is that you are aware of your child's emotional needs, do your best to fulfil them, and remember that parents have needs as well. (So don't forget to love yourself, to give yourself some pleasant, new experiences from time to time or you'll find yourself drained and depressed, and in no condition to give anything, emotionally, to your children.)

Let's have a closer look at some of those needs. *Love* is vital to children (see section on **Love**). I doubt whether any child can get too much love, so do show affection to your child. Hug him, kiss him, cuddle him, especially when he's young. Love him, and leave him be, giving him space to grow up and live his own life. While you're at it, teach him to be loving and affectionate, by being loving and affectionate yourself. *To love another human being is just as important to us as being loved.* We have to learn how to love and it is you, the parent, who is the child's first (and best) teacher. Through a loving relationship children learn to control their emotions (anger, fear, frustration) and to use them constructively. Love gives children self-respect and self-discipline.

Children (as every mum and dad knows) are gluttons for new experiences. To a baby, everything is exciting: his own toes, mother's face, a light in the room. Children of all ages like action, doing things. No doubt, you'll find this terribly tiring and my advice is to get your children out from under your own feet as much as possible. Use the playgroup, the club, the park, the neighbourhood as resources and get out and take them with you and talk about what you see. All the world, even the inside of the supermarket, is magical to a child.

While your child will need to feel that he belongs in the family (encourage this by giving him some *responsibilities* in the home even if it's only cleaning out the hamster cage or making the tea on Sunday), I doubt whether, however hard you try, your child will be absolutely, totally secure. That is why, on my list, I have included the phrase 'some security'. None of us, whether child or adult, is completely free from fears and anxiety. *The best (and probably the only real) security that you can give to your child is a feeling that he is wanted and loved.*

You may not be a Christian and you may think that, these days, since we live in a confused, rapidly-changing world, it's hard to lay down a fixed code of values for a child to follow. Perhaps so, but I think we should give our children *some* guidance as to how to behave towards others and *we should never be afraid of saying, 'That is right and that is wrong.'* Where we don't know the answer – say, on such tricky matters as euthanasia and abortion – we can at least say what we think and answer their questions as honestly as we can. I think we should have *some* values to pass on to a child: to expect them to work everything out for themselves, to behave exactly as they like, is to do them no favours at all (see section on **Over-Permissiveness**). Say what you think is right, stick by your own standards, give them a guide. Then, let them have sufficient space to work it all out for themselves. They may find that your views weren't as daft as they sounded after all.

As children get older you'll find that their needs change. Teenagers, curiously enough, have a need to be misunderstood (they don't like to think we know everything about them!). They have a need for privacy, a need to keep part of their world secret from you. They need *friendship* from you, as well as love. As children grow older we have to learn to relax our hold on them, as they fledge their wings, ready to leave the nest. If we've tried hard, done our best, they'll respect us for that and remain our friends for life.

Exam Phobia

'Exams' is a word that strikes terror into the heart of many teenagers and, if your child is amongst this ashen-faced number, there are several practical things you can do when tests and formal examinations loom up on the horizon. Exams are not the only way of assessing young people, and they tell us little about a person's character, or ability to work with other people. There have been plenty of distinguished men and women (including Sir Winston Churchill) who have failed examinations but succeeded in later life. Nevertheless, exams *are* important: the result of an exam may well determine whether your youngster can pursue his chosen career.

What do you do, as a parent, when exams (and, in particular, O- and A-levels) bring stress and worry into your home? You will, I hope, sympathize with your youngster and perhaps give him an extra ration of bacon at breakfast in the morning, and a decent meal in the evening before he disappears upstairs to learn mysterious things like the conditions of the Treaty of Utrecht. Don't just let him grab pieces of toast and make for his books, badly-fed and anxiety ridden; this is a vital time in the child's life and you can best help him by feeding him properly and staying calm and practical in the middle of all the fuss. Excuse him household chores for a couple of weeks and insist that he works in a reasonably quiet room. Urge him not to leave revision to the last minute or (just as bad) start panicking months in advance. Cut down on television-watching (no child can revise properly *and* watch TV, despite what he may tell you) and make sure that your youngster gets enough sleep. Staying up into the small hours is not a good way to prepare for a taxing examination the next day.

There are books available which tell young people how to study. These books cannot ensure that your child will pass the examination but they may help him to do his best, which is the object of the exercise. A useful book is *How To Study* by Derek Rowntree (Macdonald). Although it is aimed mainly at sixth-form and university students this book is very readable and readily understood by most youngsters in their O-level year. Some youngsters set about examinations the right way; others don't. The best thing I can do, therefore, is to give you a few tips from my own experience which you can pass on to your youngster. In giving them, I'm assuming that your child has done *some* work during the preceding five years! The child should:

Plan his revision, and do a definite amount of work each evening. Worrying about revision is more painful than settling down and actually doing some.

Look at old exam papers and try some of the questions, using an alarm clock to time himself. It is better for him to find out his weaknesses (e.g. that he writes rather slowly) *before* the exam takes place.

Use a tape recorder to learn, particularly if he doesn't find it easy to read quickly, or if he has a poor visual memory. He can play back the relevant sections during the day (even whilst in the bathroom!) until he knows them.

Revise with a friend if he finds it difficult to learn alone or if he has a tendency to read book after book without remembering anything. Active learning (question and answer, plus discussion) is better than passive learning.

Learn main points rather than try to revise everything. Jot down on cards brief headings; make diagrams and charts. Headings are easier to recall than page upon page of hastily-scribbled notes.

Use memory aids such as mnemonics to help him remember material. For example, if he wishes to recall the causes of the French Revolution, he could write the word **Knitting.** This reminds him that the King was weak, the Nobles corrupt, the Intellectuals causing trouble, etc. For most people, making notes, writing something down, is much better than sitting reading a book.

Try to 'spot' likely questions but *not* rely on this method completely. If he does, and none of the questions crop up, he will be in for a bad exam (as many youngsters have learned to their cost).

Let's assume that you've been through the period leading up to the exam and, now, exam-day has arrived. What advice can you give to your youngster to make sure he does his best in the examination room? Here are some practical points you could pass on to him:

Make sure he knows the time (and place!) of the exam. He should arrive ten minutes early and, rather than chat with friends, take a last look at his note headings. Panic is silly at this stage, as is trying to learn five years work in five minutes. This will only ensure that he forgets what he already knows.

Make sure he has two pens (one in reserve), a handkerchief (for nose-blowing, hopefully, rather than tears), a ruler, compass and any other equipment he may need.

Tell him to read the instructions on the exam paper. There's nothing worse than working like a slave and finding out you've answered the wrong questions. *Advise him to read the questions carefully.*

Tell him to plan the time available. It's most unwise to spend an hour-and-a-half on the first question and leave too little time to answer the rest. If he's short of time on the very last question he could make notes as an answer. These will gain him a few vital marks.

Tell him to answer the easiest questions first. This will give him more confidence to tackle the others.

Tell him to leave ten minutes to check through answers, to rectify any spelling mistakes and correct glaring errors. Silly mistakes lose marks, so this is ten minutes well spent.

During exams children undergo a certain amount of strain. Don't pick up their anxiety. Try to remain calm, practical and supportive rather than getting caught up in the tension. This is your opportunity to show what a lovely mum (or dad) you are. Lastly, don't forget to wish them good luck as they go off in the morning, poor souls, to sit the examination.

Extraversion
See also **'Normal' Behaviour** *Page* 159

I am quite sure that there are *some* inborn temperamental differences between children. Looking back to when my own three were babies I can remember that two were very cuddly, one was a 'wriggler'. The latter, at the crawling stage, was always off, exploring somewhere or other. Now, at fifteen, she is what might be called an extravert. Lively, outgoing, and liking other people's company, she is much more spontaneous and talkative than her siblings who are quieter and more thoughtful.

There are people who seem to be complete extraverts: show no trace of shyness, adore company, feel unhappy when they are alone, are at their best at parties, or other social situations, where they can talk to lots of people. There are very shy people, introverts, who are happiest when alone, or with a small group of familiar and well-tried friends (see **Introversion**). *However, I think we have to be careful to remember that extraverts and introverts are extremes: most of us are a mixture of both.* My extraverted daughter *can* be very shy, very introspective, at times; my two more introverted children *can* be extremely talkative, outgoing and lively if they are with people they know and whose company they enjoy. Obviously, social circumstances can alter behaviour. Identical twins *may* start off life being extraverts. If they are brought up in different environments, one may end up as an extravert, the other more introverted. We are affected by the people who surround us; our behaviour, for example, when we are abroad, on holiday, may be quite different from when we are at home, amongst people we know very well. This suggests that human beings are a little too complicated to be divided into neat categories.

Carl Jung (who coined the terms introvert and extravert) was very careful to point out that the variety of personalities which make up the human race is enormous. Adults, and children, *are* different from each other and, even more complicated, don't even stay the same – they develop, show different aspects of their personality in different circumstances and at different stages of their life. How nice it would be if we were all simple, predictable creatures! We're not.

If you have a particularly extraverted child I think that you should remember to give him plenty to do, *and remember to show him plenty of affection.* Extraverted children give the impression of independence, self-sufficiency. The truth is that they need just as much expressed affection as any other child, so don't be misled by his social skills: he still needs lots of hugs, kisses and other displays of affection. Forget about your British, stiff-upper-lip, introverted attitude to showing your emotions, and remember that an extroverted child needs just as much love as an introverted one!

Fantasy
See also **Daydreaming** *Page* 42, **Walter Mitty Complex** *Page* 261

A young child can turn himself, in his own imagination, into a lion, a car, a mother, father, king or pirate. If you go for a walk with him you may find that he's creeping along on all fours, being an Indian, or a tiger. To a child the world is magic, because a child can transform himself, and common objects such as blankets and chairs, into anything that he wants them to be. Parents may worry about the imaginations of their children and you may catch yourself saying: 'Come over here and do something sensible.' You may wonder what use fantasy and make-believe are. They are tremendously useful because a child with a good imagination (and all children seem to have marvellous powers of imagining things) can learn to sort out problems, build things, think up solutions, reasons, possibilities. He can identify with the thoughts and feelings of others, their predicaments, goals, hopes and fears. Fantasy is something to be encouraged, not stifled.

With the young child you should try to provide materials which the child can use to 'play out' the various aspects of the world he sees around him. The toys needn't be expensive. A cardboard box can become a car; your old clothes provide children with an opportunity to play 'mothers and fathers'; two chairs and a rug can become a Wendy House; an empty can, or carton, with a hole in the top can become a 'posting box'. Space, as well as toys, is important to children. Out of doors a hill can become a mountain, a small group of trees a jungle, a pond a sea on which to sail paper boats (or just twigs – which act as boats). If we give children a chance to play, they'll make full use of the experience so take them to the park and let them have a good selection of toys and 'junk' to play with at home. Don't worry about their fantasies whether it's creating an imaginary friend, playing 'nurses and doctors' or beating the world speed record in a super-charged car (another cardboard box). We can only envy them their creative gifts, their ability to make use of everything when they play. If children had no imagination parents would have an awful time in trying to keep them amused. Imagination is the source of creativity, and it is a precious gift.

What should you do if you want to develop your child's fantasy and imagination? *You can tell him stories which you make up yourself.* These home-made products (especially if the hero or heroine is called by the same name as the child) bring great pleasure to children. One or two comments on the child's quirks and behaviour can be interwoven into the story ('John loved marzipan and crisps but he didn't like washing his hands'). Children can see the humour of this, and they're easily pleased if they know you're doing it for them. The best remembered stories of my own children's early days were the ones I made up myself and, believe me, they'd win no prizes for literature.

There are now superb children's books available (if in doubt go to your local library, and ask for advice). *It's important for you to read to your children and, later on, encourage them to read books themselves.*

Perhaps you could pop into the library with your children whilst doing the Saturday morning shopping. If you make a habit of it, and start them young, they'll acquire a natural love of reading. Children love stories and soak them up like a sponge soaks up water so do give them every chance to enter the enchanted land of books.

Books aren't all. *Conversation, and listening to what the child has to say, are important too.* When you go for a walk with your child point out things of interest (in the country birds' nests, animals, houses, flowers, trees are all grist to the mill; in the town there are buses, cars, sweetshops, oranges, trains, pigeons, cats, gardens. Even a can of tomato soup in a supermarket is interesting to a child if the parent points it out and comments on it if only to say: 'That's what you had last night for tea'). In the evening, try to find a book with pictures in of some of the things you have seen and *talk about them.* Your curiosity, your enthusiasm, will rub off on your child and spark off his own imagination and thirst for knowledge. (It's a good idea to keep a few factual books in the home to encourage children to look things up. These 'general knowledge' books act as a balance to fantasy. If you can't afford them use the local library to track down what you want to know and encourage your child's current interest.)

Games don't need to be fiercely competitive. 'Grandmother's footsteps', 'What's the Time, Mr Wolf?', charades, pretending games, piggyback rides, mum being 'the teacher', all help the child to create a world which is fun and limitless (there is no end of roles to play, people to 'be'). Sometimes you may think that your child is going too far in his fantasy (e.g. if he 'shoots you' or says that he ate a tiger on the way to school). You can deal with this by smiling at him and saying, 'Only pretend.' If a child offers you a 'pretend cake' to eat you should make a great play of munching it. He knows (and he expects *you* to know) what is fantasy and what is reality and he will soon realize that adults who are imaginative and who can enter into his fantasy world (for the duration of the game) are greater fun to be with.

Don't scold your child if he exaggerates and lays it on a bit thick. Just indicate that you know that he's exaggerating, by smiling at him or saying, 'That's something you would wish to happen.' You know the boundary between fantasy and downright lies (see section on **Liars**). Do discourage lies; don't discourage your child's fantasy.

Don't tell your child stories that frighten him or with alarming themes (e.g. monsters, werewolves, Dracula) that the child is far too young to understand aren't real. Similarly, don't let your child watch programmes on TV that alarm him. Children like to be frightened but only within limits when they feel safe. Don't overdo it by presenting them with horrifying stories or TV programmes and expecting them to be able to cope with them when they're too immature to do so.

With teenagers, you may want to encourage them to join a dance or drama group, or an art class (or even join the Scouts or Guides or other organizations where there is scope for imaginitive activities). At home, if a youngster is presented with an old sewing machine, or allowed to use dad's tools in the garage, or bought a rug and an embroidery needle (or materials to make puppets, decorative candles, or a couple of knitting needles and a supply of wool) the young person will be given a chance to do something creative and avoid the cry which goes up from many teenagers: 'I've got nothing to do.' (See section on **Boredom**.)

All children are creative. What we have to do, as parents, is to spark off their creativity, their curiosity. With younger children, a cardboard box, a tin and a few wooden blocks may keep them going for hours. With older children we have to be slightly more resourceful in thinking up ideas (and anything from science fiction to dress design is fine, so long as it interests them). What we have to remember is that fantasy is great fun, and it is a very good road to learning.

Fathers
(For Parents)

A family should be a shared enterprise; dads are just as important as mums. The days of those bossy, self-centred fathers of Victorian times are, I hope, over. These days, fathers have an active, contributing role to play in the family whether he works and you stay at home or, as sometimes happens, *he* stays at home and you go out to work.

Start off as you mean to go on and share things together, the good experiences as well as the bad. Perhaps your husband may want to be present at the birth of your baby. If so, well and good: for quite a few men this is a marvellous experience. (Some, it has to be said, *don't* relish it.) Be that as it may father should have his turn at bathing the baby, changing nappies, cuddling the baby. If he gets to know the infant during this stage he'll find it much easier in relating to him later on. There's no good reason I know of (providing that he's there, and isn't a long-distance lorry driver, a travelling salesman or doing some other job that keeps him away from home) why *father* shouldn't be a dab hand at giving baby a bottle, or why *he* shouldn't get out of bed at night when the baby is fretful.

Recently, I saw a women's Morris Dancing team. One of the dancers was the mother of a baby whom dad was looking after while both of them watched the dancing. The man, a tall, bearded gentleman, was absolutely marvellous with the baby. I was watching him as he fed the child, changed a nappy, talked to the baby and played with him. They were having, both of them, a good time. Also, there's a lot of hope for that little family, I'd guess, because they have a flexible attitude towards roles (it *isn't* always mum's place to look after the children) and dad was actually enjoying himself with the baby. He did not look upon the child as something 'not really to do with me'.

A child gains a lot of security from playing with dad, being cuddled by him or being carried on dad's shoulders when out walking. It isn't unmanly, these days, for a father to push a pram, dress a toddler, and play with his own children. The participating dad is in; Andy Capp dads are out. The secret is *sharing*. For example, when your children are of school age make sure that you attend parent-teacher association meetings together. If only one of you can go, take turns. Get your husband to look after the children whilst you go out for a drink, or to do some shopping, with a friend. Join an evening class. Leave him with the children and he'll appreciate the hard work involved so the earlier you start on this one the better. Don't establish a pattern where *you* have total responsibility for the children whilst he goes out drinking with *his* mates. He's missing a lot of fun while you'll be becoming more and more resentful. Don't become tired and washed out so that he has a good reason to head to the nearest pub. Share the chores; share the good things.

79

Dad can play with the children, teach them games, help them with their reading, their hobbies or just talk and (equally important) listen to them. If your husband's away a lot he could still promise to go swimming or bowling or cycling with them once a week (providing he keeps his promise). There's not much point in a man working to death for his own family if he never takes time off to go out with his wife and children. Many dads have to work very hard. Children can understand that but they like to feel that dad has *some* time left over for them.

If you're one of those very maternal ladies who loves children don't hog the whole limelight. You'll want to do everything yourself: particularly when your child is young. If you do you are depriving your child of another human being he can relate to and you're not giving yourself a break from baby (and your baby a break from you!). Some women won't, or can't, let their husbands help simply because they resent anybody else interfering: they think that the domestic front is their kingdom and don't like anybody else muscling in. Other women, probably because their mothers took a centre-stage, maternal role or because they didn't have very good mothering themselves, are determined to be extra good mothers with their own children and hold the children close to them. Both these attitudes are very understandable but they can make dad, at least some of the time, feel an unwelcome intruder.

If you're like this you will, I hope, see the drawback. Later on, when you want dad to participate and would appreciate a bit of help, he'll be a stranger to his own children. So start early, and let your children have a chance to make friends with dad. Ask your husband's advice about the children; encourage him to talk about them. Otherwise, he may become more and more of an outsider in his own family. I know that some men work long hours, and are tired when they come in; too tired to play with anybody. That's a modern problem. Do you want more money or more time spent together? It's a problem that only you, in your family, can talk about and come to your own decision. If your husband is out of work, or works shifts, he could perhaps help at a local playgroup. Young children love talking to a man. It makes a nice change from all those women around them!

Marriage is a partnership. If you don't work closely together, take decisions together, have responsibility for the children together, you'll find that you're heading swiftly for the rocks. These are difficult days, confusing times. The only way you can match up to the age, and the difficulties, is to make your marriage a joint enterprise.

A word, now, to single-parent mothers. You may worry about your child not having a father-figure to whom he can relate. You should inform the school that the child doesn't have a father and perhaps one of the men teachers could build up a relationship with your child. Boys can be encouraged to join a local youth club, or the scouts, or some sports organization, where they can meet men who would act as suitable father-substitutes. Girls miss their fathers, too, but perhaps your daughter can also join a club, association or youth club in which she would come into contact with older, caring male adults? Mother and children joining a group together is useful since it brings the children into contact with a variety of adults, and provides them with a better idea of what grown ups, including men, are like.

Two national organizations that deal with the problems of single parents are:

Gingerbread, 35 Wellington Street, London WC2 (If you write to them please enclose a stamped, addressed envelope.) Tel No: 01-240 0953

The National Council For One Parent Families. 255 Kentish Town Road, London NW50 Tel No: 01-267 1361. (Reverse charge calls accepted during office hours, Monday to Friday.)

Fears
See also **Anxiety** *Page* 8, **Nervous Children** *Page* 154

My youngest daughter, when she was an infant, seemed to have few fears. She climbed high trees (she wasn't afraid; I was!), jumped off high diving boards, liked new faces, new places, dogs, cats (she wanted to stroke the tiger at the zoo), the sea, plus the Big Wheel, the Big Dipper and the Waltzer at the annual visiting fairground. She is now (as a teenager) a member of the British Gymnastics Squad and it doesn't surprise me. Some fearless children become fearless adults; most of them learn fear and anxiety (anxiety is fear 'spread thinly') from life and from the people around them. We know from research that some children are born more sensitive than others and, later, these children will pick up fears more easily than other children. However, no child is born afraid. Fear is something that the child learns from his parents, his brothers and sisters, his friends, his teachers – *from other people*. We learn what we live. If we live with people who are optimistic, courageous, we learn to be brave; if we live with people who are fearful, we learn to be afraid.

Because we don't live in a perfect world, however, most children have fears. If you make a loud noise behind a small baby (or pretend to drop him – not that you would, I hope!) he will show fear. At six months of age (when the infant begins to grow into a real person and to make some important 'Me-Not Me' distinctions) he *may* show fear of separation from mother, or fear of strangers. (Though, not necessarily. If you prop him up in his pram, so he can see strangers all the time, take him to the park just to watch the people going by, and maybe see the ducks he'll soon get used to new faces and unfamiliar sights.) At the pre-school stage the vast majority of children (ninety per cent of them, according to one study) have fear of *something* – usually something specific. It may be of 'bogeymen', 'witches', dogs, cats, the dentist (but not if the child is taken along *as an infant*, to a good preventive-minded dentist and gets used to the surgery and having his mouth examined), the dark (see section on **Dark – Fear of the**), baby-sitters (but, again, not if the child meets and gets used to the person *before* he or she sits for you), and (last but not least) being abandoned or not wanted. As John Steinbeck says in *East of Eden:* 'The greatest terror a child can have is that he is not loved, and rejection is the hell he fears.' So you must never say to your child: 'I won't love you any more,' or, 'I'm going to leave you there and go home,' or, 'I'm going away and not coming back.' Children can't tell that you don't mean these things and threatening them with loss of love, or abandonment, really *does* frighten them.

As children get older they usually have less focused, less specific fears. They have instead (rather like adults) nasty feelings of anxiety about this and that: 'things that worry them'. As we get older it is the unknown, the possible, that makes us anxious rather than the things we know. Children of ten to fourteen, for example, may be afraid of horror movies, hospitals, going away to camp: these are things they don't know too much about and they can't fit into their day-to-day experience. Adults fear the unfamiliar in a similar way. When something happens we usually cope. Sometimes, the fear of the 'awful event' is far worse than the event itself.

What can you do, in practical terms, to make sure that your child doesn't grow up into a fearful adult? *You should try not to be too anxious about each and every thing your child does but save your energy for really dangerous situations.* Fear, like courage, is catching and (sometimes) you have to watch with your heart in your mouth as your child goes up the slide, or paddles in the water. *He* has to conquer his fears; you can only give him the chance to do it, sometimes when you're a little bit afraid yourself. If your child has a particular fear, accept it. Say: 'We're all a little bit afraid of something.' It's no more than the truth – I'm scared stiff of heights. What we have to do is accept our fears, try to overcome them.

The thing to remember is that, in these matters, *familiarity breeds courage and confidence*. Another vital point is to start early. The infant who is used to dogs (you may not want a puppy of your own but you can find a neighbour with a friendly one) gets to know how to let them have a good sniff, how to approach the dog, how to stroke it. The infant who has been taken along to the local swimming baths and taught to swim is not going to be afraid of water and is less likely to be scared of the sea. (I admit the sea is choppier but most children soon get used to the small waves.) A toddler who has been to the swings with other children or to watch the men working on a nearby building site is not going to be afraid of noise. With mum, or dad, alongside him as his 'safe base' he can learn that many situations, which might appear frightening at first glance, are not frightening at all.

Remember that a certain amount of nervousness is quite normal so let your child decide what physical feats of daring he wants to attempt. Don't put him off before he starts and don't (just as bad!) try to 'toughen him up a bit' by urging him to do things he can't manage. Commonsense is useful in preventing fear. A young child shouldn't be allowed to watch films that scare the living daylights out of him: he's too immature to distinguish fantasy from reality. Neither should dad or mum read children stories that are too scary. Children like to be frightened *a little*. If we overdo it, then they become fearful of their own fantasies and imaginings.

You may have real-life situations which are potentially frightening to a young child (though they needn't be, if you handle them well). If you have to go into hospital, tell your child well in advance; give him some 'special jobs' to do while you're away and *say that you are coming back*. (If possible, say when.) Tell your child about visiting, *why* you're going (not too much detail) and what the food arrangements are whilst you're away! It's what they don't know that scares hell out of children (just like it scares hell out of adults) so be open, matter-of-fact and don't show any anxiety. It's the same with holidays. You can go away and leave your children with people they know, and they'll accept it – providing they know what's going on *and* when you're coming back. Curiously, these separations (rather than giving rise to great anxiety) bring out the best in some children and they seem to mature, and behave much better, whilst mum is away. It's expected of them, and they rise to the challenge.

If your child has to go to hospital (or away to camp, or on holiday) without you, again, be matter-of-fact about it. If it's hospital, he'll want you to explain why he's going, when you'll visit (always keep your promise on this), when he's coming out, what he'll do while he's there. It's surprising what children *can* cope with providing that you remain the child's 'safe base' and don't try to 'protect' him (by gilding the lily or telling lies) from things which, with your support, he can face up to anyway.

If you put a child who is afraid of rabbits in a room with another child who's never seen a rabbit the second child picks up the first child's fear. Fear *is* contagious. That's why you and me, the poor old parents, have to try to be brave.

Football Hooligans

Bill Shankly, the ex-manager of Liverpool FC, once said: 'Some people think football is a matter of life and death. It isn't. It's much more important than that.' An exaggeration, I know, but to some supporters football is a substitute for religion: they go to watch their local team as the devout go to church. That's fine except that, for a minority of supporters, football is not a substitute for religion, it's a substitute for war. They go about the country, like private armies, urging on the team and willing to do battle on the terraces with anybody who doesn't happen to support their own particular side.

Most football supporters, despite what you may read in the press or see on television, are ordinary, normal people. However, there are some of them, mostly teenagers, who are absolute fanatics and who see Saturday afternoons as an opportunity to get up to a bit of mischief and, sometimes, a good fight. One sociologist has divided these anti-social supporters into three sub-groups: nutters, rowdies and hooligans. The last two (the rowdies and hooligans) are the ones who are not averse to making a noise on the streets and doing damage to property. The nutters take it a stage further. They don't shrink from physical violence and, in some cases, have been known to throw bricks, bottles, darts (even petrol bombs) at members of the opposing team's supporters.

That's all very interesting, you say, but what do I do (as a parent) when my teenage son or daughter is a football supporter and wants to go to the match on Saturday afternoons? What do I do (you might ask) if I find that my own son or daughter is in danger of becoming a football hooligan? There are three practical steps you can take:

Go with your youngster to the game. The more law-abiding adults there are about the better and the less chance the rowdies have of affecting the behaviour of other youngsters in the crowd.

Insist that your youngster only goes when he can afford to sit in the seated accommodation (and/or goes with an adult). When football grounds consist solely of seated accommodation (with refreshment facilities, of a high standard, for all the family) the game will be less marred by teenage 'warriors' more interested in fighting each other than football.

Try to divert your youngster's need for rewards and excitement into more positive channels. There are plenty of young people who *play* football (or rugby, or some other game) on a Saturday. There are clubs and associations for them to join (ranging from motor-bike scrambling to youth hostelling). Isn't it better to participate rather than be just a spectator?

If none of these ideas work and if there is a lot of violence at your local football ground, *simply forbid your teenager to go.* A parent does have the right to say NO occasionally. The violence at matches seems to escalate season by season. If Team A's supporters are beaten up by Team B's supporters one year then, the following year, Team A's fans are determined to get their own back the next time the two teams meet. Often, the fans form a 'reception committee' to 'welcome' the opposing supporters outside the ground, in the streets, or at the local railway station. The violence and vandalism spills over into the journey there and back. Trains are wrecked, shops are attacked, local people are terrorized by gangs of youngsters roaming the streets looking for a fight, or something to vandalize. My advice is: don't let your youngster have anything to do with this. I know that football hooligans get a lot of attention from the papers, and from television. This encourages the hooligans to see themselves as heroes. I don't think they are heroes. Violence, even if perpetrated in the name of a football club, is still violence. Each team's official supporters club should be held responsible for the behaviour of all the fans who belong to that club, and should work with the police to stop the violence. However, that's the Football Association's problem, not yours or mine. If your son, or daughter, is in any danger of becoming a football hooligan (or being attacked by football hooligans) you should say: 'Stay Away.' And mean it.

Friends

See also **Lonely Children** *Page* 137

Friends are important to both children and adults. Friendship provides a shoulder to cry on; somebody to talk to (and talk to us); somebody to go out with and do things with; sharing; safety; and a feeling of belongingness. But as Aristotle wrote many centuries ago, 'Wishing to be friends is quick work but friendship is a slow ripening fruit.' We have to *learn* how to make friends and the best time to learn is when we are very young.

For a parent with a young child I suggest that you take your baby along to a Mother and Toddler group. There, your infant will have a chance to get used to, and play alongside, other children. Between the ages of three and five children learn how to play together and share with each other. These are vital social skills (and they enable the young children to adjust to big school more easily). They are best learned in a playgroup or nursery class where the children can interact with their peers. So, if there is a community playgroup, nursery school, or nursery class in your area, *do take your child and enrol him.*

For mothers with older children there are a number of things that may worry them about friendships. What do you do if your child goes through a patch when he seems to have no friends at all? I think it's useful to remember that many children go through lonely patches. It doesn't mean there's anything wrong with your child, or the way you've brought him up. Your job is not to cajole or bully the child into relationships but to encourage hobbies and interests, to take our children to places where they want to go (anything from museums to sports centres) where they can develop a skill and meet other children who have common interests, common goals. *It's useful to remember, too, that children – even children from the same family – vary enormously in their social needs.* One child will stick to the same friend and have a lasting, close pal for years. You shouldn't suggest that he doesn't have enough friends. You may have another child who, in contrast, has a wide range of friends and who seems to move in and out of friendships very quickly. Children are temperamentally different and you should interfere in their choice of friendships as little as possible.

What happens if your child chooses a friend who you think is unsuitable? The rule is: only forbid a friendship if it's absolutely necessary (e.g. if the chosen friend is very aggressive, anti-social, a thief or, if a teenager, takes drugs). Here you may have to say:

'I'm sorry but I don't want you to go around with....' That said, let me stress that generally it's better for youngsters to make and break relationships themselves. A good mix of friends, going to clubs and sports centres where a wide choice of friends is available, enables the child to sort out the wheat from the chaff *himself*, and to understand that certain friendships offer more to him (and are more acceptable to his parents) than others.

If your child is shy you could encourage him to play with younger playmates, so that he can learn to help, lead and advise children younger than himself. Later on, having learned these skills, he'll gravitate towards his own peers. A shy child can help a younger child to make a model, read or ride a bike; he is doing things with, and for, other children. Give him time and he'll naturally gravitate towards children of his own age.

If your child is bright you could encourage him to play with some older children where his ideas are better understood and where he will have a chance to be a subordinate, a follower, rather than being the leader all the time. The main thing is to try to get your children to places (whether it's the local park or a local club) where there's a good mix of other children and then leave the choosing to him. Children seem to choose companions that contrast with, or complement, their own social skills.

Don't forget to provide lots of support when friendships end or falter. A close friend means a lot to a child and – whether through moving away, or an argument, or change of school – it's a big blow for a child to lose a good pal. You could say: 'You must feel very sad and lonely now that you don't see John any more.' Add that he'll make other friends (and take him to places where he *can*) but don't expect him to get over his loss too quickly. What he'll want from you, during this period when he feels at a loss, is real sympathy and not an attempt to play it down.

Thousands of books have been sold which offer (or seem to offer) a quick way to friendship. I think that friendships have to be worked at, whether we're children or parents. We parents can't wave a magic wand to make our children sociable, born leaders and very popular. We can, however, take certain steps to help them to make friends.

I suggest that you:

Avoid – if you're about to start a family – calling your children exotic, esoteric names e.g. Aloysius, Folly, Psyche or Zog. (Or calling boys Vivien or Evelyn.) Children have enough to put up with without having a name they may have to be embarrassed about all their lives.

As far as is possible, keep out of children's friendships – and their quarrels. If quarrelling starts, stop play until tempers have cooled, but let them sort it out. If children are over-tired and have played too long, call a halt to it. Apart from these commonsense limits let them handle their own friendships; they have to learn sometime.

Don't criticize neighbours (and their children) all the time. Your children have to live in the area, make the best of it, so don't fuss, criticize or set too high standards. Encourage them to go out to play, and let them get on with it.

Try to avoid (if you can) changes of area and of school when your children are teenagers. With a dad, or mum, seeking promotion in a job a few changes of address are inevitable. Do it when the children are young; try to keep the home as a safe base when the children are of secondary school age and when close friendships are very important to them, and less easily made.

Remember that children are great conformists. If all the other children wear jeans and T-shirts don't send your child out to play in a party frock or velvet suit. *Try* to dress your child like (and give him the same privileges and pocket money as) the other children in the school or neighbourhood. Children don't like to be different so don't set too high (or too low) a standard for them.

Have a few friends yourself and invite them home where your children can see you relating to them in a warm, informal, friendly way. They'll soon get the idea so don't forget to set a good example in your own friendships.

Frustration
See also **Aggression** *Page* 3, **Destructiveness** *Page* 53

In the face of frustration some of us regress to an earlier, more childish, stage of development. I have a friend who, some years back, was putting up a kitchen cupboard. I watched him for a while (an enormous pleasure: he is the only person I know who is worse at DIY than me) and then went home. I returned to my pal's house later that day. The cupboard lay in the back garden – smashed to pieces. 'That'll teach it,' said my friend, darkly.

I act childishly sometimes, too. Once, my wife asked some visitors, a whole gaggle of them, to stay with us. The visitors extended their stay and I found it impossible to do any work for more than a week. I was frustrated, fed-up and furious. For three days I went around the house in a black mood and my wife (and kids) took care to avoid me. They knew, at the drop of a hat, that I'd take it out on *them*. Quite irrational, since they had nothing to do with it, really, but they knew enough psychology to realize that, when a person's frustrated and annoyed, it's often the nearest person available whom the anger is vented upon. Finally, ironically enough (considering that kitchen cupboard of my pal's), I spent an afternoon in the garden chopping wood, and felt much better.

I know what frustration is, and so do you. You know, like me, that it can lead to anger, fury and irrational behaviour. It should be no surprise, then, to find that children react to frustration too, and they can show great anger, get into a mood and have a tantrum just like us. Children can be frustrated by toys, by other children and by adults – especially when adults interfere with, or bring a premature end to, their games.

We've all seen children frustrated by toys: 'This won't screw in'; 'This wheel doesn't fit'; 'This glue won't work'. A four-year-old, building an aeroplane, throws down his model and stamps his foot in frustration. A child is riding a tricycle at playgroup and having a marvellous time. He turns his back for a moment and another child takes the bike. He howls out of sheer and utter frustration. 'Interference' is another source of great frustration: another child 'messing about' and spoiling a game, or an adult calling out 'Time for tea' just when whatever the child was doing has got to the most interesting stage.

With good management, and a bit of observation, it should be possible to avoid quite a bit of frustration when it comes to your own child. Don't give him jobs to do that he just can't cope with; like a good teacher, don't interfere too much when he's getting on with something but step in if you see him in obvious difficulties. It won't encourage his determination, it will just make him frustrated and angry. With children in groups – and I'm thinking about that playgroup tricycle – the fairest thing to do is to have 'turns each', so many minutes at a time, so that everybody gets a turn. A few rules, a routine, an adult there to whom they can appeal as referee avoids a great deal of frustration when young children are playing together. Say what you want beforehand ('No fighting; no taking anybody else's toys') and leave them to get on with it.

It's wise to keep a weather eye open for any frustration that your older child may feel in school. If, for example, he can't read and everybody else can, he's going to feel frustrated. Do go up to the school and ask for remedial reading help for your youngster. If your child is very clever he may be bored in school: boredom can be a source of great frustration so contact the school and have a word with the teacher about the situation. If your child is a teenager and simply isn't getting very much from the classroom do have a chat with the teacher about it. Your youngster's timetable may be altered – he can, perhaps, drop a subject and take another, or spend more time doing a subject he really enjoys. This isn't interference. It's doing something about the apathetic, or down-right unpleasant, feelings that your child has about his lessons, and his sense of frustration that the school isn't developing the talents he does have but merely harping upon his weaknesses.

Try to encourage your children to talk about their feelings. Don't have a family atmosphere where feelings are bottled up and never expressed (this, in itself, can be a source of frustration). Where children can openly say how they feel (it's the same with adults) they are less likely to smash up the furniture, have tantrums or lash out at another innocent person. I used to work with a colleague who, whenever she felt frustrated, would take hold of a cushion, punch it relentlessly and shout out, many times: 'Christchurch Priory.' In some Japanese factories they have, I'm told, a room with straw dummies in it so that workers can hit the dummies with large wooden poles when they're feeling frustrated. I'm not certain that you'll want either of these two solutions in your home. What you should have is a clear understanding that every member of the family can express their frustrations, verbally, rather than keeping it all locked up inside.

Really, it's a question of attitude. Some degree of frustration in life is inevitable. A toddler is going to feel frustrated because of his size, and the sheer number of things he'd like to do, but can't. A teenager is going to feel frustrated if he's doing badly in school and (even more sadly) if he can't get a job. Adults meet minor frustrations every day. The right attitude is to accept that life involves regular frustration, to talk about your feelings, to have a sense of humour about it all, and to find areas in which you can succeed and find that sense of competence which is so important to us all. If you react to your child's frustrations by taking practical steps to help him by giving him toys which he can cope with rather than ones which totally baffle him; keeping in touch with the teacher when your child is at school; if you can keep *your* sense of humour; if *you* can learn to bounce back after frustration then the chances are that your child, whatever his age, will learn to bounce back too.

Fun

The Greek philosopher, Epicurus, believed that pleasure was the aim in life. (He also believed in moderation in all things: if you overdo anything, your pleasure suffers from the law of diminishing returns.) I'm quite sure that *one* aim in life is to be happy; whether it's by helping others, seeking amusement or just sitting and thinking, is up to you. The trouble is the more you chase happiness, and fun, the more it seems to elude you. It seems to come from doing things together with people you like; it's a by-product, not an aim and it needn't cost money.

So much for philosophy, you might say, when I'm worried sick about my mortgage/overgrown garden/slates falling off the roof/the incredible price of everything these days. We're living in the age of anxiety. *Everybody* I know seems to be worried about something. There just doesn't seem to be much *fun* about. 'Every minute you spend being miserable is sixty seconds when you could have been happy,' I told a friend. 'I don't want to know that,' he said. 'We're here to help others,' I suggested. 'What are the others here for?' he countered. So many people, nowadays, are wary, cynical and pessimistic.

That's no good to youngsters. The idea of having children is to enjoy them while we have them: they grow up, believe me, only too quickly. Children want to enjoy themselves, to enjoy life. Lucky the child who is born to parents with a sense of fun. Let's look at young children. What would they define as fun? *Movement* is fun (e.g. crawling, hopping, skipping, running about in an open space); *getting dirty* is fun, for many young children; *getting wet* is great fun for infants, it makes them laugh, gets them animated (though some parents would define youngsters who are splashing each other with water as being anti-social); *being swung in the air* by dad, or *tickled,* by mum, can be great fun (if you don't overdo it); *making a noise* can be fun; *going for a walk*, or *swimming*, or *making music* can be fun. I'm sure you can think of your own list of things that young children would regard as fun.

Fun is vaguely anarchic. When youngsters are having fun, some parents think they're 'not really doing anything'. That misses the point. All human beings (including adults) need to have some fun, sometime. With children, their fun is more uninhibited than that of adults; it can be noisy or quiet; it doesn't depend on having expensive educational toys. A tree, a cardboard box, a hill can each be a source of lots of fun. What you have to do, as a parent, is to spot the potential for fun in a situation and not worry if your child gets a bit wet/dirty/noisy/excited. Having fun is an exhilarating business.

There are parents (a lesson to us all) who seem to have boundless energy, and a terrific sense of fun and imagination. One mother I knew took a group of under-fives into the garden, where there was a table and chairs. She took a spade, dug up a spadeful of earth, and placed it on the table. Then she gave each of the children a magnifying glass. 'Let's look for creatures,' she said, as they peered, through the glasses, at the great mound of earth. Good fun, but let's be realistic. We can't all be perfect parents. What we can do, with young children, is get them into the open air, give them lots of chances to play with other children, give them a break from us from time to time (neighbourhood child-minding groups and playgroups provide, amongst other things, this necessary relief from each other's company) and *remember to have a bit of fun ourselves*. If your attitude is that life can be (and should be) enjoyed, your children will enjoy it; if you go through life with a permanent 'Let's get through Monday' outlook, you'll pass on your grumpy philosophy to your offspring.

Older children, like younger children, want *action*. Sitting around, discussing the price of fish, isn't fun. When children are at that lovely stage of development between eight and twelve years you can still have fun with them (join in their games, take them to interesting places – and enjoy them yourself – suggest ideas as to what they might like to do). Brass rubbings, potato prints, cooking, crazy golf in the garden (with margarine tubs as holes, build your own obstacles), archery, building a go-cart are fun. Sitting about, doing nothing isn't (and is ultimately more tiring for parents than listening to children complain that 'there's nothing to do').

With teenagers, discos, squash, swimming, playing in a group, just 'messing about' in the street can be fun. Probably, at this stage, they won't want you to share in their fun (though you can still do some things with them such as swimming, dress-making, model-building or going to the shops). What you have to do is to realize that the inordinate amount of time they spend just talking and chattering on about this and that, is a preparation for adult life, for mixing with others, as well as a search for identity. It may strike you as a waste of time. It isn't. It's part of the task of coming to grips to the world and it's fun – although you may think that they'd be better employed doing homework. If you allow them fun and have a sense of fun yourself, it makes it much easier when you want them to do something. 'He's great. You can have a bit of fun with him but he's strict underneath.' Thus, a youngster described his youth club leader to me. Discipline is easier to accept when it comes from somebody who has the humanity to realize that everybody, but especially youngsters, need occasionally to relax and have fun.

If you're reading this and feeling totally washed-out, exhausted, despirited and dismayed you won't be impressed with this emphasis that I've placed on fun. 'All I get is hard work,' you'll say. 'Where's the fun in that?' Don't worry. None of us have fun all the time and some of us have no fun any of the time. What I want to do is to stress the importance of having a bit of fun just some of the time. Here are a few rules of having fun with your own children:

Have some fun yourself. A sense of fun is infectious. So is gloom and despondency. Get up, get out, and remember that you (quite apart from your children) are a real person, who needs fun.

Don't be a Smother-Mother. Children are precious but they are also tough, resilient, washable and born with a sense of wonder. So *don't* molly-coddle them and keep saying, 'Don't do that.' Let them run about, get a bit dirty, have fun. They'll learn more and they'll enjoy their childhood more.

Put young children in sensible clothing. They can't have fun if you insist on dressing them like Little Lord Fauntleroy or sending them out into the street (or nearest field) in party frocks.

Get into the great outdoors with your children, or into the local park, or even supermarket!

Let teenagers have fun (as long as it's not anti-social) without too much criticism of their choice of amusement. They live in a different world than the one we were brought up in. The best contribution you can make to their happiness is to have lots of interests yourself, and not lose your own sense of curiosity, or fun.

Remember, life is short, and we all take ourselves too seriously. Enjoy life while you can.

Gangs
See also **Friends** *Page* 86

Up to the age of two children play (mostly) by themselves or (sometimes) in pairs. When they go to playgroup or nursery school they begin to play in larger groups and to show awareness of group belonging. During the ages from six to eleven they are into gangs and clubs. A group of children may form a secret club, with special badges and, perhaps, a den with a sign over the door: KEEP OUT. THIS MEANS YOU. The gang provides the child with companionship, a chance to organize projects and a feeling of independence from adults and from 'the others' who don't belong to the gang. This is the start of that 'group identity' which is such an important part of adult life – with its associations, societies, luncheon clubs, sports clubs, trade unions, political parties, 'old school ties', T-shirts, uniforms, badges and styles of dress: all of which emphasize group belonging.

By the time that children are eleven- or twelve-years-old, groups, clubs and gangs (or cliques and teams) are of major importance in their lives. What is noticeable is that most of these groups are sex-segregated: boys go with boys and girls go with girls. Whilst girls may look upon the group as a loosely (or tightly) knit network of intimate friendships, boys are keen to emphasize that the group comes first and individual feelings and aspirations second. Again, this clustering into same-sex groups, sharing friendships and intimate secrets only with members of the same sex, is to be seen amongst adults in our society and is, perhaps, the result of sex-segregation (and the male chauvinism) that goes on at earlier stages of development.

Groups *do* offer support to children. By doing things together, discussing things together, children can come to terms with their anxieties (about themselves as people, or about growing up). By the time they are teenagers children may feel the first stirrings of independence. The teenage gang is a kind of refuge, a last outpost, before the growing youngster is faced with the adult world. In the gang, he can be with his peers and (if he wants to) reject adults and their values for a while before he, inevitably, has to join them. Gangs *can* have a bad influence on the youngster: they can lead him to over-value such things as pop music, fashionable clothes, in-group loyalties, or to swear, smoke, or take drugs; they can over-emphasize the importance of 'being like the others' – rather than being an individual, being oneself. Too much peer group orientation can drive a wedge between the youngster and adults (so *whatever* the adult says is wrong). In our society, teenagers get a great deal of attention. They make a great deal of noise; they have their own music, fashions and pop stars. Yet, when all is said and done, none of these things last very long. The teenage gang (and the teenage culture) should be seen for what it is: a useful opportunity to learn to learn to live in a group, a half-way house between the joys of being a child and the worries of being an adult. Conformity to teenage peers is, whether we like it or not (and whether we think teenagers have to much to say, or not), a normal part of growing up.

If you find that your child is a member of a gang (i.e. a group which meets regularly) what should you, as a parent, do about it? My advice is to:

Try to find out what kind of gang it is. It's sad but true that youngsters sometimes join gangs who bully younger children, or steal, or indulge in other forms of anti-social (or criminal behaviour). You are entitled to express your views about this and also to suggest that your youngster might be better employed (and happier) being in a group which helps other people rather than takes advantage of them.

Encourage your youngster to join a group of which you approve. (It's always better to say 'Do this,' rather than 'Don't do that.') Young people need involvement, status and an opportunity for social growth but they can get them from a sports club, a youth group (or by starting up a group of their own) rather than joining a delinquent group. Boredom is the enemy and the bored youngster is in greater danger of finding a delinquent group.

Encourage them to bring friends home. The gang *is* a refuge from adults but the separateness of children and adults shouldn't be over-emphasized. The family is (or should be) the safe base from which they can spring forth to tackle the world so don't let them live in two worlds – theirs and yours. Try sometimes to bring those worlds together.

Give them some space in which to lead their own lives. If you pry too much, don't give them any freedom and don't trust them, children (and especially teenagers) will resent it very much. Too much interference will drive a wedge between you and make them more (rather than less) secretive about what they are up to.

Go along to school parent-teacher meetings and to other events which your child wants you to attend. Heaven knows, children don't always want us; teenagers invite us to partake in very little of their world. They're desperate to keep it to themselves. So, if they do want you to go to something make sure you go. The more displays of 'family solidarity' the better.

Try to do some things together, as a family. This is easier with young children: teenagers, mostly, want to do their own thing. (Our own teenagers won't come on holiday with us – they claim it's boring – but they *will* come to the cinema, for a meal, or to the pub.) I know it's hard but do go out together occasionally, even if you have to drag yourself to the speedway or to a pop concert that you don't particularly like.

Accept your child as he is and show him affection. Treat him like a real person. The more acceptance, and love, the child finds in the home the less he'll look for status, identity and belonging outside the home. Accept, however, that you can't give him everything. Whatever you do, he's going to be influenced by his peer group – those of his own age – but he'll modify his views later on. After all, we did. Young people need to rebel against parents and question adult values. Later on, they realize that adults are not quite so awful as they thought they were.

Treat your growing teenager as a friend. He'll still need other friends but he'll look upon his home as a safe base and somewhere he can come back to after all his wanderings. That's what a home should be.

Generation Gap
(For Parents)

If you think of life as a journey, we parents are obviously further along the road than our children. This doesn't necessarily mean that we've seen more than they have (*that* depends how much you keep your eyes open) but it does mean that our experience and our expectations are different from theirs. When you're young you want the moon, you have plenty of energy and you want lots of excitement and new experience. Life gets harder as we grow older. Our bones get creakier, we realize that there are a lot of ambitions that we are not going to achieve. Nevertheless, I don't think we should go about the place spreading gloom and despondency in the presence of our youngsters. Let them hope, let them dream, let them work it out for themselves. They'll discover their own limitations, and the realities of life, soon enough.

Like birds, the aim of young people is to fly the nest, fend for themselves. Bearing that in mind I think a generation gap (but not too wide) is necessary. Your youngsters will want, sooner or later, to make the break and stand on their own two feet. 'The Gap' is a kind of half-way house where they prepare to think for themselves and be real people in their own right. I think we should recognize the gap but build a few bridges over it, mainly leaving the choice of *which* bridges to *them*.

You could start off by *negotiating* with them about certain perennial bones of contention. All of these are to do with the concept of 'freedom'. This is a very important notion to teenagers. (They don't know, but they'll learn, that there is no absolute freedom in life since our actions always have some kind of effect on other people. Responsibility is less popular than freedom but it's more crucial to our all living together.) Let's say you'd like your daughter or son to be in by 11pm. She thinks curfew should be midnight. If you make a big performance out of it ('I said eleven and eleven it is.' 'You can't make me.' 'Oh, yes, I can …') you'll be destroying a vital bridge rather than building one. Why not talk, sensibly, about last buses, what time the dance ends or the youth club finishes? Say you don't like to see him or her looking too tired. Talk it out, settle for 11.30pm. It's your attitude that counts. If you're reasonable on this (and on the other bones of contention such as driving the family car, choosing clothes, parties or pocket money) it's another bridge built. Stay your ground on your side of the gap ('I know best.' 'You're too young to know anything.') and you'll find that the gap widens and it will become more and more difficult to cross it.

We live in an age-stratified society – that is a society where babies play together, young children go to school (and play) with other young children, teenagers stick together and adults stay in their own groups. We think of senior citizens as yet another group apart. This, of course, is quite wrong. We're all human beings (admittedly at different stages of the life cycle) and we ought really to mix together more so that we benefit from the vivacity of those who are younger than us (and the courage and liveliness of those who are older).

Infants like older children to play with them; older children learn a lot from playing with infants. Some teenagers are marvellous with toddlers and with senior citizens. What a pity that we all keep in our own little world when we would have a lot more fun (and learn a lot more) by being together. It *is* harder in a nuclear family – all of us in our own little boxes, with our own children. It *was* more natural in the extended family setting when we had aunts, uncles, grandparents, cousins, young and old, all about us. When big families were the order of the day older children looked after younger children, and younger children learned from older children. Now, parents and children are thrown together far more. Is it any wonder that they get on each other's nerves? Is it surprising that the youngsters insist on being (or looking) different to emphasize that they need some space in which to lead their lives, learn to grow up, make a few mistakes, *away from the parents?*

It isn't easy, in our tiny houses, living on top of each other, to avoid frequent quarrels with our children. Here are a few things we can do to make sure that the generation gap doesn't become a chasm and the skirmishes that we're bound to have with our children don't develop into a full-scale war. I suggest that you:

Say what you think on such matters as dress, homework, choice of friends and hair-styles, but play it cool. The more fuss you make the more inclined your youngsters will be to dig their heels in, disobey or think up something really bizarre just to annoy you.

Expect some quarrels. They're part of life and of living together. You're bound to disagree over some things but compromise cements the underlying relationship while making a big issue of every little disagreement erodes it.

Expect to win a few, lose a few.

Realize that they need you. They'll argue with you, defy you and annoy you (on principle). They're learning to spread their wings. The odd thing is that they respect you more than you realize and lean on you, want you to need them, more than you'd think.

Erect a sign in your head: NO PARENTS BEYOND THIS POINT. Leave their letters, and their personal friendships alone. *Some* privacy and trust is vital to young people: without it, they can't grow up.

Have some sympathy for them. Can you remember being a teenager? Would you like to go through that again?

Keep talking. Whilst you're talking (and, I hope) listening to them, whilst you're discussing things with them, the bridges are going over the gap. When they're adults the gap will be much narrower and it'll be easier to see the other's point of view, and to be real friends. All that hard work will have been worth it.

Avoid being misled. Teenagers look self-assured, sophisticated. Underneath, they are far less confident than they seem. You are the safe base from which they set off to explore the world. They need you more than they'd be prepared to admit (to you). They may not, at times, want you to talk to them (or talk to you). They *want* a generation gap. They don't want a chasm. Don't disappear but don't get too close. That gap is very useful, to them and to us: it gives us a rest from each other.

Gifted Children
See also **Precocious Children** *Page* 175

What is the best way of giving gifted children a square deal? There's no simple answer since the children concerned may be very different in their abilities, social adjustment and emotional needs.

Whatever else we do with gifted children we should always treat them as individuals and assess their own particular gifts (and weaknesses?).

Anybody with experience of a number of gifted children will realize that it is silly to put them under the same umbrella. This child is a good all-rounder; that child plays the violin like an angel; this one is brilliant at chess (and, curiously, poor at school subjects); this one over here is a marvellous ballet dancer.

The distinction I would make would be to separate those children who have a special talent from those who seem to be able to cope outstandingly well with a variety of tasks, and who are generally (rather than specifically) extremely able. Each child has to be treated as a unique case and advised accordingly.

If you have a gifted child you will know that some of them can be extremely demanding and tiresome. Few parents see, straight away, that what they are faced with is a one-in-a-hundred oddball child who needs and deserves more stimulation than other children and, even more difficult for the ordinary parent, *stimulation of an appropriate sort.*

This is where you need professional advice, and you need that advice *as early in the child's life as possible.* After a diagnosis of giftedness has been made you, at least, know what you're dealing with. I'm stressing this because I've come across cases of gifted children wrongly diagnosed as 'maladjusted', 'lazy' or 'eccentric'. The main enemy as far as gifted children (and their parents) are concerned is boredom. Not a few gifted children have ended up as lost souls simply because their special talents were never recognized by their teachers or their own families.

Teachers can do an awful lot for the gifted child; point his nose in the right direction, lend him books, set him interesting, mind-stretching tasks for homework and put him in touch with libraries, professional societies and clubs where he can mix with, or correspond with, older people who are not over-daunted by the youngster's knowledge.

Programmes of 'enrichment' have to be worked out carefully in the context of the whole child. Otherwise, we may produce a child who has too many peaks and troughs: who, for example, has the intellectual ability of an adult and the social and emotional skills of an eight-year-old. A boy may be able to write to the alumni of an astronomy society and understand the esoteric debates; that doesn't mean to say that he shouldn't join the cub scouts and learn something alongside the less-gifted children of his own age. In adult life, after all, the gifted person has to mix with the rest of us.

In some areas there are Saturday clubs where gifted children may communicate with other youngsters of similar ability. However, these clubs often entail a certain amount of travel. More locally, there may be free music tuition (from the school orchestra, local bands), cycling badges to be gained, swimming, athletics and gymnastics badges, cubs, scouts, the church choir. Gifted children are often brimming over with physical and psychic energy: it makes life much easier for all concerned if school and parents can work together to keep them busy.

Educationally speaking, we need more classes for gifted children and more specialist teachers who could devote time to encouraging particular talents. Those children who are backward or severely retarded get a very square deal in our educational system. Why should gifted children get less than they deserve?

We mean by a 'gifted child' somebody with an IQ of 140 and above. I have seen an eight-year-old boy with an IQ (I estimated) of 250. He scored so highly he was 'off the map' as far as the test was concerned. The intelligence test, often carried out by a school psychologist, can also tell us what the child is good at and what he is less good at; it can give us a profile of that particular child's abilities.

This individual assessment is crucial. Your gifted child may be outstanding at gymnastics; mine may be a brilliant musician. Their social, and educational, needs will be quite different, though their *emotional* needs will be similar. Whatever their gift they will need constant love, friendship and emotional support. The main job of parents of gifted children is to love them. It cannot be stressed too highly that *all* human beings (including children of outstanding ability) need demonstrated love. They need to feel, in the middle of feeling 'different' that they belong, somewhere.

Here is my ten-point plan for parents of gifted children. If you follow this you have a chance of ensuring that the child isn't misunderstood or bored out of his (or her) mind:

Have your child assessed by the school psychologist. Is the child within the gifted range? If so, in what particular areas is the child gifted?
Liaise closely with your child's school and ensure that the child is given *individual work* appropriate to his intellectual abilities. Encourage the child to do projects, or pieces of research, using the local library. The child could report back to his class thus enriching their experience as well as his own.

Place the child in a class above his own age group for particular subjects e.g. maths but consider carefully whether you want your child permanently in a class where the children are older than he is. Only do this if the child can cope emotionally and socially.

Find out whether there are any special classes or schools) for the gifted in your area. If not, get in touch with other mothers of gifted children and start up a Saturday club.

Find out what facilities are available for children with special gifts i.e. those children who are outstanding dancers, musicians or mathematicians. Sometimes, scholarships are available at boarding schools catering for gifted children. Before you make any decisions, however, *see the school*, and make sure that you think your child will be happy there.

Encourage the child to learn a foreign language, and to learn something about other countries. Also, introduce them to subjects not in the school curriculum but which may interest them such as astronomy, philosophy, archaeology and ethics.

Teach the child how to play chess, or bridge, or some other game which may stretch him intellectually.

Encourage wide reading (it doesn't matter whether it is fiction, or non-fiction).

Let the child set his own pace. Your role as a parent is mainly one of a *facilitator,* who can put the child in touch with (either personally or via a written correspondence) with those people who have the skills and knowledge to help him.

Last but by no means least, *try to provide a loving and understanding home background.* If you're not in the gifted range yourself don't try and ape your child. What he wants, most of all, from his parents is that very vital ingredient to human happiness: love, without strings.

Further advice can be obtained from The National Association for Gifted Children (NAGC), 1 South Audley Street, London W1Y 5DQ.

Guilt
(For Parents)

Whatever you do, don't make your children feel guilty. The best way you can do this is not to feel too guilty yourself. You may not be a perfect mum or dad but, come to think of it, who is? Your child isn't, as a result of all your efforts, perpetually happy. Which child is? You can feed your child, provide shelter, give him love but you can't protect him from *some* pain, *some* hurt, *some* disappointment. He will, believe me, take all those setbacks providing that you tell him that you love him, and are not afraid of showing him lots of affection. Love is like armour to children: nasty things still happen to them but, with love, it doesn't matter quite as much.

If you have a difficult child and you're not coping very well, don't feel guilty about it. It happens to thousands of mothers and fathers. Do your best; that's all you can do. If you find that you love one child more than another, accept it – there's nothing you can do about it anyway – but be fair to the child you love less and try to build up a 'special' relationship with him. There's not much point in feeling guilty about your feelings; you can, though, go out of your way to like a child and to be friends with him. Be positive, don't analyse your every emotion and motive. Whilst you're sitting there, moping, life is passing you by and you're spreading guilt and despondency on to those around you; especially your children.

I, to be honest, have no time for guilt. What's done is done. We'll do better next time. No sense in spending a lifetime punishing ourselves for our mistakes, or the 'bloomers' we commit in bringing up our children. If I were to give myself detention for every mistake I've made with my own family I would not set foot out of the door. Bringing up a child you'll experience disappointment, alarm and failure. If you're optimistic, tough and cheerful, if you bounce back when those little disasters hit you, you'll pass on those, very useful, qualities to your child. If you're pessimistic, gloomy and broody your child will catch that from you. In families, emotions are caught, not taught.

Whatever you feel guilty about, don't allow yourself the luxury of those totally wasted feelings. If you feel guilty about something in your past, forget it. It's got nothing to do with your child and why should you pass your guilt feelings on to him? If you make a mistake with your child say you're sorry it happened. Don't buy him a present to propitiate him and don't feel guilty for months. Terrible things happen in families as well as at sea. I remember my mother giving my rugby shirt – my best one – to the 'rag-man' by mistake. 'Not much I can do about it now,' she said, as I tried to make her feel guilty about it. 'I don't even know where he lives,' she added. Don't use the technique of making people feel guilty. Your children will try this tactic out on you. Don't fall for it and don't use it on them.

Some mothers (and fathers) have had very unhappy childhoods. You may have had an unhappy – or totally disastrous – childhood yourself. Don't worry. Many of the very best parents I know had awful childhoods: *they* are determined to give a better deal to their children than they had themselves. So write off your past to experience and never live in the past. If you had a lot of misery when you were a child say: 'The misery stops here.' Don't pass it on to your child. You needn't, if you don't want to.

Lastly, accept your own limitations, life's little ironies. Few of us get quite as much as we'd hoped for. The most precious thing that a parent can pass on to a child is a sense of fun, of sheer gladness to be alive. So, don't tell them lies, tell them the world can be a nasty place, and tell them it can also be very beautiful.

Guilt is a most destructive emotion. Have nothing to do with it. Accept your mistakes. I'll bet I've made more than you. That doesn't stop me being convinced that the world is a beautiful place and I belong in it. I, like you, have a right to be here. So why feel guilty about *that?*

Handwriting

Children, I think, take a pride in work which is neatly presented; the appearance of their written work is important to them, and to their teachers. Also, it's important for children to be able to read what they've just written. You'll find this hard to believe but some infants arrive in school without being able to hold a pencil or crayon. (I'm not talking, here, about physically-handicapped children but about normal youngsters who have never had a chance to develop their manual dexterity and their hand-eye coordination.) Young children, before they go to school, should be encouraged to play with Plasticine and other modelling materials, to paint with large brushes, use a hammer and saw, cut out shapes with scissors and play with simple jig-saw puzzles, build 'houses' with Lego and 'towers' with wooden bricks (as well as scribble on paper with a pencil or crayons).

Motor movements in the young child develop in sequence: going from large to small movements. The child needs to learn to walk, run, hop and skip before he can be expected to develop the pencil control that is necessary for writing. The under-five who can ride a three-wheeler bike, or catch a ball, is usually able to write more neatly than his friend who can't do either. In infant school it is the teacher's job to teach the child, first, to print his own name and simple words and sentences. Usually, the teacher writes a word or sentence (sometimes under a picture) and the child traces over it.

103

You, the parent, can help at this stage by encouraging the child to draw, to trace over pictures or around templates (shapes, in wood or plastic, of animals and common objects), to tackle puzzle books (sold in Woolworth and W. H. Smith), to play cards (especially snap) and to copy sequences of beads, straws, shapes, and letters.

Sentence completion, or missing word games, are useful, too. You should write out the sentence (use 'printing' in lower-case letters, not capitals, and not 'double-writing') and outline the missing word with dots. Your child joins the dots to complete the sentence. (This join-the-dots technique can also be used with drawings: you draw a dog, cat, house or church etc and the child traces the dotted path to complete the drawing.) Some educationists frown on the use of templates, and on tracing; personally, I don't see why these approaches shouldn't be used, provided your child is also allowed to paint and draw freely when he wants to. (To be given too much freedom of expression, too much 'do your own thing', is as bad for your child as being given no freedom at all.)

When the young child has reached the stage where he is to learn 'proper' or 'joined-up' writing the teacher will choose from the main writing styles: cursive, round and italic. Some schools teach the Marion Richardson handwriting style (rather like round-hand) whilst others may choose a modified form of italic. It is at this stage that things may start to go wrong for your child and he may start experiencing difficulties with writing. If he does, what do you do about it? You must teach your child to:

Sit up properly, with back straight and both feet on the floor. The paper (or book) should be moved to suit the posture and not the other way around. (Some children stoop over the paper, face screwed up, feet under them. Don't encourage this.)

Hold the pencil or pen correctly, not too tightly and about an inch from the point (an elastic band can be used to indicate the correct place). Elbows should be held slightly away from the body, not tucked in, and wrists and forearms supported by the desk or table.

Form basic patterns (e.g. lines of m's, o's and w's) and join letters together. Practise these patterns with your child.

Use a decent pen. Platignum offer a wide range of pens and nibs. Mentmore (Platignum House, Six Hills Way, Stevenage, Herts SG1 2AY) sell instruction leaflets on the main styles of handwriting together with copy books and an attractive lettering kit.

Re-vamp a deteriorating writing style. You could buy your child a Platignum fountain pen with an interchangeable nib unit. Many children like italic nibs: they encourage a neat, attractive, clear style. Buy a copy of Tom Gourdie's *Learn About Handwriting* (Ladybird Books) and get your child to write a little each day in this rather stylish modified-italic style. Don't overdo it and you will find that the child quite enjoys seeing how well he *can* write.

Keep to the lines. If your child is having difficulty here (wandering above and below the line) you could draw faintly-pencilled lines across the page to guide the lower-case letters. Some exercise books sold in W. H. Smith have a faint blue line which serves the same purpose.

Understand why writing is better when it's neat. With an older child (and many teenagers have problems with handwriting) a certain amount of sensitivity and loads of praise are necessary if the youngster is not to become demoralized about the whole business.

If your child's difficulties persist you should go to the head teacher at your child's school and ask for an appointment with the educational psychologist who will be able to advise you further.

Useful books are: *The First Reading and Writing Book* by Margaret Hooton (Heinemann & Shepheard Walwyn) and *Nelson Handwriting Workbooks,* Books 1–4 (Nelson).

Hatred
(For Parents)
See also **Intense Dislike of a Child** *Page* 120

In every relationship there are ups-and-downs. Sometimes we think everything our friends say or do is wonderful; the next day we're squabbling like alley cats. These disagreements and quarrels are part-and-parcel of any worthwhile relationship. If we can't tell the truth and be ourselves (warts and all) with a friend who can we be truthful to?

With parents and children there will, similarly, be periods of closeness, and times when we seem to be growing apart. There'll be flashes of anger, even hate; this shows, I suppose, that we really care. When you stop caring, you don't bother to argue, or to hate. Sometimes, with parents and children (emotionally speaking) the going is rough; sometimes it's smooth; it's all part of that mysterious thing called family life.

What happens, though, when the going is never smooth? Some parents do have an animosity towards a particular child (see section on **Intense Dislike of Child)**. There are a few parents, too, who hate a particular child, not for a day or a week but for years and years. In a few cases, the hate seems to be a permanent, inbuilt part of the relationship. This, for both parent and child, is a very sad state of affairs. Hate takes effort. What a pity that all the energy expended on hate couldn't be spent on an emotion a little more productive and positive – such as love.

I knew a little girl, aged ten, called Tracey. In school, Tracey was a super-thief. She stole everything that she could lay her hands on: paper, pencils, money, food, clothes, even the blankets out of the medical room. She didn't try to sell any of the stolen goods or eat the food. It all went home as a gift to the family from her, Tracey, with love.

Tracey kept the family together. She cooked, bought food, sewed, did the washing, cleaned the house, as well as reading to her four younger brothers and sisters before they went to bed. There was no father; he had run off with a woman who had lived in the next street. Tracey's mother was there, but she did very little because she was so depressed. One of the things that kept mum going was her hate for Tracey. 'She's got the same nature as him,' (her husband) she said. 'She's lazy, idle and you can't trust her. She's dirty too.'

What this mother was saying about her eldest daughter just wasn't true. The girl *wasn't* lazy and she was terribly loyal to her mother. Tracey stole from school, admittedly, but only for the family. Tracey's thieving was based on selflessness; she loved school and was reasonably bright but, to her, the family came first. She was a miniature Florence Nightingale. The mother saw her as a slut and a villain. Why?

My guess is that mother disliked Tracey because Tracey reminded her of what she could be, i.e. courageous and competent, if she tried. She reminded mother of the good times she had had in the early days of her marriage. Mother, in my view, was doing two things wrong. She was colluding in Tracey's thefts – criticizing her for stealing but encouraging her to do so by accepting the stolen items into the home – and blaming Tracey for what had happened to the family and using her eldest daughter as the scapegoat (see section on **Scapegoat Children)**. In fact, Tracey was none of the things mother thought she was. Tracey was a heroine; she deserved a George Medal for the way she cared for her brothers and sisters. Mother simply needed somebody to hate. She chose Tracey.

It's very odd when a mother hates a perfectly natural, likeable child. I've heard a mother describe her teenage daughter as, 'the incarnation of evil, monstrous, vile,' just because the girl, aged sixteen, got herself a boyfriend whom mother didn't like! What this mother couldn't cope with was her daughter growing up into an attractive, sexually-aware young woman. It was jealousy that lay beneath the hate she showed for both the boyfriend and her daughter. As soon as this mother gained some insight into her own feelings she began to see her daughter as a real person and was capable of liking her for what she was, an extremely pleasant (and very moral) young woman.

John was a similar case. John was illigitimate: a product of one of mother's teenage liaisons. Mother had married at twenty and had three legitimate children: two girls and a boy. Mother suffered a tremendous amount of guilt over John and was wracked with remorse about her teenage behaviour (and the birth of John in particular). Her husband knew all about her indiscretion and had long ago forgiven her for it; he loved his wife deeply. This didn't seem to make much difference to mother or to her relationship with her first-born. Everything John did, as far as mother was concerned, was wrong. It was only when she described him as a 'nasty, evil, dirty boy' (John was aged twelve, and quite charming) that she (the mother) began, slowly, to get some insight into the fact that the boy represented what she saw as the nasty, irresponsible side of her own nature. As time went on she learned, at last, that she had no reason to dislike herself so much and not to love her son.

Perhaps it's true that we are capable of hating someone simply because they remind us of something that we don't like (or hate) inside ourselves. The only thing we can do in the face of these emotions (and hatred is a waste of time – it is undignified and does nothing for the one who is hated and even less for the one who hates) is to realize that we are being unfair and that the reason for the hatred lies within ourselves. It *is* normal to hate a person from time, for a short while (this includes hate for a husband, a wife, a child). It isn't normal (it certainly isn't fair) to hate a child permanently. If you do this, you must ask yourself, fairly and squarely: am I blaming this child for something which is really my problem?

Accept that you may have a difficult child; accept that you'll have family arguments and fall out with a particular child; but *don't* accept that you should hate or reject one particular child for a long, long time (or for ever). It's unfair. It says more about you, and your own personality, than it does about the child. Don't try to *like* the child if you can't; yet, you should try to *love* the child, and go out of your way to show that love. Love is the other side of the coin from hate. If you care enough about somebody to hate them, you care enough about them to love them. Try it.

Homework

It is doubtful whether schools have the legal right to set homework. In 1884, in the only recorded law suit about this issue, a child had been punished for not doing his homework; whereupon the parents sued the teacher for damages.

The court's decision was that the parents did have a duty to send their child to school but any orders to the child to do lessons at home were *not* authorized in law. Nevertheless – before you tell your child the glad tidings – I should point out that a modern court of law would *probably* (and nobody I know has put it to the test) find that the setting of homework, in moderate amounts, to children of *secondary* school age, is legal. Also, as many teachers will tell you, it is almost impossible for children to complete present-day examination syllabuses unless they do homework.

You may agree with me when I say that a great many youngsters (especially those approaching their O- and A-level examinations) work far too hard. Six hours at school is tiring enough; on top of that some teenagers do as much as four hours' homework (a ten hour day!) when they need to be with their friends, relaxing. Let's be realistic and admit that homework (set in moderate amounts) is inevitable.

The main arguments for homework are:

It encourages children to work on their own: an important preparation for adult life where we have to get on with it, (often) without supervision.

It extends the time available for learning: the child can learn French vocabulary, or write up notes, rather than take up precious time in school.

It is expected by many parents. Some primary schools set homework, some don't, and you (the parent) may become worried if you find that your child is *not* set homework. This may be more to do with the policy of the school rather than your suspicion that only brighter children are given homework.

The arguments *against* homework are:

The child who is obsessed with homework has little opportunity to talk, in a relaxed way, with parents or with friends.

108

Outside activities may have to be curtailed. Yet, it is in the brownies, cubs, guides, youth club or local sports centre (or coffee bar) that a young person can learn the social skills which come from mixing with others of his own age.

It is difficult to say what is a 'moderate' amount. A bright child, or somebody particularly interested in, say, maths, may take half-an-hour over a task. Another child may face two hours of anxiety and hard work to do the same job.

What can you, as a parent, do in the face of the strain that homework imposes on some children? What can you do to make sure that it is done properly and with the minimum of fuss? I suggest that you:

Discuss homework at parent-teacher association meetings and find out what the school is hoping to achieve from it. Have a word with your child's teacher and take advice on the best way for your child to set about doing his homework.

Impose a limit on time spent watching TV and try to get the child into a *routine* of doing his homework at a certain time every evening.

Save some time for the family to be together and to talk about things other than school. Homework *shouldn't* dominate family life quite as much as it does. You could, for example, ban any discussion about homework at weekends or during family meals; otherwise, there is never any spontaneous, open-ended conversation at mealtimes.

Ask the school what time should be allowed for the child to follow his own interests, particularly where he has a demanding hobby such as music, gymnastics or any one of a thousand things that interest children.

Make sure that the child has somewhere quiet to work: away from the television, and the family hustle and bustle.

Go to the school and see the child's teacher if the homework set is too hard or if it is causing the child chronic worry and strain. After all, it is your child who is under stress, and your family that may be disrupted by ill-considered homework tasks.

Sadly, with examinations around the corner, it would be a foolhardy child who refused to do homework; the options that he has on his future depend upon exam results. You have to put up with homework, like your child, but every school should have a sensible homework policy and it is your job, as a parent, to find out what it is. Where school and parents liaise there is less strain on the child, and fewer tempers flaring (and insults flying) when homework is done quietly, conscienciously, and with the support of everybody at home.

Hyperactive Children
See also **Boisterous Children** *Page* 19

'Hyperactive' is a word applied to those children who are fidgety, restless and always on the go. You'll know the ones I mean: their emotional elastic is wound up at breakfast time and, whoosh, off they go through the day, like a balloon that somebody has let the air out of. They leave, in their wake, a trail of exhausted adults. What makes children like this? The cause can be *emotional*. The child is chronically anxious and his anxiety expresses itself in incessant chattering and moving about. The child may find it hard to concentrate; anything that happens round about him is likely to distract him. The other cause is *temperamental*. Some babies, even in the womb, are much more restless than others. These children, as babies, do not seem to want to be cuddled; when they're older they seem to have great difficulty in sitting still for more than a few minutes. The last (but not least) cause is *boredom*. There are perfectly normal, healthy children who are restless for the simple reason that they are bored out of their minds and have insufficient scope to use up all their surplus energy.

If you have one of these hyperactive children (I've seen quite a few and, believe me, they *are* tiring) what can you do about it? Here are a few ground rules:

Keep cool. Don't pick up the child's anxiety and become fidgety and restless yourself (I know this is easier said than done!).

Have a routine for the day. A restless child responds best to a predictable pattern of activity where he knows what's going on. Don't add to the child's difficulties by being inconsistent yourself (making promises and not keeping them; saying one thing and doing another). Have a pattern to the day or (if the child goes to school) the evenings, or weekends. Try to keep meals, bedtimes and outings regular so your child knows what to expect.

Give the child something to do but take into account his limited attention span. Research shows that a hyperactive child needs highly-structured, planned activities; he should be given realistic, short-term tasks to do, in a calm atmosphere. *Do* give the child a chapter of a book to read, a few jobs to do in the house. Allow him to bake a cake, mend a bike, do a few sums in his maths book. The idea is that these activities have *definite goals*, and last for anything from ten minutes to an hour. Don't say: 'Here are a few crayons and a book so get on with it, and don't fidget.' Do say: 'I want you to colour in this picture for me and make a nice job of it.' (This is a *specific* goal.)

Learn to reward the behaviour you want (and to ignore (if you can!) the behaviour you don't want). The temptation (see section on **Reward and Punishment)** is to pay attention to the child when he's playing up, being naughty, and to ignore him when he's good. This is exactly the opposite of what should happen.

Since hyperactive children can be utterly exhausting, and a very real problem to the busy mother, I would like to suggest a method of dealing with them based on re-inforcement (i.e. reward) procedures which you may find helpful. Make two lists. The first list is of everything that the child does that you find annoying e.g. moving about all the time, chattering, calling out when other people are talking, scratching himself, restless movements and so on. Next, make a separate list of the kinds of behaviour that you would like to see more of (e.g. sitting still, getting on with his play, no talking and so on). Then, you must reward the behaviour that you want. You can do this quite simply by smiling at the child, or by a word of praise, when he has (for example) managed to do a job for you without making too much fuss about it (or even sat in his chair and read for ten minutes without becoming restless and fidgety).

If you want to introduce a little variety into the rewards that you use you could give your child a little note book and stick in a coloured star, or an ink-stamp made with some distinctive design; alternatively, you could use tokens which can be exchanged for a special treat when the child has collected ten or twenty. Again, a reward could be a special privilege such as the child staying up later on Saturday evening or being allowed to cook a tray of biscuits. To be effective, the reward must immediately follow the good behaviour: don't give him his token, or stamp, days after the event!

If your child responds to this method you can reward him after longer and longer intervals: the rule is to reward frequently at first and then tail off the rewards as the child learns to behave sensibly without them. I'm a bit averse to using reinforcement procedures with children but, in the case of the hyperactive child, I think

111

they're justified even if they only teach us to be calm, systematic and logical in our approach. The hyperactive child needs to know what's allowed and what isn't; he needs the emotional security that comes from a calm atmosphere, and plenty of praise.

Finally, an example. John, aged nine, was put on a simple reinforcement schedule for a month. His mother used gold stars in a note book as rewards. Ten gold stars could be exchanged for a 'treat'. The chart below shows the decline of undesired behaviour during the first month of using these rewards:

	Moving from chair	Fidgeting	Interrupting others' conversations	Disrupting others' play
DAY 1	6	22	5	8
DAY 19	—	10	—	3
DAY 30	—	2	—	—

As John's unwanted behaviour decreased in frequency so the incidence of acceptable behaviour increased as the following chart illustrates:

	Playing for ten mins. or more	Finishing a job	Sitting still	Reading ten mins. or more
DAY 1	—	—	—	—
DAY 19	5	3	3	2
DAY 30	12	6	14	3

Do you notice, though, that I haven't said all this need not be fun. With hyperactive children, as with any other child, you certainly need a sense of humour. Try a systematic, sensible approach but be affectionate, and calm, in the middle of it all. Don't pick up your child's bad habits. Nobody wants you to end up as a hyperactive mum, zooming your way through the day, like a balsa-wood aeroplane fired from elastic. One hyperactive person in a family is quite enough!

If, despite all you do, your child remains hyperactive it would be wise for you to go along to your family doctor and discuss the problem with him. If your child is of school age you could see the school psychologist and ask for advice (an appointment can be made via the headmaster of your child's school).

The Hyperactive Children's Support Group (write to 59 Meadowside, Angmering, Sussex, BN16 4BW) exists to give advice and help to mothers of hyperactive children and to put them in touch with other parents with similar problems.

Inferiority Complex
See also **Uriah Heep Complex** *Page* 253

When I was a boy I disliked my oldest brother intensely because he was better-looking than me, cleverer, *and* always seemed to have more money. I spent a great deal of time, as a child, trying to out-do him. Now, as an adult, I like him a lot. We both do our own thing. I don't feel inferior to him, nor he to me. We don't see life as a competition between the two of us. Life is to be lived, to be enjoyed; it isn't the Olympic games. The trouble with competitions is that there's only one winner. I won't deny, however, that there is some competitive element in life. In applying for a job, for example, we may not get it, somebody else may be chosen, and there's no hiding the fact that we're disappointed. It's what happens next that counts. We can say, philosophically, that 'you can't win 'em all' (and make sure we do our best the next time) or we can take our non-selection as a sign that we're inferior, inadequate and not up to the mark. In life, it's not so much what happens to it that's important but the use that we all make of our experiences (see section on **Attitudes**) and our ability to 'bounce back' after disappointment.

It was the psychologist Alfred Adler who coined the term inferiority complex. Adler, like me, had an older brother of whom he was jealous and whom he said, as an old man, was 'still ahead' of him. Without going into it too much, Alfred Adler was a very odd-looking child (he looked a little bit like Miss Piggy in 'The Muppets') and his face, and short stature (plus his handsome brother) led to his having something of a complex about the whole thing. 'To be a human being,' wrote Adler, years later, 'means the possession of a feeling of inferiority that is constantly pressing on towards its own conquest.'

That's fine. Or is it? We all know people with an inferiority complex, children who seem to have no real confidence in themselves. However, most of us know adults with plenty of confidence, and children too: the curious thing is that individuals with plenty of self-respect are *not* always beautiful, clever or rich. In fact, some of them are downright ugly (or of only average ability, and perhaps quite poor). Their confidence comes from inside: it's a state of mind, an ability to live with, and accept, themselves and their own uniqueness. It's a realization that, though we have to compete, we don't have to spend our lives trying to be better than the Jones', or come out on top, all of the time, at any cost.

The question is: how do we develop this feeling of self-confidence in our own children? How do we give them a sense of their own individuality, their own worth, so that they're not for ever comparing themselves to other people to their own detriment? I think we should try to encourage our children to:

Work hard for the goals that they have set themselves. It's rare to achieve anything without a certain amount of sustained effort.

Not be too disappointed if they don't come first. Learning to lose, without too much heartbreak and bitterness, is an important lesson in life.

Not compare. Children should try to set good standards – within their own capabilities – and go for them. They will, sooner or later, come up against somebody who's better than they are. It doesn't really matter so long as they feel they've done their best.

Not be too perfectionist so that they never reach their goals and spend their time making excuses, being ill, or feeling bad, because they never 'succeed'. Success is relative: children should have realistic targets and try, very hard, to attain them.

Develop a sense of cooperation, as well as competition. Most of the goals we reach in life we reach by working with, cooperating with, other people. We can teach children to work together on joint projects at home – even if it's only washing the dishes and tidying the table – and we can encourage community feeling, especially in older children, by getting them to help younger children, or handicapped youngsters, or by visiting old people. It is this sense of community (and a family *is* a small community) which is the royal road to mental health and the main cure for unhappiness.

Accept themselves, for what they are. Nobody who spends his life wanting to be somebody different, longing for what he isn't or what he can't have, is likely to be happy.

The main way that you, as a parent, can get your child to accept himself for who he is is for *you* to accept him for who he is. Don't always compare him with his brother or sister. Don't imply that you could love him more if he was cleverer/more handsome/more polite. Love him for who and what he is. Then he can, from a basis of security and confidence, go out and face those two imposters – failure and success.

It's rather sad that, when we have a chronic feeling of inferiority – like Kaiser Wilhelm II with his withered arm, like Hitler, and like Napoleon, with his funny, Corsican accent and his humble background – we are often led to spend our lives *over-compensating* for our feelings, trying to prove to others what marvellous, infallible human beings we are. Often, this can be at tremendous cost to other people – as in the case of the three men I've mentioned. What we should be doing is leading our own lives, getting on with the three life tasks of love, work and friendship. If we're aware of the feelings of others, we can succeed much more easily. If we are obsessed with our own feelings of inferiority life is much harder.

One of the greatest gifts we can give to a child is a feeling of self-respect. We can do that by letting our child be himself and by loving him through the good patches and the bad, and showing him that we do love him. No child who is loved has any feelings of inferiority. No adult who feels loved ever feels inferior.

Insecurity
See also **Anxiety** *Page* 8, **Nervous Children** *Page* 154

I don't know anybody who is totally secure: life is full of risks, of set-backs, of disappointments. The only thing we can do with our children is to teach them to be adventurous and to take reasonable risks, to try and overcome set-backs and to face up to disappointment with courage and optimism. If we, the parents are courageous and optimistic the chances are that our children will be too.

There is a great deal of uncertainty in life but, with children, I don't think we should make life more uncertain, more confusing than it already is. We should, from an early age, put them in the picture, tell them what's going on, have a routine in the home. It's what they don't know that hurts children just as it's fear of the unknown that frightens adults. We can stand up to quite a lot if we know what's going on, know what to expect. It's when things change, when we can't see any recognizable pattern, when we can't trust what's going on around us (see section on **Neurotic Children**) that we become unsure of ourselves and of our perceptions.

How do you give your child security? The obvious thing to do is to show him plenty of affection and tell him that you love him. Don't be all gooey about it but do tell him from time to time. Forget all about the taboo on tenderness which exists in the British nation. Everybody needs some show of tenderness, and particularly children.

The way you speak to your child is important. A lot of the time you'll be in a hurry, trying to get things done but I hope you'll take time off to have some real conversations with your child. The magic phrases are: 'Tell me more about it.' 'I'm listening.' 'What do you feel about that?' 'Go on. That's really good.' All these open the door to what your child is thinking and feeling. The non-magic phrases are: 'Not now, I'm busy.' 'Later, darling.' 'Oh.' 'You did, did you? Trust you.' They close a lot of doors. Why should your child take the trouble to talk to you, tell you what's happened and describe how he feels when he never gets any response from you that could be called a response? If you are busy (and most of us are) institutionalize your sessions together. Call them 'talking times'. One a week is better than none at all and certainly better than you being lovely and sympathetic one minute and telling him no, you haven't got time to talk to him, the next.

What gives a child security is a consistent framework to his life. Don't over-emphasize discipline for discipline's sake. Leave some room for compromise, for working things out together; that's good training for the responsibilities of adult life. However, do have some rules, so that the child knows what's expected of him. The rules are an essential part of the framework: they should be based on commonsense and consideration for others. Don't have too high standards for your child. Nothing makes a child more anxious than perfectionism, where nothing the child does is good enough, where whatever he does is criticized. Ask him to make decisions, take some responsibility; a family is a joint enterprise; let your child be a real part of the group and a person who is consulted, respected.

It may be as well to explain to your child that everybody who is trying to achieve something gets anxious and jittery from time to time. Without some anxiety we would never get up in the morning or get anything done. New situations (and, for a child, going to a party, a new school, the house of a new friend are all potential anxiety-making situations) do make many of us anxious. We have to learn to live with it. Tell your child about worry, about 'nerves', about having the shakes before some big event. If you don't, he'll think he's the only one in the whole world it happens to!

When tragedy or crisis strikes your family you have to remember that children like to know where they are with the adults who surround them so honesty is always the best policy. If you are separating from your husband/wife (or have separated) you run the risk of causing emotional pain to your children. On the other hand, you can minimize that pain by telling the children, openly, what's happening and by assuring them that both parents still love them. Not every marriage breaks up with awful consequences for the children: if adults can remember that the differences are between two adults and children should never be used in the quarrel. 'I love somebody else.' 'I want to live by myself/with somebody else.' That's true. It can be said, and accepted, however reluctantly. It's out in the open. To wage war, with the children in between two quarrelling adults, is very unfair, and very damaging.

If you have a bereavement in the family you are entitled to show your grief. Say: 'I'm very sad.' 'I feel miserable.' (See section on **Bereavement**.) With children it's never a good idea to feel one thing, say another. They then feel insecure simply because they can never de-code your messages and know what's going on inside you.

It always struck me how confident and lacking in anxiety the astronauts were when they landed on the moon. It was a risky thing to do. Still, they knew what the odds were and what they had to contend with. It's the same, for me, with watching horror movies. If I know that it's silly (monsters all over the place, a hero who isn't afraid of creaking doors, not to mention Dracula or Frankenstein) I quite enjoy the film – if I'm in the mood – but it doesn't frighten me. The only films I have seen that scared me were those (like some of Alfred Hitchcock's) where I'm not sure of what's going on or what's happening. It's like that with children and parents. When you tell your child what is going on inside you, build up a consistent routine for him, make sure he has a framework, a pattern that he can recognize and in which he knows what's expected of him, you are ensuring that he'll be as secure as any human being can be. In life, things we know (like a dentist's drill, or a bump on the head, or a kick on the shin) can cause us pain. But what causes us most pain and anxiety is uncertainty, not knowing.

Intelligence

In our society, *language* is the key to learning. *Words* are the exchange currency in the home, in school, and in many jobs. Without them we would find it difficult to express our thoughts and get our ideas across to others. So, my first piece of advice, if you want to bring up an intelligent child, is: *talk to him.* The earlier you start the better. There is a theory that fifty per cent of a child's development takes place before the age of four years. We, don't have to put a figure on it. What we do know for certain is that the early years (from birth to, say, five years) are vitally important in laying down a good groundwork of words, ideas, and hunches upon which the child can build when he goes to school.

My second tip is: *develop your young child's curiosity.* Go for walks together and discuss the things you see (whether it's a number twenty-three bus or a cow). You can go for a walk up the street together; it doesn't matter where you go as long as you talk together as you're strolling along. The parents are the people who determine the child's learning. If they are enthusiastic, interested, curious to find things out, then their child will be too.

In the early years (see section on **Under-Fives**) nursery rhymes, songs, music, rhythm and, of course, the reading of stories are all vital. Parents are there to point out that the world is a wonderful place. Enjoy your child, encourage him to play, and to talk. These are the magic years: *so do start early.* Talk to the baby in the pram, it's all interesting to his developing mind, even though he won't understand everything you are saying. Point things out; say what you're going to buy for tea. Language is the key to learning, and intelligence.

Of course, I'm not saying that words are the only part of intelligence. As your child gets older you should keep an eye out for particular abilities including such things as verbal ability (good with words, whether spoken or written); numerical ability (good at maths); spatial perception (good at seeing the relationships between shapes and the different parts of the whole; good at dressmaking, jig-saws, maps, painting, design, hairdressing); manual dexterity (good with his hands); mechanical aptitude (good with machines, at mending bikes, toys, motor bikes and motor cars, or – more up to date – electronic equipment); musical and/or artistic ability. What a good parent does (like a good teacher) is to set about building up on the child's strengths (the things he's good at) while giving him a bit of help with his weaknesses (the things he's not so good at).

What I've noticed is that a child's intelligence improves (i.e. his IQ goes up) when he is genuinely interested in something. I met a boy whom the school described as dull who was the Robin Cousins of the internal combustion engine: what he didn't know about cars, and motor bikes, wasn't worth knowing. He, with my help, got himself a job in a garage. He now owns his own business and earns more than his former headmaster! On a more homely level, I taught an eight-year-old who couldn't write essays for toffee. One weekend his mother took him to a fete and, reaching into a bran-tub, she lost her diamond ring. The boy put his hand into the barrel of sawdust and rescued the ring. He wrote about his visit for me and the writing was superb.

Every child is good at something; we have to find out what that something is. Children, to learn, need stimulation. You and I can give them that stimulation, by taking them out to interesting places,

118

getting them to join the local library, getting them to 'read up' about things they are interested in, and listening to them when they want to tell us about what they have been reading, and doing.

Every child is an individual, each with his own talents and that's why I'm not happy about intelligence tests which place children on a scale of IQ from mentally subnormal to gifted. The IQ – or Intelligence Quotient – is arrived at by the formula $\frac{MA}{CA}$ x 100 where the MA is the youngest's mental age on the test and CA is his chronological age. We multiply by 100 to make it into a round number. All this sounds very scientific but it has great dangers. We *can't* sample a person's abilities adequately in the time it takes to give an intelligence test. We don't want to imply that, if you're not academic, you're no good. This country needs young people who are good at practical things, as well as academically-inclined youngsters. What we should do is to have a clear idea of the strengths and weaknesses of the particular child and, as I've said before, build up on his strengths. When you're helping your child, forget the 'IQ'. Ask: what is he good at? What is the best way I can encourage his interest(s)?

In order to develop your child's intelligence, and curiosity, you should:

Play with your baby, and talk to him. Give him plenty of toys to play with.

Develop your infant's imagination by looking at picture books together, playing imaginative games (play with the dolls, or tot trucks and cars together); finger-paints, Plasticine, wooden blocks and crayons and paper all help to develop imagination and learning.

Have a word with your local children's librarian about picture and/or story books for children. These days, there are some marvellous books for young children and (borrowed from the library) they cost nothing.

When you take the child out, do talk together.

Take your child to a playgroup when he's about three-years-old. There he'll find plenty of stimulation, he'll learn to play with other children and you'll get lots of ideas from the other parents.

When your child goes to school take an interest in what he is doing (but don't get too anxious about it all!). Visit the school from time to time, talk with the teacher, go to Parent-Teacher Association meetings. Your active interest in the child's life at school is likely to make him want to do his best while he's there.

Get your child to join a few clubs. Being in the cub-scouts,

scouts, youth club, sports club or church group helps to develop a child's all-round competence, and confidence in himself.

When it comes to the time for your child to choose a career, seek advice. Schools have careers masters and mistresses; each area has a youth employment officer. Weigh up what abilities your child has and make sure he uses them. You don't want him to end up frustrated, under-stimulated and a square peg in a round hole.

The main thing that you can give your child, when it comes to developing his abilities and furthering his intelligence, is a sense of curiosity in, and wonder at, the world. It's your attitude that counts. If you are lively, interested, willing to have fun and to find things out, then your child will be too.

Intense Dislike of a Child

(For Parents)
See also **Hatred** *Page* 105, **Scapegoat Children** *Page* 192

You'll know, like me, families in which dad is potty about a favourite son (or daughter); this favourite child is 'the apple of father's eye'; he (or she) can do no wrong. The same applies to mothers; they, too, can have favourites. One mother will find a daughter 'easy to talk to' or a son that she is so proud of that she could burst. 'I'm very close to my eldest daughter,' a mother will tell me. 'My son and I just have a lot in common,' a dad will say. Usually, the child and parent have interests in common, like to do things together, enjoy each other's company and (last but not least) don't get on each other's nerves. What is nice to see is a parent and child who have spontaneous, easygoing fun together (see section on **Fun**). Whenever I spot this kind of thing it reminds me that one of the main reasons for having children is to enjoy them.

There is, however, another side to this optimistic picture of family life. There *are* parents who dislike one of their children, don't seem to get on with a particular child at all. 'We rub each other up the wrong way,' a mother told me of her son. 'We've never got on together,' said another mum, of her daughter. 'Quite frankly,' said a father of his youngest son, 'I just don't like him. I don't know why it is and I feel guilty about my feelings but whenever we're alone together I feel uncomfortable.'

Whether we like it or not we just have to accept the fact that we may like one of our children more than another. We try to love them all equally but it's not quite as simple as it sounds. If you've

120

wanted a boy and have a girl (or vice versa) you may be disappointed and find it hard to respond to the child in quite the way you would if he (or she) hadn't been born the 'wrong' sex. The fact that this is grossly unfair doesn't make it any easier to signal, in subtle kind of ways, your feelings of disappointment.

Sometimes, a mother will tell me that she feels no mother love at all. 'I lack any maternal instinct,' said a young mum to me. 'It's like when people tell you it's a beautiful sunset but you don't feel anything at all when you see it. I'm that way about babies, they simply don't call up any response, any warmth, from me in any way.' That particular mother, when her children were older, got on with them fine; it was the babyhood part she couldn't cope with. On the other hand there are mothers who are absolutely marvellous with babies but seem to lose interest once the children are gaining their own personalities and reaching out for independence. These mothers would have been quite at home eighty years ago having a baby a year and letting the older children look after the younger ones as they join the family.

To complicate matters even further there may be one of our children whom we like enormously who goes through a stage of development which seems quite abysmal and which seems to alter his personality (and spark off a dislike of him on our part). Mothers are always telling me, of teenage sons: 'I used to like him so much. Now I can't abide him. He's so rude, monosyllabic and downright boring. I'll be glad when he leaves home.' It seems a shame that, having had a pleasant relationship with a child and having put in so much work on that relationship, the youngster seems to undergo a sea change and what was once a pleasant friendship is now a bickering, fraught, edgy relationship.

Sometimes (though this is hard to admit) it's quite possible for a mother, or father, to hate a particular child. I knew a woman who lived on the top floor of a block of flats. One sunny afternoon, when her baby was three-months-old, she held him over the balcony and thought of hurling him into the concrete courtyard many feet below. Something inside of her prevented her from doing so. 'I love him now,' she told me but her apologies weren't necessary. I understood that she was under tremendous strain, emotionally and financially, when the balcony incident occurred. Any of us (given sufficient stress) are potential baby batterers. Out of desperation, exhaustion, anger, depression, worry, a baby's face is bruised, an arm broken. In the darkness of temporary insanity a limb is shattered, a death occurs. Baby batterers may not be any different from the rest of us; there, but for the Grace of God, go us all.

Besides enormous stress another potent reason for hating a child (see section on **Hatred**) is the psychological mechanism of *projection*. We hate (or dislike) the child because he reminds us of somebody else we hate or dislike or because he reminds us of *parts of ourself* that we fear, loathe, or despise. Thus, the poor child becomes the recipient of many of our nastiest and least generous feelings not because of what he is but what he represents in our minds. The child becomes, in the family circle, the one who gets the blame (see section on **Scapegoat Children**) not only for what is going wrong with our lives there and then but (even more unfairly) for things that have gone wrong: all the sorrows, disappointments and frustrations in the past.

What can you do as a mother, or father, when you suffer from negative feelings like those I've described? I think that the following are the important points to remember:

Nobody can prove that there's a Universal Maternal or Paternal Instinct. If you don't have it, you're not the only one. It's something that, hopefully, grows as you and your child get to know each other. When you're less weary, less care-worn, as your child gets older, you'll feel more positive feelings towards him.

Don't harbour resentment. Perhaps you gave up a career to have your child. You may have had a hard time when the child was born (or simply found that being a mother didn't bring you any of the rewards and pleasures that other people had told you it would). None of this is the child's fault. Rather than blame him it would be better to get as much help with your child as you can and to look forward to resuming your career, or taking a part-time job, as soon as you can. Don't feel guilty about this. We're told that we're supposed to adore motherhood or fatherhood but not all of us do. It's like that sunset: you must try as hard as you can to like it but there's no point in blaming yourself (or your child) if you don't.

Ask yourself why you dislike a certain child so much. Is it because he reminds you of Uncle Arthur or, more likely, parts of yourself that you don't like? If so, it's not fair to punish him for that. He is a real person, not Uncle Arthur, or you. So (I know this is hard) do try to be fair and to remember that the child can't help being who he is. The last thing he wants is for you to project all your hates, dislikes, frustrations and anger upon him.

You can't like everybody but you should try to love people. If you don't like a particular child you may have to go out of your way to show positive discrimination because of that dislike. You have to say: 'You're special.' If you go out of your way to love the child, give him extra-special loving care, you find (curiously enough) that you'll grow to like the child much more.

Even the best of friends have patches of indifference, or dislike. If you run into a bad patch in your relationship with a child, be patient, hang on, keep talking, ride the storm; there could be smoother seas ahead. Most parents have moments (or months, or years!) when they go off a particular child, especially a teenage boy. Keep trying. Most teenagers, surprisingly, grow up into charming, attractive, intelligent adults.

Introversion

See also **'Normal' Behaviour** *Page* 159, **Shyness** *Page* 206

In contrast to the extravert (see section on **Extraversion**) the introvert is not interested in other people – except, perhaps, a few close friends. An introverted child may be happy with just one friend. Sometimes, the child may not have *any* friends and may seem quite content to read a book, pursue his special hobby or just watch television by himself. To other children the introvert may appear reserved, aloof, stand-offish, anti-social or 'snobby'. Those that know him better may say: 'He's a sensitive boy and he doesn't seem to want, or need, the company of other children.' However, you may worry if your child is very withdrawn and wonder whether you ought to try to make him a little more outgoing and friendly towards other children. There are two important questions that you should ask yourself (see section on **Shyness**). *Can the child join in with others when he wants to? Is the child happy when he's by himself?* If the answer to both queries is yes then I should leave the child alone. Children are born with different temperaments: some like the bright lights, being with others, being 'where the action is'; others are more introspective, thoughtful, less in need of the stimulation which comes from having lots of friends. *These differences of temperament have to be respected.* It's silly to try to make an introverted child into a raving extravert.

Let's imagine that you have two teenagers. One of them is always out at the youth club, at discos, calling on friends. He's interested in the latest fashion, in pop music, in looking smart and impressing others – his acquaintances of both sexes. This particular youngster never stops talking. He's very popular with his peers (and liked by adults); he pursues one madcap scheme after the other and seems to find everything in the teenage world interesting. In particular he seems to need to be with people; he wants an audience, he wants friends to talk to; he's never happier when it's noisy and he's surrounded by people. Your other teenager is quite the opposite: he's quiet, prefers his own company, isn't interested in clothes (though he's very 'into' motor bikes, cars and anything to do with machinery) and is happiest when he's tinkering about with an old car engine, dressed like a tramp, his hands covered in oil. (For motor bikes, substitute foreign stamps, reading books, model gauge railways or a hundred-and-one other pursuits which are indulged in alone or with just one friend.) Is teenager A more 'normal' than teenager B? I don't think so. Teenager B is temperamentally different and we ought not to compare the two to the detriment of either. If we get over-concerned about Teenager B and start saying: 'You should get out more,' or, 'You really ought to make a few more friends,' we merely devalue his personality, his own social inclinations and suggest that there is something wrong with him merely because he doesn't fit into a pattern that we think is 'right'. A better approach would be to show approval of the way he spends his time and suggest ways such as clubs, associations, classes where he can extend his expertise in the things that interest him and, incidentally, meet people who have the same hobbies.

The main things to remember about your introverted child are:

Let him do 'his own thing'. Don't put pressure on him to be the same as more outgoing youngsters (especially more sociable brothers and sisters).

Encourage him in his hobbies, praise him for what he is good at. With all of us praise and prestige work better than nagging and criticism.

Don't let the squeaking gate get the most oil. Give each of your children a role in the family, and recognize (and respect) the differences between them. It would be a very dull world if we were all the same.

If you think your child is lonely, take some practical steps to help him to meet other children (see section on **Shyness**) *but don't try to change his basic personality.* He'll become less introverted when he feels more confident and when he's in the company of people he likes and feels comfortable with as we all do. So don't force him into awkward situations or into meeting people he doesn't want to meet.

Lots of people are basically shy. With praise, sympathy and not too much pressure to be other than what they are, they learn to overcome it and to attract lasting friendships. With a bit of encouragement they'll make friendships, which can be, in contrast to the more superficial and volatile extravert, lasting and deep.

If you are very worried about your introverted child then go to see your family doctor, or the head of the child's school, who will arrange for the child to see a school psychologist if he thinks it is necessary. If your child is utterly miserable don't say: 'He'll grow out of it,' but try to do something about it yourself – or with the child's school – before you call in further professional advice.

We live in a noisy, fast-moving, competitive world. Surely, in that world, there is a place for the child who is slightly quieter and more introverted? I think there is, if we respect the differences between people – and especially between children.

Jealousy
See also **Differences Between Children in the Same Family** *Page* 55, **Sibling Rivalry** *Page* 209

I used to know a family with two boys and two girls. The mother had a marvellous relationship with one of the boys, her eldest, and with the girls. The dad had an extremely close friendship with his eldest son. I was asked to see the youngest boy because he wasn't doing very well in school: he lacked confidence and his work was well below his potential. I found that the boy was consumed with jealousy of his older brother. Yet, is it any wonder? The brother was the apple of his parents' eyes, in the family he could do no wrong. The younger boy wasn't a victim (see section on **Scapegoat Children**); he was simply ignored, not given half as much attention or affection as his brother. His jealousy preoccupied him. When I asked the boy, after seeing him a few weeks, what he thought of his older brother he said, quietly: 'I could kill him.' He meant it. Jealousy can be a very powerful emotion.

What is jealousy about? It usually starts from a knowledge that somebody has got something that we desperately want (whether it's love, a new dress, good looks or a bigger piece of cake). It can also spring from a fear that somebody will deprive us of something that belongs to us: love, status, a boy friend, a girl friend, a better-paid job. It can arise also, not from real things, but events that we imagine might happen: that somebody will do better than us, or love somebody more than us, or be more popular than we are. Jealousy can make us sad, or bad (it can also drive us mad); it can make us chronically resentful of others; it can lead us to restrict (needlessly) another person's freedom. Jealousy is an extremely *self*-destructive passion indeed. It destroys affection, distorts our perception of others: it's rather like being infected with a nasty bout of 'flu which you can't shake off.

How can you avoid jealousy in your children? There are certain family situations where a weather eye has to be kept open. Let's have a look at some of them:

The arrival of a new baby which takes up a great deal of the mother's love and attention. An older child (especially if he is a toddler) will need extra reassurance and loving at this time. The child who helps with the new baby, is given a practical part to play and allocated specific jobs, will feel less excluded. Say: 'New babies can mean a lot of hard work. We'll all have to help.' See the newcomer as a start of a *family* enterprise and not a disruptive event. Talk about the baby but, when visitors arrive, don't forget to talk about (and give some attention to) your other child; he may feel, especially if he is still an infant, deprived and insecure. Don't leave him out, then he'll feel proud, rather than jealous.

Favouritism One little girl once told me: 'Sue is daddy's favourite. Ben is mummy's favourite.' I asked her what about her? 'I'm nobody's favourite,' she said, forlornly. Be absolutely honest with yourself. It isn't easy to avoid favouritism. Sometimes, dad will like a girl more, or mother a boy. Sometimes, a scamp or mischief in the family is a favourite. This has nothing to do with the intrinsic merits of the children. 'I just find it easier to love him,' the mother of that older brother told me. Maybe she did (and some of us do find one child easier to love than another) but it's still *unfair* and it leads to very understandable jealousy. What can you do about the injustice of it all? You can have a heart and think what it feels like for a child who is less loved (or thinks he is) than another child. Believe me, he really suffers emotional pain (which is just as bad, if not worse, than physical pain). You can also stop trying to love your children equally but love them *uniquely,* as individuals. It's the quality of love, that counts, not quantity. Don't share it out. Give all you've got, to each one, since each one is a real person and needs to be loved. It's the withholding of love that wears us out, not the giving of it.

Competition Avoid your children competing for your love (as though they were in a race with only one prize for the winner). Each child in a family tends to think that the others get more than their fair share of your love and attention. The solution? *Tell* them: 'I love you all in different ways.' They'll understand then that it isn't the hundred metres sprint, or the high jump. They'll have, without the competitive element, a better chance to be themselves.

Roles Think of your family as a small repertory theatre. When you dish out the parts, be fair, and don't hog the centre of the stage yourself. Allow for development, give somebody else a larger part (or to be the star for a day) whilst you play the third soldier on the left, carrying a spear. Do it as they did in Shakespeare's day with everybody having a go at something different. Don't get yourselves into stereotyped roles; be flexible; change places occasionally. You go to the PTA and let your husband do the dishes or (better) get a babysitter and both go ballroom dancing. Give each child a chance to shine, everybody in the family a chance to say their lines, and to grow.

Age differences Age, with children, usually brings new privileges: staying up later, more pocket money, going into town alone, having a 'two-wheeler' bike and perhaps going off for a week camping or holidaying with friends. Age *should* also bring more responsibilities within the family: jobs to do, errands to run, perhaps the odd meal to cook. So, if a younger child complains about the privileges of an older child, you should say (respecting what he *feels* about it): 'You wish you were a bit older,' or, 'It looks to you as John gets all the good things.' At the same time, make sure that more responsibility *does* go with age or the younger children will rightly think that being younger means the rough end of the stick *all* the time. Don't forget to give younger children a treat occasionally – just to set the record straight!

The best way to avoid jealousy is to realize that nobody really owns – or should try to possess – another human being and understand that each and every friendship we make adds to us not detracts from us. We need a large variety of friends (including our own children) and as many warm, positive relationships as we can create. So, don't ration it, dole it out; love each person with generosity, for himself. And, should one of your children be feeling particularly jealous, especially low and demoralized, take him into a corner *by himself* (once a day, once a week, once a month – so long as you do it) and tell him how special he is. Give him the Good Treatment, your undivided attention, even if it's just for five minutes. Who's counting? Certainly not the children. They'll be quite happy if they get the Good Treatment at some time or other. It's when it never happens to us (as we all know) that we really get jealous.

Kleptomania
See also **Stealing** Page 221

Kleptomania is the name given to a compulsion to steal. The objects stolen may be valueless, trivial; they may be of no use to the person who has stolen them. Shoplifters, and thieves in general, will usually steal something that they want, or something that they can sell. A teenage girl suffering from kleptomania will, in contrast, steal dozens and dozens of one particular thing (e.g. bottles of perfume) or scores of articles of which she has no particular need. She may steal pencils and rubbers from school and hide them away like a magpie in her bedroom or some other hiding place. She may go into department stores and steal items of clothing that she will never wear. She may go to the supermarket and steal food (which she doesn't eat) or visit the library and steal books (which she never reads); she may steal teenage magazines which she could afford to buy. The girl is not motivated by dire need, or even by greed: she simply has an irresistible impulse to steal whenever she can.

Teenage boys can suffer from the same impulse, and be equally undiscriminating in their thefts. With boys, sometimes, there is a sexual component to the stealing: the boy may steal articles of women's underwear either from shops or clothes-lines in gardens. He may steal semi-pornographic magazines from shops, or women's shoes, or items of jewellery. More often, a boy suffering from kleptomania will, like the girl, steal an amazing array of items most of which are of no practical use to the child and which he has no intention of selling to make a profit. It is as though (see section on **Stealing**) the child has something to prove to himself – and signal to others – through his thefts.

The indiscriminate stealing observed in a child who suffers from kleptomania represents two very urgent needs: *the need for help with his problems* – the stealing is a sort of Mayday distress signal; and *the need* to express an unfulfilled desire: the stolen articles represent the child's needs to be 'rated', to feel valued as a person. Some children steal so blatantly and so frequently that it is almost as though they want to be caught, and punished. They know what they are doing is wrong; they haven't the will-power to stop themselves.

128

There are plenty of people about us who are dishonest; there are an appalling number of shoplifters, or thieves. However, it is important, whilst not condoning dishonesty, to realize the difference between theft for gain, or excitement, or out of a lack of morals, and thefts which are the result of a recurrent compulsion. If you have a child who is a compulsive stealer – and if you suddenly find that your child has a hidden store of stolen articles – you should *not* punish the child. You can tell him that, although you cannot approve his actions, you still love your child and realize that he has a problem that he cannot solve. If he wants to talk over the problem with you, be patient and receptive. Don't reject the child; that is the last thing that he needs. Having not over-reacted to your child's problem – and having got over your feelings of shame and embarrassment – you should seek professional help by contacting your family doctor who will give you a note to go along to the child guidance clinic. Make sure that your child knows you are doing this as a positive move to help him – and not to punish him. At the clinic, the whole matter can be discussed. The compulsive stealing will quickly clear up if the child is given an opportunity to talk to a skilled, professional person who is not shocked at the behaviour and is sensitive enough to elicit the – often quite unconscious – reasons for it.

In the cases in which I have been involved it is very rare for court action to be taken against the child as a result of the stealing. Your best insurance against such action is to get your child to see a doctor, or a children's psychiatrist, who will ensure that the behaviour is seen for what it is: a compulsion, a temporary aberration of the mind, which will quickly clear up with the right kind of help. The three things to remember are: don't punish your child; don't make too much fuss; and take your child along to have a, completely confidential, talk with the family doctor.

Lazy Children
See also **Under-Achievement in School** *Page* 246

I'm very sceptical when a mother says to me of her child: 'He's bone idle,' or, 'She's just lazy.' The Concise Oxford Dictionary defines laziness as: 'averse to labour, indolent, slothful'. In my view there's no such thing as a lazy child. Children are naturally dynamic, active, curious; to them, it's a fascinating world and they want to find out as much about it as they can. That's why I'm not convinced when I read a termly report (see section on **School Reports**) and it says: 'This child is lazy and doesn't seem to want to do anything.' The child may be bored, or lacking in motivation or simply not well but *not* lazy. It's adults (and I include parents and teachers in this) who are lazy in using such an easy word to describe a child's behaviour instead of looking for the real causes which underlie the youngster's lack of zest and enthusiasm.

There may be physical reasons for laziness and you should look out for tiredness, refusal to feed, and general 'scratchiness' on the part of a baby or young infant. *The health visitor or the doctor should be consulted, to check the baby's general health and his diet.* No infant should show constant lethargy and/or lassitude. The normal baby, during his waking hours, likes action. If you think you have a permanently 'tired baby' you should see the family doctor.

Young children who are just starting infant school (and/or who have a long bus journey to school) may be exhausted by it all. There's no point in saying they're lazy when they're sluggish and lethargic because they're tired out. Similarly, youngsters who watch too much late-night television, or just go to bed too late, may be thought of as being lazy in the classroom. They're not. They're too shattered to do any work in school. Moral? Get them to bed at a reasonable time.

With older children, commonsense has to be used. Teenagers (according to a lot of mothers I know), 'hang about the house all day listening to pop records'. This is a stage of development rather than laziness. If, however, you have a youngster who was formerly lively and who suddenly becomes sluggish, apathetic and withdrawn it will do no harm if you have his health checked by the family doctor.

In school, if a child is reported as being lazy, it's as well for the parents to ensure that his hearing is good (can he hear what's being said?); his vision is satisfactory (can he see what's written on the blackboard?); and that he's eating proper meals. These days, lots of youngsters are on stringent diets, or go to school without any breakfast: this isn't a good idea when you consider the demands of the school day (plus homework). If your child's 'laziness' is radically affecting his school work, his job, or his friendships do first of all ensure that he is in a reasonable state of health and eating proper foods.

On an intellectual level there are two things to look for rather than accuse the child of being lazy. Is he understimulated and therefore bored? If he is ahead of you, and of his teacher, it's just as well to seek advice from an educational psychologist. Nothing is worse than being understimulated, day-in, day-out (see **Gifted Children**).

If your child is over-extended, or being pressurized (at home or at school) to do work he cannot cope with, he will very likely give up trying altogether (and have to face accusations of 'laziness'). Why not have his abilities assessed by the school psychologist so that you know what sort of standard he *is* able to cope with in school?

Praise works, pressure doesn't: and neither does anxiety. Take a mother who complains that her infant suffers from 'lazy speech'. What does that mean? Usually, that the child talks less distinctly than her neighbour's. (Or, perhaps, has started late, or still persists in using 'baby talk'.) Some mothers, in this situation, put pressure on the child to talk by resorting to bribes, threats and anxious pleas. The truth is (see **Reluctance to Speak**) that there are enormous individual differences in the rate of speech development *and* in the ages at which children first start to speak. With late-developers, what is needed is lots of patience and encouragement, not over-anxiety. What is required least of all is the facile remark that the child is 'lazy'. Such comments, such unsympathetic attitudes, further impede the child's progress in acquiring language.

In school, the child's attitude towards the teacher (or to that particular subject) can greatly affect his achievements. If you think that the teacher is setting too high a standard – or too low – and/or if you think your child is frightened of the teacher you should arrange to visit the school so that you can have a chat about the matter. Often, a visit to the school (evidence to the child of a genuine and useful concern on your part) is far more constructive than putting even more pressure on your child by accusing him of being lazy.

Parents, too, can set too high a standard. Let your child decide whether he or she wants to become a doctor/concert pianist/famous footballer/Cambridge Don. If the talent is there, with your encouragement and support, it will win out. Pressure, too much pushing, will kill your child's enthusiasm. Nurture, don't force. Don't call your child 'lazy' if he decides, off his own bat, that he doesn't want to become a concert pianist after all. Discuss it all with him, let him make the choice; what he wants from you is support and friendship not dismissive diagnoses like: 'You're lazy.'

Don't resort to bribes, or threats. What a good parent does is build up the child's strengths and try to bolster up any weaknesses. Look for any areas of special interest, or talent, and encourage your child to join a club, read, go on visits: do those things which will develop his special interest and build up his competence in that area. One area of competence, a skill acquired, a hobby encouraged, is worth a thousand words of advice. It's certainly worth more than shouting at the child and accusing him of 'never moving out of the house' or (equally popular with distraught parents) being 'totally idle'.

Children are naturally curious, and imaginative. Appeal to their imagination and they will not regard lessons, or the pursuit of a hobby, as work. Look for an interest, look for a special talent within your child, and encourage it. That's the answer to laziness. 'Lazy,' as you've gathered, is an adjective I seldom use about children though I have been known to use it to describe teachers and, sometimes, even parents.

Left-Handed Children
See also **Clumsiness** Page 33, **Crossed Laterality** Page 37, **Dyslexia** Page 62

You should *never* force a child who is naturally left-handed to use his right hand. You should also *never* assume that a child who is left-handed is going to inevitably experience difficulty in school: look around you and you'll find plenty of eminent, successful left-handed people.

Left-handers are as good at most things as their right-handed peers. Their handwriting, maths, language development is, on average, equal to those of right-handers. However, *some* left-handed children do experience difficulty with writing, with reading and/or motor coordination, so let's look at these one at a time and see how we can help them.

Writing Your child's writing *may* be slow or untidy and he may have a tendency to get tired, or bored, of the whole business. This *could* lead to a life-long distaste for written work. In addition, he may (when writing) have adopted an awkward position known as 'the hook', i.e. he writes with his arm curled round, elbow pointing away from him, so that his hand is above the writing and the pencil tilted towards the body. This contorts the arm (and shoulder muscles) and results in fatigue. If he writes for long periods he may get cramp and, if he uses ink, he may smudge the words he has just written.

What to do about it? Your child should be encouraged to sit in a comfortable position with the top left-hand corner of the writing paper slightly higher than the right. The paper should be positioned slightly to left-of-centre of the body. An untidy writing style can be revamped (see section on **Handwriting**) especially if a left-handed nib is purched for the child and reference is made to Tom Gourdie's inexpensive little book *Learn About Handwriting (Ladybird Books)*. Try to get your child to take a pride in his writing and to practise each day: twenty minutes at a time is quite enough. *Don't* over-do it, and *don't* get anxious about it. Make it fun.

Reading To help a young child to prepare for reading you need to develop day-to-day hand/eye skills such as tying shoe-laces, tying a knot in a tie, fastening buttons and cutting out simple shapes (using left-handed scissors). There are shops (e.g. *Anything Left-Handed Limited,* 65 Beak Street, London W1) which specialize in selling left-handed scissors, irons, potato-peelers and pens. If your child is left-handed and right-eyed (see section on **Crossed Laterality**) he may be a little bit clumsy: model making (either with wood or plastic), ball games, playing a musical instrument, learning to ride a bike, to skate, ride a scooter or swim will all help to develop his motor coordination and build up his self-confidence. For better perception, and to help him with any directional confusions (i.e. to stop his eyes scanning from right to left instead of the other way round), I have found that 'join the dots' puzzles are useful, together with mazes, simple crossword puzzles and inexpensive puzzle books from Woolworth's. For younger children, games such as 'I Spy', 'Simon Says' (and, if you have the energy, the Hokey Cokey!), all help to build up the child's perception and motor movements. Older children may enjoy playing word bingo and using a dictionary: both activities which help them to familiarize themselves with the shape of words. A wall blackboard, with chalk handy, or a 'wall memo pad' will (especially with teenagers) encourage writing things down: it's almost impossible to use the hook style on a vertical surface! Further advice is provided in another inexpensive book, *Teaching Left-Handed Children* by Margaret Clark (Oxford University Press).

Motor Coordination Left-handers form one in ten of the population and, believe me, not all left-handers are clumsy. Many of them make first-rate sportsmen playing tennis, golf, cricket and many other games with distinction. So *don't* expect your child to be clumsy or he'll live up to your worst expectations. For hand-eye coordination games like dominoes (where looking and matching are involved) and simple skills such as learning to sew, knit or crochet are all very useful. With pre-school infants

133

encourage the child to run, skip, hop, balance on a box, go on a slide or a swing, throw and catch a ball. One session in the local 'swings' or on the beach with a beach-ball is worth a thousand derogatory remarks. Playing with dough, clay, papier-mâché, finger paints and building blocks help both manual dexterity and spatial ability (besides being great fun!) Why should you expect your child to master the complicated motor skills of reading when you haven't taken him out there, in the open air, where he can learn to throw a ball, or ride on a tricycle? Big motor movements precede smaller motor movements (see section on **Clumsy Children**). It seems an odd thing to say but, when you teach your child to use his hands, his eyes and his body, you are in fact preparing him in the best possible way for the motor control, and fine eye movements, involved in the reading task.

Older children can be encouraged to take up a game for enjoyment or encouraged to play a musical instrument such as the recorder, or the guitar. (Yes, there are left-handed guitars.) The left-handed youngster, a member of a minority group, needs practical help and reassurance. Wherever we find something for him to do (whether it be playing squash, or chess, or learning to cook, or looking after his bike or motor-cycle) we are building up his confidence and saying, in effect: 'You're very much like the rest of us.' Let's hope you never regard your child as being clumsy, or odd, just because he's left-handed.

Liars

When I was about six I had a friend who was a terrible liar. He told me his dad was a Spitfire pilot in the Royal Air Force (his dad, actually, was a corporal in the Army). Then, he told me that Joe Louis (then, the heavyweight boxing champion of the world) was his uncle. He was lying *to gain attention* but also because, at the age of six, he knew what the truth was but – like a lot of five- and six-year-olds – he didn't always tell it. It's not until the child is about eight that he really and truly sorts out the difference between what *is* and what he'd like to be.

Last year a girl of seven showed me her painting in school: a large, crimson blob. 'It's a red bluebottle,' she said. Actually, it was lovely and, to her, it looked like a blue bottle. She wasn't lying: she was using her fantasy and imagination to give meaning to what was going on around her. So children, up to the age of eight, can often compensate for the dullness of the world around them by telling stories. I wouldn't classify them as lies. I'd just say, at that stage, that the child has a vivid imagination.

After the age of eight children can lie, and know they're lying quite deliberately. They may lie to avoid social embarrassment, as when a child tells his pals that he gets as much pocket money as they do. He can lie to gain revenge on an enemy or to salve a guilty conscience. ('Yes, I *did* tidy my bedroom. Somebody must have gone in there and made it untidy again.')

Children can certainly lie to attract sympathy. I remember one beautiful, blue-eyed ten-year-old coming in to see me and telling me that her mother suffered from an incurable disease and had to go around all day long in a wheel chair. When I saw the mother in the clinic she was a well-built, sun-tanned woman, absolutely blooming with health. Her daughter *had* got my sympathy (but not for long!). It's when a child goes on lying – despite having been found out – or lives in a dream world of fairy stories and fantasy (here, I'm talking about older children) that the youngster needs help.

There are some teenagers who never stop romancing about this and that. They may claim to own a pony, live in a grand house or have an offer to be a model, or film star, when they leave school. Mind you, you have to be careful. A teenager told me she'd just been to Las Vegas *and* spoken to some famous film stars. She had too: her parents had just won the football pools and all the family took off for an American holiday. It was next week, when the girl brought in all the momentoes of her visit, that I realized that she was telling the truth.

Obviously, young children should be allowed (as long as possible, in this cynical age) to believe in Father Christmas, and in fairy stories. They'll meet harsh reality soon enough. Fantasy is a good way for young children to make life exciting.

To stop an older child lying you should try to be as honest as possible with your own children and tell the truth yourself. The best ways to stop your own children from telling lies are for you to:

Set a good example. If you cheat the tax inspector and boast about it, or cheat business colleagues and brag about it, you can hardly expect your children to respect honesty.

Try to make your child feel safe with you. No child who is loved should need to lie. If he does lie we can indicate to him (perhaps by a knowing smile or a remark such as: 'I'm surprised you don't trust me enough to tell me the truth') that we don't like being lied to but we still like the child and believe in him as a person.

Don't cross-examine your child. A 'district-attorney' approach may make him lie even more. Cool it and try to build up the child's self-respect rather than break down his alibi.

Give honest answers to questions about sex, death, your own feelings and illnesses. Honesty on important matters leads to honesty in the day-to-day contacts with others. If you're truthful and straight, your child will learn that nobody who has confidence in himself has any reason to lie.

Don't pry too much into your children's lives, especially if they're teenagers. Most children, as they get older, have secrets which they wish to keep to themselves. Respect this privacy and learn to trust the child to act honourably: children have a curious knack of living up to our expectations.

Praise your child and give him jobs to do about the house. Lying is one strategy used to gain prestige and maintain self-esteem. Show the child, in a practical way, that your approval can be gained without him having to resort to lies.

If disaster occurs, and he does break your vase or best coffee pot, *be angry, say you're annoyed, and tell him that you will get over it.* Don't make a war of attrition out of the incident; otherwise, you'll encourage your child to tell lies when he is next confronted by the slings and arrows of outrageous fortune.

It's wise, with your child, not to ask daft questions. 'Do you love your baby sister?' for example. If he says, 'No,' and he's being honest, you may show annoyance, but what else do you expect him to say if he can't stand the sight of the baby? If you do find out that your child has been lying to you, *don't* blow a fuse or he'll lie to you again simply to avoid your angry reaction. With young children give them a chance to distinguish between truth and fantasy. 'I've got a million pounds,' your infant says. 'You wish you had,' you can say.

Don't make out you're perfect. If you do tell a lie occasionally, admit it, but tell your child it's better to tell the truth because, if we lie regularly, nobody will trust us. Sometimes, children feel that adults *aren't* honest. If you're honest, then your children are likely to be honest too. And don't forget lies can be of omission – not telling the whole story – as well as commission – deliberately distorting the truth. Lastly, if your child is rather insecure and given to chronic lying you should seek professional help. Go to your family doctor or ask the head of your child's school if you can have an appointment to see the child psychologist. Do all you can do, yourself, before seeking professional help.

Lonely Children
See also **Friends** *Page* 86

The best way to make sure that a child isn't lonely is to be sociable yourself. *You* can make efforts to get out, meet other people. Single parents will gain emotional and social support by joining *Gingerbread,* a country-wide organization for one parent families (you can find out who is the secretary of your local branch from your library or by writing to *Gingerbread,* 35 Wellington Street, London, WC2). You will be at your most vulnerable, your loneliest, when you've just moved house and are living in an area where you don't know anybody. You must conquer your shyness, go out and meet people. There's no easy cure for loneliness. The best way to tackle it is to offer to help: whether it's at the playgroup, or at the school jumble sale, or in organizing a sponsored walk for the handicapped children in your area. There's always somebody that needs your help: so do volunteer. Doing things together for other people is the best way of making friendships I know.

Don't be ashamed of inviting people into your house. It may be like Steptoe's Yard (see section on **Tidiness**) but that won't bother potential friends: they'll probably be relieved to see that you're even more untidy than they are. It's good for children to mix with adults, on their own territory, in their own home. It gives them a chance to get used to meeting strangers, to get over their shyness and to learn – by watching you – how to make friends with people. Don't push your child to join in, act a part, do anything other than say 'hello' and do his own thing. He'll join in when he's ready and when he's relaxed enough. So you relax and enjoy the company and let your child take from it what *he* wants.

The aim with your child is not to produce the most popular youngster of the century. As long as he has one or two children to play with, to talk to, to share his ideas with, that is quite enough to give him the social skills that he needs. If you have just moved house, or live in a road where there are no other children of your child's age, you will have to go out and forage for other mums whom you like with children of the same age. You can meet them in the shops, at the park, outside the school gates. Invite her and her child around to tea, or say you'll see her the next day/next week. Work at friendships; it's for the good of your child, and it's good practice

137

for you (and for all of us, since most people I know are basically very shy).

Concentrate on one or two close friendships for your child: he can expand out from these if and when he wants to. Don't worry if he spends a certain amount of time alone. We all need a bit of peace now and then. If he can make friendships when he wants to (see section on **Shy Children**) *don't* think he's inevitably lonely just because he's by himself and don't push him into a whole network of friendships that he'd really rather do without.

The things to remember about loneliness are:

You are the young child's doorway to the world. If you are lonely and isolated, he can't be expected to go out and explore.

If you have small children you must make the effort – if you feel the need and if your house gets you down – to get out and meet people.

Being alone doesn't mean being lonely. If you're alone and happy, don't think it's odd. At the same time, remember that children can learn a lot in other children's company so do see if you can find one or two friends for your child to see from time to time.

With teenagers, expect a certain amount of 'keeping to oneself'. It's part of adolescence to be very sociable and, at the same time, feel very lonely. Don't be too analytical; get on with being reasonably happy and contented yourself and your teenager will get over his recurrent bouts of cosmic misery and loneliness.

Keep the lines of communication open between you and your teenager. Young people do sometimes feel isolated and lonely. The worst loneliness of all is to be rejected by friends, and not to be able to talk to your parents.

You can snap yourself out of your own loneliness. There's always a person, or some organization, that could do with your help. Nobody should ever be lonely. There is, if we look around without selfishness, too much to do. If you're friendly and outgoing your child will be too.

Love
(For Parents)
See also **Mother Love** *Page* 147

Love makes the world go round and, certainly, it's a vital ingredient in marriage and in being able to form and maintain relationships, both as a child and an adult. Who teaches a child to love? His first teachers are the parents (or parent-substitutes). If he doesn't learn love from them he finds it more difficult to love, and to be loved, than those fortunate children who have been shown lots of affection from babyhood onwards.

What is love? What it isn't is amateur psycho-analysis: worrying about whether your own psychological hang-ups are going to inflict lasting traumas on your child. It isn't smother-love: loving your child so much that he never gets a chance to grow up and become a person in his own right. Loving is doing things for your child, being there when he needs you, listening to him, talking to him, not rejecting him even though you go through patches when you dislike, or even hate, him. Love is constant. And with children, love is hard work.

I went to the retirement celebration of a nun who had been headmistress of a primary school for nearly thirty-five years. She stood up to make her farewell speech. 'Thank you,' she said, 'for giving me a chance to be happy.' She spoke of the school during the Second World War, with bombs raining down all around, of the hard work, and then she said what a privilege it had been to serve the children.

Love *is* a privilege. It isn't a right, it isn't possession. We chose to have our children; to love them is our duty, our happiness. We shouldn't expect (though we often get) a great deal back for the privilege of loving them.

Children who lack love can be found anywhere. Deprivation is no respecter of social class. Many poor children are unloved but so are many rich children. Some rich parents think that material possessions – a new bike, a video-tape recorder, a lot of pocket money – can make up for the love they don't give to their children. They can't. Children need love as plants need water; they don't want to be drenched in the stuff but, if they don't get some, it makes it very difficult to grow up and be courageous, optimistic and loving.

You'll have your favourites. You'll 'go off' a child for a time and you'll worry about not loving all your children equally; but children want to be loved uniquely, for themselves, rather than equally. They want you to love them in a unique relationship – for themselves, for who they are and not what they achieve. Love is like a petrol pump with a limitless supply of petrol; if you dish out love, you're not going to run out of supplies or make yourself bankrupt. To give a child love is a marvellous – and inexpensive – thing because the child can grow up and say 'I am loved'.

Where there is love the bond between a child and a mother is remarkably resilient. Love for an infant is like an overcoat: it will protect him from the harshness, the coldness, of adult life and from the disappointments, taunts and set-backs he is bound to meet as he makes his way in the world. It is *physical* affection which is so important to a young child – touching, cuddling, snuggling up to somebody – as well as the spontaneous expression of joy, happiness, amusement, contentment.

You'll find, as your child grows older, that he won't want this physical display of affection. It will probably embarrass him. The British, particularly, are reticent about showing physical affection. What older children do want, however, is love and friendship expressed in a different way. Talk to them about their interests, listen to them, be around when they need you. Believe me, they'll need you for years – even when they're grown-ups.

The main things to remember about love are:

Love your child – and I mean hold him in your arms – as much as possible during his first six months. Keep loving him and showing lots and lots of affection during his first five years. After that, you can relax a little. The battle's over, or nearly. You've given him a sufficient supply to carry him a long, long way. Now, knowing how to love and be loved, he should be able to get 'topped-up' by other people besides yourself.

The child who is loved grows up confident about his own loveableness and able to respect the loveableness of others.

Human beings cannot live without love. It is a vital human need, so don't be shy or embarrassed about expressing the love you feel for your child.

Don't be too sentimental about love. It is, for your child, much too important for that.

Love and let go. Love shouldn't be choking, suffocating. Your eventual goal is a genuine, warm friendship and we don't suffocate our friends.

Maladjustment
See also **Eccentric Children** *Page* 68, **'Normal' Behaviour** *Page* 159

We're all a little bit maladjusted from time to time, especially on Monday mornings! I think as long as we can *cope* (i.e. with our work, our loves, our friendships) then we can regard ourselves as being at the right end of the scale of adjustment. With children, what counts is the *intensity* and *duration* of their maladjustment. If your child has bouts of aggression, that's normal; if he chases you or his friends with a meat cleaver, *that's* maladjustment. Similarly, with duration. It's normal for a child to go through a quiet, withdrawn phase; if, however, the child refuses to talk to anybody for month after month *that's* maladjustment. You should ask yourself, of your child's behaviour: how bad is it? (compared with other children, or even yourself as a child!) and, how long has it lasted? It's the second question that's more important since maladjustment, in my experience, is rarely a permanent state. Most children are going to show *some* signs of stress, sometime on their road through life.

Basically, your child has three modes of defence against the feelings of loss, pain, guilt or isolation that accompany 'maladjustment': *fight, flight* and *imitation.* Your child may fight back against a world that has hurt him; he may 'run away' by withdrawing, turning into himself); or he may pretend to be somebody else. Of this trio I think pretence or imitation is the worst defence. If we don't have the courage to be ourselves we are going to have less chance of fighting back against stress, less chance of making genuine relationships with others. Your main task, therefore, is to give your child self-respect. We can't prevent children from running into some of life's slings and arrows but we can give them that love and security which will enable them to deal with life's slings and arrows as they come along.

Here are the Ten Commandments that have to be observed if we are to survive our contact with the odd, the moody, the aggressive, the naughty or the withdrawn – our own children.

Listen to the child more. It's easy enough to talk but how many of us know how to listen?

Give them something to do. Unless children have some responsibility in the home, some job which is their own and which they know must be done, they will mistreat the home and despise us for being too lax and 'free and easy' with them.

Have rules (not too many) of courtesy and behaviour and stick to them. Don't forget to tell your children what the rules are – and observe them yourself!

Respect the child and don't over-react to his difficulties. Most problems clear up if parents can manage to 'play it cool' and have a sense of humour.

Keep your word. It's better not to make any promises, than to make a promise and break it. Children, like elephants, have very good memories.

Don't pick up the child's feelings. If he is miserable, depressed it will only make things worse if you are miserable too. If he's aggressive it won't help if you lose your temper and become even more angry than the child. A soft voice and a calm manner (if you can manage it!) will, honestly, achieve more than too much thoughtless shouting.

Be firm. What children often need, when they're upset, is stern kindness, *not* being allowed to do just what they want to do. They like to feel that parents are safe, that there are limits to how far they can go, and that the parents are not frightened of saying, 'Enough is enough.'

Show affection. What point is there in loving the child, not to mention working hard for his benefit, if you never show that love, openly and without embarrassment. Why not say those words to the child, words which are so important? 'I love you.'

Get your child to join clubs and other organizations. Do not have them 'under your feet' all the time: the best of us (if we see too much of each other) can get on each other's nerves.

Care. The greatest antidote to maladjustment is that somebody, somewhere, really cares about us.

Just a word about school. It may be that your child is having trouble at school, either with lessons which are boring or too difficult, or perhaps with other children who are making his life a misery. It is vital that you take an interest in your child's schooling and *liaise closely with the school.* Many, many children have spent months of misery about some problem in school simply because their parents didn't know what was going on. It is your job to know, to go to school meetings, to give the child support by your physical presence at school functions. This is, believe me, greatly reassuring to children: it's been shown that the children who do well at school are those children whose parents go out of their way to keep up the contact between home and school.

If your child's problem persists you should go to the family doctor and ask for an appointment at the child guidance clinic *or* if your child has a school problem which is severe or persistent, go to the head and arrange an appointment to see the school psychologist, who will interview you and the child either at home or at the school.

Before you call in professional help, however, do try to do the things I've suggested. Then, you'll be able to say, hand on heart, that you've done your share to *make sure that the child is getting lots of love,* sufficient to make him face life with courage and to look the inevitable stress, strains and worries of living right in the eye.

Messy Play
See also **Under-Fives** *Page* 249

Play is essential to children. Through play children learn to build up a model of the world and how it works. Through play, they learn something about their own identity and the identity of others. Through play, children can come to terms with their own feelings: whether they be of fear, anger, joy or sadness. It is this *emotional* aspect of play – play acting as a means of giving expression to various emotions – that is so important in messy play. Young children love to play with water, with sand and clay. They like to take some mud and squeeze it in their hands; they love to dig in soil, or on a beach. These activities seem to enrich their spirits: make them tougher, more resilient, happier. Children get as much satisfaction from making mud pies, digging holes, mixing sand and water as adults do from eating a Cordon Bleu meal or falling in love. Who would deprive them of such happiness?

Just a minute (I can hear you saying) I let my children get dirty sometimes *but* messy play means a messy, untidy house and it's me that has to clean it up. This is understandable. None of us wants to live in chaos; we all want a little bit of order in our lives and have *some* part of the house which isn't a complete mess (see section on **Tidiness**). All the same, if you wish your children to be entranced, absorbed, thoroughly involved in what they are doing (and hence, for the moment, out of your hair) I think you'll find that messy play can be *managed* so that your nerves don't become too frayed about the whole business. All it takes is goodwill, plus common sense.

Let's look at the practical side, under some relevant headings:

Where to Play A garden is ideal, if weather allows, especially if you can keep your eye on them through the kitchen window. Even the smallest garden can have a sand-pit (plus bucket and spade – both cheap to buy) tucked away somewhere. A room for messy play, with a trestle table and/or sand tray is ideal: if you don't run to that, a corner of a room is quite sufficient. Cover the floor with an old plastic tablecloth, a ground-sheet, or some old lino and try to choose a spot where other people (especially adults) are not trooping back and forth – and carrying mud and paint on their shoes as they go!

Clothing Make an apron or (better) a long smock for your child. If he's playing with water make sure it's waterproof. An old

143

dress or mackintosh can be used to make these special (and very) cheap 'dirty play' clothes for the child.

What to Play With *Dry sand:* bucket and spade, plastic pots and containers, spoons. *Wet sand:* old pans, yoghourt containers, shells and pebbles. *Water play:* bowls, washing-up liquid containers, plastic bottles (*not* glass), plastic tubes to blow through, plastic cups, sponges. Also, bits of smooth wood, boats, corks (things that float) and large pebbles, heavy objects (things that sink). *Don't* leave your child alone when he is playing with water. *Mud* (soil and water): preferably in the garden! Bucket and spade, old cooking utensils, toy plates and cups for making cakes. *Finger-painting:* use an old table with a plastic surface, plus powder-paint, thickened with flour. Encourage the child to make patterns in it with his hands. He'll love it. Make a design of hand patterns on paper. *Modelling with playdough, Plasticine or papier-mâché.* (You can make this yourself using a bucket, old, torn-up newspapers and wall-paper paste. *N.B. Make sure that, if you're using a cold water paste, it does not contain fungicides.* Ask at the shop.) *Blowing bubbles, painting* and *cutting and sticking* (even if it's only sticking different coloured squares on to a large white sheet of paper using paste and brush) are all activities dearly loved by most young children.

How Long For Let your child play – barring meals, and visits to the toilets – for as long as he is happy. When he is bored, stop. Don't over-do the activities or they will lose their magic. Half-an-hour may be enough, two hours may find him still happily playing. The rule is to get him to stop while he's still interested, and before he over-does it: rather like you at the dinner table.

You'll find your children will quickly become absorbed in mucky play so it's well worth the effort involved, and the mess. The benefits of messy play to children are that they can explore with their hands different kinds of material; experience new feelings and sensations; indulge in imaginative games on their own and express their emotions by handling a variety of materials. Sand and water (and mud) are 'magic substances' to children with limitless possibilities for exploration and manipulation.

When I am worried or upset, I wash every dish and pan in sight (my wife encourages this). When my daughter is upset she goes upstairs and plays with soap and water. We both find our own particular form of therapy very soothing! When I taught mature (i.e. adult) student teachers and they were tense and worried about exams I used to let them have an afternoon of finger-painting and clay. It was surprising how soon they all relaxed and talked to each other chirpily. Playing with the materials I have mentioned *is* very soothing, for children or grown-ups. It seems a shame to deprive young children of that experience.

If you simply haven't the space (or the patience) for messy play, then make sure that your pre-school child joins a playgroup where he can join in with other children in these activities.

If you run out of ideas for messy play have a word with your local playgroup leader. She'll have plenty! Or, write to The Toy Libraries Association, Seabrook House, Wyllyotts Manor, Potters Bar, Herts, EN6 2HL, and ask them to send you their booklet *Mucky Play* by Kay Mogford which contains lots of practical suggestions.

Morality
(For Parents)
See also **Values** *Page* 255

What should you do, in a rapidly-changing world, to ensure that your child grows up with some idea of what is right and what is wrong? The best way you can start is to encourage him to be helpful and think of others in the family situation. Even a child of between two and three can do little jobs for you; fetch something, carry something. A slightly older child can help to whisk a cake-mix, tidy up his toys. Both jobs will take longer with him than without, but never mind; you're doing something together and he's 'helping'. Children of five can set the table, do some cleaning jobs, a bit of polishing. By the age of eight, they can do some really useful tasks around the house: including making you an early-morning cup of tea. (If you're worried about them using boiling water from the kettle leave out a vacuum flask of tea and trust them to pour it out and carry it up to the bedroom.) Teenagers should have some responsibilities in the home: if you're keen to avoid arguments work out a roster so that one person, usually mum, doesn't get left with all the dirty work. It's useful, too, for teenagers to do some voluntary work where they can meet people – like the handicapped, or the elderly and infirm – who are not so lucky as themselves. Even a paid, part-time job puts them in touch with a wide variety of people. The aim is to train children to be sociable and not to think about themselves the whole time.

What we have to do is to teach our children to think of others, behave towards them with kindness and respect. The best way to achieve this is:

Show lots of affection to your child. Knowing that he is loved gives a child self-confidence so *don't* undermine him by threats of withdrawal of love ('Do that again and mummy won't love you') or by looking hurt or by sulking. Just say, briskly: 'Don't do that.' It's usually enough.

Be cheerful about morality. All we're concerned with, really, are simple rules for living together. So don't walk about the house spreading guilt all over the place. ('Who stole the biscuits?') None of us, but especially a child, should feel guilty about being alive. None of us should be made to feel permanently guilty about minor transgressions. It's more useful to say: 'Do better next time.'

Avoid extremes. Don't be too strict or pretend you know everything. On the other hand, don't be too lax, let your child do what he likes. The middle way is best: your rules should be based on commonsense, family convenience and a genuine concern for others.

Show concern for others yourself. You can do this by discussing problems of the community, or the world, with your children. Even better, you can help out at the local playgroup, or at the school's parent-teacher association, or by serving on local groups and committees. With children, as with adults, actions speak louder than words.

With teenagers, make some rules but don't be too rigid and overbearing about them. Don't forget to discuss things with your teenagers. It's the middle way, again, that's needed: if you're too permissive, too democratic they won't know what the limits are and they won't know where *you* stand. If you're too autocratic, it doesn't give them a chance to develop their own personalities and to work out a system of rights and wrongs which works, and which is *still* applied when nobody's looking.

Don't resort to threats, punishment or bribery to get your own way. Use rewards (and your own approval, expression of pleasure) is the best reward. As the child grows older, and he knows that you care about him, he'll do things not because he is going to be punished if he doesn't, or rewarded if he does. He'll do them because that's the right thing to do: the thing which harms others the least, or helps others the most – which is true morality.

Be yourself and be honest. No child expects his parents to be

146

saints, but every child expects love and a little bit of guidance and friendship. If you give your child these three fundamentals, he'll work out the rest for himself. Friends don't (or shouldn't) hurt each other. Whatever you believe in I think you'll agree that respect for others – including our own children – is the only way to happiness. And survival.

Mother Love
(For Parents)
See also **Love** *Page* 138

Before we have a closer look at mother love, let's just draw attention to three things that you, as a mother (or father), are likely to be suffering from:

Feelings of Inadequacy. I'm not doing what the experts say I should be doing (or I'm trying to, and it isn't succeeding). I never look like those glamorous, unruffled mothers on TV. Everybody else seems to be able to cope, so why can't I?

Guilt. It's my fault that my child is too thin/too fat, not clever enough, aggressive, timid, short-sighted, shy, boisterous, a boy/girl. (Many mums believe or are told that, whatever happens to the child, if it's bad it's mother's fault. It isn't.)

Lack of Praise. You're more likely to be praised for being a business executive, or a saleswoman, or doing some kind of a job in the 'outside world' than you are for being a mother. This, despite the fact that we have always, since the days of Mary the Mother of Jesus, sung hymns of praise to the whole idea of motherhood. You may find, when motherhood hits you, that there's plenty of hard work and criticism but not much praise or support.

There's no doubt that your child wants love, and plenty of it, from you, the mother. Children who don't receive love spend the rest of their lives looking for it, in one form or another. Those who are given lots of love face life with optimism and courage, and a deep-down sense of security that comes from being able to say those three simple words: I am loved. The love you give to your child is, emotionally speaking, money in the bank as far as he is concerned, the one certain investment for his future. Love is a vital ingredient in the human cake-mix. The trick is to give it, and get something from giving it – to be a mother and still remain a viable, interesting and fulfilled person *in your own right*.

We have to learn to be brisk about love. And having a first baby, bringing up a first infant, can be an anxious business, and you may think you're too busy, or exhausted to worry about love but we live and learn, and what we *should* learn about love is:

To have fun. Enjoy your children while you have them. Life is short. Instil in them a sense of enjoyment of life which they'll carry with them always.

To be consistent and reliable. Love doesn't mean a gooey sentimentality. It means being there when the children need you, wiping their noses, listening to them, playing with them, talking to them. And it means saying to them: 'No, you mustn't do that.' When we genuinely love another person we raise our own standards, and expect them to treat us as we treat them: with affection and respect.

If you love your children, say so, and don't be afraid of showing them affection. The words 'I love you' mean a lot to children. A hug, a cuddle, are the best antidotes to many of the world's woes.

Don't try to love all your children the same. Love each one as a unique, one-off human being. Try to spend a few moments each day, a half-hour each week, with one child. Moments that are shared, when the child has your sole attention, are deeply treasured by children.

Move from love towards friendship as your children grow older. When your children are young they are very dependent upon you, they need your love, you are the main person in their lives. As they grow older they should lean less on you (and you on them) although they still need your emotional support. What they want to see, as they grow up, is that you are a real person with a personality, a life and friends of your own, apart from them. Love them, but leave them space to lead their lives. Try not to be too dependent upon them for your emotional rewards.

Never use the threat of withdrawal of love as a weapon. Don't say: 'If you do that I shan't love you any more' (children take these threats seriously). You are entitled to say instead: 'I'm angry with you for doing that.' Just because we love somebody doesn't mean that we can't, occasionally, be really angry with, loathe, dislike or get very irritable with that person whether it's an adult or a child.

Don't worry if you 'go off' your child from time to time. We all do (especially when they're teenagers!). If you feel that you are rapidly getting to dislike your son or daughter the only

148

consolation I can give you is that we've all been through moments, days (or weeks) like that – even though we love the child dearly.

Don't worry too much about what experts say – they've been wrong before, and they'll be wrong again. Trust your own deepest instincts, and try to join a group where you can meet other mothers with children of the same age where you can swop experiences and discuss, in a commonsense way, the kind of problems (including tiredness) that most mothers have.

Have a break from your child. Little absences make the heart grow fonder. Join a group of mums so that somebody else can mind your baby whilst you have your hair done, or go shopping. When the child is old enough, take him along to join a playgroup. He'll enjoy the different faces; you'll both enjoy a rest from each other. When your children are teenagers encourage them (they'll probably insist on it anyway) that they 'do their own thing' regarding holidays, and you do yours. When you come back, you'll have something to talk about to each other. My own experience, with infants and with teenagers, is that I enjoy them more if I don't see them *all* the time. What's true for fathers, in this respect, is just as true for mothers.

It's a tough job being a mother but to raise a reasonably happy child is, in my book, one of the greatest, most satisfying achievements of which human beings are capable. It is certainly on a par with writing a book, painting a beautiful picture or (dare I say it?) holding down a highly-salaried job. It's about time we gave mothers the praise and recognition they deserve for all the hard work they do. Love is hard work, but it's worth it.

Motivation

See also **Emotional Needs** *Page* 70, **Reward and Punishment** *Page* 185

There's no doubt that *the fear of punishment* does motivate children, especially infants, and I cannot see any harm in a sharp word, a tiny tap on the wrist, if your toddler, say, plays with the electric plugs or does something else that's dangerous. A tiny smack, when children are young, providing it's done against a background of love, isn't going to do a child any harm. It may be the timely, salutary warning that the child needs at that particular moment. However, punishment as a way of life, and as a main prop in your dealing with the child, seems to me quite wrong. There are much better ways of getting children to do things than punishing them and, as children grow older, this appeal to their better instincts should, in my view, be used more and more.

To find out what does motivate youngsters we ought really to have a quick look at some of their basic needs. I'll just say a few that come into my own head. Praise; a sense of belonging to a group; adventure; self-esteem; to be thought highly of by others; to build and make things; new experiences and new ideas; a certain amount of independence (especially in older children); an element of danger (again, especially with teenagers); to be with other people and to cooperate in joint enterprises with them; to be secure; to be loved. This list isn't definitive. No doubt, you can add a few needs that you think are important to children (and, incidentally, adults!).

Let's just take the first of these needs: praise. I find – and I don't know how it works with you – that praise acts like a charm on me. If I'm praised for something I've done, or something I'm doing, I try harder. In contrast, punishment has never worked very well on me. At school, unwilling and unable to eat my lunch one day, I was caned quite savagely for refusing to do so. I still didn't eat the lunch. I hated the teacher who caned me because I thought the whole business was rather silly and exaggerated. As an adult, teaching small groups of poor readers in the child guidance clinic, I've found that what applied to me as a child applied to them: punishment was irrelevant and solved nothing. Praise and encouragement brought out the best from them (see section on **Reward and Punishment**).

If we look at the other needs we can see an emphasis on belongingness, on groups. *Children want to feel part of a group so do let your children contribute to the family, make suggestions and be involved.* Don't do everything for them since this does nothing to build up their self-respect. Give *them* some responsibility (another human need) and they'll respond. Don't give them jobs to do that they can't manage; 'bring them along' steadily giving them more and more responsibility and more of a place in the group. This is good preparation for adult life where we have to work alongside others.

Set your standards and don't set them too high or (just as bad) too low. Nothing's worse for a child than to be faced with an impossibly high standard, where everybody around him is just too good to be true. On the other hand don't take the attitude 'Anything Goes'. Children don't like that: it gives them no security and it's no compliment to anyone to expect nothing from him.

Explain what you want and why you want it, especially as your children get older. If you are doing things in a way that involves everybody – and in a way which you think is right – you should be able to talk to the others involved and decide, together, what you want.

Give your child a few challenges. Teach your young child to swim; let your teenager go off walking in Wales or help to build an adventure playground. Sports present a challenge, competition within fair rules. Even things like collecting stamps present a challenge in getting to know more about a particular subject. Give them a few goals to aim for. Don't set your goals too high or they'll get anxious; don't set them too low or they'll become bored and fed up.

Doing things *for* children motivates them. The main thing to do is to create, or take them to, an interesting place where they can learn something, make something, build up their skills, scaffold their understanding of the world. Doing things *with* children motivates them. It appeals to their instinct to cooperate with others. *Listening to them, talking honestly to them, giving them some of your time* motivates them. *Rewards* motivate them but the best rewards of all cost nothing: words of praise from those we love and/or respect and – just as important – a sense of achievement in creating something near to the best of our ability. Twenty pence can be a powerful motivation to a child but the words 'Well done', said sincerely, can be even more powerful.

The main point to bear in mind is that what motivates you is probably what motivates your child. If you're anything like me the things that motivate you are praise, words of thanks, courtesy, affection, goals that can be reached and bring a sense of satisfaction – in fact, most of the things mentioned in my list of needs.

It's exactly the same with children. To motivate them be aware of *their* needs, their hopes and aspirations. Before you punish a child, ever, ask yourself, fairly and squarely, does it work? Did it ever work with you? I think you'll agree with me that it must be used sometimes as a last resort but it's a poor way indeed of motivating children to contribute what they have to give to you and to your family.

Nail-Biting

In the 1950s I read a survey which said that one-in-ten primary school children had the habit of biting their nails. Now, it seems, more than a third of young school-children bite their nails. Perhaps we live in anxious times! Nail-biting *is* a habit: it can start by the child chewing at a nail, finding this comforting, and persisting with the behaviour. It can start by copying another child at school or when the child is worried, excited or feeling particularly shy in company. Boredom, tension or fear (say, when watching a frightening television programme) can all spark off a bout of nail-biting. When the excitement, or boredom, is over the child stops. What happens, though, if the child doesn't stop? With a girl of school age you can use the incentive of buying her a bottle of nail varnish. Teach her to varnish her own nails and say something like: 'My, you've got really pretty nails.' You can, if you wish, buy her a bottle of colourless nail varnish for school (and, if necessary, tell the teacher what you're up to) and another bottle of coloured nail varnish for weekends. The main thing is to get your child to take a pride in her nails. Buy her a little manicure set if you think she would like one. You are appealing to her vanity and using the fact that she can 'show off' to friends and tell them that she is allowed to use nail varnish.

Before we go on to mention other techniques for stopping nail-biting it might be a good idea to say that, in most cases, the best approach is to ignore it, or simply say: 'Don't bite your nails. It's not a habit I like, and it makes your fingers look unattractive.' After all, so many children do bite their nails that we cannot claim that they're *all* neurotic, or born worriers, or highly strung. Most children do grow out of the habit so your best approach is to signal your disapproval but play it cool and don't make too much fuss. Nagging doesn't help; punishment is quite wrong since, half the time, the child is quite unaware that he *is* biting his nails.

If you do think that your child is biting his nails because of worry over something it is a good idea to be supportive and sympathetic rather than critical. Are you too strict with the child? Do you set too-high standards for him (and yourself)? Is the child worried about any aspect of school work? (If so, do go up to the school and have a chat with his teacher.) If some programme on TV makes your child twitchy and nervous then don't let him watch it. It's not much use complaining that your nine-year-old bites his nails if he stays up late to watch the Midnight Horror Movie. In the same circumstances, at that age, we'd bite our nails. With a boy you can try rewards (bribes?) and say: 'You get 5p for every day that you don't bite your nails,' (or whatever you can afford). The sight of a child's chewed nails isn't pleasant but, having tried bribes – and praise when he *doesn't* bite his nails – there is probably not a great deal more you can do about this messy habit.

Some people advocate bitter medicine on the nails as a deterrent. There are several brands of these nasty-tasting substances available from chemists. Before you go along to your local Boots, however, you should ask yourself whether, with your child, this is likely to put a stop to the habit or simply make the child more defiant. You may be paying too much attention to it and making too much of a problem out of it. Certainly, in my view, it's not worth spoiling a good relationship with a child by a squabble over his nails. It's better to ignore the nibbling and hope that it will – as it does in most cases – go away.

If your child does stop biting his nails for a few days it's as well to call attention to the fact, say how pleased you are and perhaps give him a little treat or reward (e.g. buy him a cake that he particularly likes or give him 2p for each finger, or thumb, that looks neat and tidy!) The best reward of all is your words of encouragement and appreciation. With children – as with adults – this approach works better than criticism and threats. Remarks like: 'My God, look at the state of your fingers,' do no good at all.

With teenage girls, some people advocate using false nails (placed over the real nails) which gives the youngster's nails a chance to grow and then, after the nails have grown, coating them with a protective, hardening substance to strengthen them and discourage biting. This nail-strengthening solution, again, can be obtained from your local chemist. However, before you do this, do consider whether a straight appeal to your recalcitrant daughter's vanity (by offering small monetary rewards you might also successfully appeal to her greed) might not be a better approach. Again, the more fuss you make, the more attention you pay over and above a word of disapproval, the more you build up nail-biting into a tremendously important issue rather than an annoying habit (of which children and young people have many).

If you think that your child's nail-biting is a result of persistent worry and anxiety you could have a word with your family doctor or perhaps get an appointment to see your educational psychologist and ask him to assess whether your child is, in fact, over-anxious and unduly tense. However, before you make too much out of nail-biting in itself, it's as well to remember that nearly half of the primary school population bite their nails at some time or other. You may worry about it. The habit may disgust you. The two shreds of consolation I can offer you are that nail-biting, like a lot of other things, passes away and, second, you are *not* alone.

Nervous Children
See also **Anxiety** *Page* 8, **Fears** *Page* 81, **Insecurity** *Page* 115

There's nothing mysterious about anybody being nervous: if you or I were in the Chamber of Horrors alone, at night, a certain amount of nervousness wouldn't be at all surprising! In fact, very little could happen to us but that would be small consolation: our worst fears are often quite irrational. It's the same with children, who can be – and often are – nervous about a number of things including dogs, spiders, meeting new people, going to new places, being asked to stand up in class and, sometimes, even going to places or meeting people that they know perfectly well.

Nervousness, as we all know, can be lessened by experience. The first time I ever gave a lecture I was terribly nervous; now, after years of lecturing, I'm always surprised when people tell me that something routine like that can make them feel apprehensive. We tend to forget our own early reactions to new experiences and to underestimate the fear that certain situations can evoke in other adults and, especially, in children.

Children who are nervous can be made more confident. In a famous experiment with an eleven-month-old boy called Albert the child was allowed to play quite normally with a pet white rat. What happened next I think is rather cruel. Every time that Albert reached for his white rat the psychologists made a very loud noise behind him. Albert started to be afraid of the white rat – and of things which resembled the rat such as little furry objects, balls of cotton wool, white rabbits. His fear was subject to *generalization,* in the same way that a child at school who fears the, say, maths teacher may begin to dislike all the other teachers or be put off school altogether.

The way to cure Albert was simple: to let him play with the white rat and *not* make the noise, so that he re-establishes a relationship with his pet. Better, after a while it would be possible to give him a piece of chocolate each time he was given the white rat to play with. Providing the noise wasn't made again his fear of the pet rat would fade away or *extinguish*. In other words, he would modify his behaviour in the light of his experience and his confidence would be built up again. It would be possible, if he'd been made very afraid of the rat, to start gradually by giving him balls of cotton wool, or white fluffy objects, to play with first (along with the chocolate and without making the loud noise). This slower process

154

of building up confidence by giving the child similar objects to play with is sometimes called *de-sensitization.*

You can see from this that, if your child is, say, afraid of dogs it might be a good idea if you bought him a puppy to play with (or at least, take him to a friend's house where there is a nice, friendly, not-too-large dog that would help to build up his confidence). Similarly, children who are afraid of going to parties, or to school, should be given more experience of relating to other children – and to adults – in smaller groups. It's silly to inflict on a child a large social gathering – such as a party or going to 'big school' – if he hasn't had a chance to lose his fear of mixing with people early on in life.

Nervousness can affect a child's level of achievement – just as it can affect an adult's. The nervous child in school, for example, may not be able to concentrate on his work; he may be worried, easily distracted; the teacher may say of him, 'He's terribly fidgety,' or, 'His mind always seems to be elsewhere.' Quarrels at home, too high expectations on the part of parents, jealousy of a younger, or older, sibling, worry about somebody who is ill at home, or about a threatened separation of his parents can all make a child nervous. If you feel that your child is very 'jumpy' and if you find that his work in school is rapidly deteriorating it may be wise to contact the child's teacher and ask to see the educational psychologist, who is trained to assess your child's intellectual ability and to diagnose and treat learning and behaviour problems in school.

Of course, it is possible that your child's problem doesn't affect his school work but does affect his relationships in the home. Perhaps, at home, your child is moody and withdrawn, or very easily hurt, or 'flies off the handle' at you with very little provocation. You may be worried about a child with eczema, or frequent headaches, or who frequently complains of aches and pains. Or, you may find that your child is painfully shy and refuses to go out in the evening to mix with other children. If you really are worried about your child's nervousness you should go along to your family doctor and ask for an appointment to see the children's psychiatrist at the child guidance clinic. The children's psychiatrist will *not* pronounce your child 'mad' or 'put him under the bright lights' or lie him on a couch. What he will do is to discuss the problem with you so that, together, you can find out what is the cause of your child's nervousness and do something, together, to put it right.

However, before you call in an expert, there are a number of things which you can do to help your nervous child.

Try to be consistent in how you behave towards your child. If your child never knows what to expect from you it's no wonder he's nervous.

Take into account that some children, from birth onwards, are more sensitive than others. Shouting at your child won't help, neither will nagging or over-harsh discipline. An approach based on lots of praise, drawing him gradually into the group, and encouraging the child's own interests and hobbies is far more likely to succeed. Don't smack your child or try to 'jolly him out of it'. Nervous children need their confidence built up slowly and steadily.

If your child is nervous about school talk gently to him about it. There may be a bully at the school, or a dog he encounters on the way to school, or a teacher, or lesson, he doesn't like. Don't say: 'Snap out of it.' If he could, he would. Just as important, don't accuse him of being 'lazy'. Keep in touch with the class teacher so that you can both help the child in the best way.

Don't be too critical of your child's accomplishments. Your job is to build him up, not put him down.

Take your child out, especially encourage him to go to the houses of friends. To cope in a small group is good practice for coping in a larger group and having to face up to unfamiliar situations.

If you are involved in marital strife make it clear to your child that, whatever happens, you love him. Never use your child as a weapon and never quarrel with your partner and expect the child to support you in your hostilities. Nothing is more calculated to make a child unhappy and nervous than to be caught between two warring parents. It's an adult matter so do try to deal with it as far as possible without harming your child.

Persist in caring, and showing affection. Most children, at sometime or other, show symptoms of nervousness, about something or other. Most of these signs of nervousness pass as the child grows up. Do all you can and, having done that, you should go to your family doctor and seek expert help and support.

Neurotic Children

What does neurotic mean? In the way I'm going to use the word here it means 'of abnormal sensitivity'. These children are sometimes described by their mothers as 'jumpy', 'on edge' or even, less elgantly, 'all of a twitch'. I think what you should be careful about is the tendency on the part of some mums (and dads) to accept complete responsibility and blame for producing an over-sensitive child. In fact, that's silly because there are children who are born much more sensitive than others. They're quicker to react – to pain, to disappointment, to happiness. They're like instamatic rolls of cameras, with a never-ending supply of film: everything that happens to them they seem to react to and record; events – whether good or bad – make a greater impact on them; they may take things a little too seriously. 'You want to calm down,' a mother will say, or, 'There, things aren't as bad as all that.' When you're a child, and extremely sensitive however, they might well be.

If you have one of these very sensitive children, don't think that your handling of the child has made him that way; he was probably that way from Day 1. Nevertheless, there are some practical things you can do to help the child; there are ways of behaving which you should avoid if you want to make your child more confident, more at ease, less volatile in his emotions. What you should do, first of all, is try to be consistent in your own behaviour. You've probably been told this before so I think it might be a good idea to explain why consistency on the part of mother and/or father is so important.

In an experiment referred to in my book *Tom Crabtree on Teenagers* (Elm Tree Books) rats were trained to jump to a black circle, where they obtained food, and to a white circle, which was fixed and immovable so that the rat bumped his nose against it. The rats, as you might guess, quickly learned to jump towards the black. The next part of the experiment was very mean. Both black and white circles were made immovable so that, wherever the rat jumped, he would bump his nose. Then, the reward of food was 'randomized': sometimes it was the white circle behind which the food was hidden, sometimes the black. The rat didn't know where he was; he didn't know what was expected from him; he usually ended up on the floor, running around in circles, emitting little squeaks, totally neurotic.

You've heard the expression: 'I like to know where I am with people.' Many adults do. They want to be treated consistently and know what to expect. Not many of us like people who treat us well one day, and badly the next. We accuse them of being two-faced, or just not caring about us enough to respond to *our* needs and interests. It's exactly the same with children, especially as regards parents. They don't want to be punished for a piece of behaviour one day, have it ignored the next, punished for something they didn't do the following day and rewarded for bad behaviour (since we give them more attention sometimes when they behave badly (see section on **Reward and Punishment**) the day after that. All children ask is that we have a discernible pattern of reacting to them. If we have no consistency they cannot, like those rats, make out what is going on, nor what is expected of them. If you're rejecting one day, loving the next, if you accept certain behaviour one time, 'clamp down on it' the next time it happens, you can't really be surprised if your child ends up baffled and slightly twitchy!

Don't tell your toddler to tidy up his toys on Tuesday and let him leave them in a mess on Wednesday. Tidy them up, together, every time. Don't let your ten-year-old run through the front door in muddy shoes today and yell at him for doing the same thing tomorrow. Don't give your teenager tea with dirty hands now and shout at him for sitting at the table, unwashed, some time in the future. What is it you want? Which way do you want your child to jump? That's up to you but, whatever you want in the way of behaviour, give out clear signals. Do the same emotionally. If you're feeling happy, say: 'I feel really good.' Don't say one thing when you're feeling another. Children can put up with an awful lot, providing they *know* what's happening. Don't make the world a more confusing place than it already is. I used to know a teacher who from time to time would say to his class: 'I'm in a bad mood today so ...' He didn't need to say anything else. They knew where they were, those kids. There was no messing about on his 'bad days'. Children are very good at reading adult moods but why should they be asked to do that kind of deciphering? Why not tell them exactly how you feel, how the world is with you. All of us, adults and children, wherever we are, have a need to know what's going on, have a need to structure our world so that we can make sense of it. You're not Greta Garbo. Don't act. Just be honest about what you want, and how you feel. It makes life easier for everybody else, particularly your child.

The rest of what I have to say is merely commonsense. If you have one of these over-sensitive children, don't feel guilty; it's not your fault! He was probably born a tizzy baby, has remained sensitive, and will probably be a little more sensitive than others when he grows up. All you can do is give him lots of love and expressed affection while he is a child, which is when he most needs it, and don't try to make him 'tougher' than he is, or compare him unfavourably with more boisterous children. Build him his self-esteem (don't call him a 'cissy') and give him praise when he tries hard at something, and succeeds or when he tries very hard and just doesn't manage to pull it off. We can't all be rough, tough, hail-fellow-well-met, hearty, back-slapping extraverts. Who would want *that?* It's the differences between children – and between adults, come to that – which make them so interesting.

Nightmares
See section on **Disturbing Dreams** *Page* 60

'Normal' Behaviour

The best way to understand 'normality' is to think of height. Most men in Europe and America are between five feet, five inches and five feet, ten inches tall. This is the 'normal' height for men we would expect to meet. (Normal, here, is a statistical concept meaning within the observed range.) It would be unusual, when you're going around observing, to come across a man who was seven feet tall. Such a man would be abnormal.

I'm not going to say there is no such thing as abnormal behaviour: there obviously is. I'm saying, really, that *there is a very wide range of behaviour that falls within accepted limits and, with children's behaviour, there are enormous individual differences.* What we have to do is to look at the whole child, take into account the good behaviour and the bad, and realize that *at some stage or another most children show some signs of abnormality.* Bad behaviour seems to come in patches and, as you'll well know, some patches are worse, or last longer, than others.

In one family I know very well, one in which the children are now teenagers, the eldest daughter went through a patch of two years or more where she couldn't make friends, the son wet the bed for five years, the youngest daughter was extremely aggressive and always arguing and quarrelling with her playmates. Now, the oldest girl is outgoing, friendly, very popular. The boy no longer wets the bed. The youngest girl is one of the most charming, well-mannered (and non-aggressive) youngsters you could wish to meet. With children, periods of maladjustment, 'bad patches', come and go like the tides.

What you may not know, as you worry about your child's potty training, the bed-time battles, his eating faddiness, is that most mothers worry about these things (or other aspects of the child's behaviour). Mothers worry about two-year-olds throwing temper tantrums but (in my experience) it's *normal* for two-year-olds to behave like this. Mothers worry about teenage sons and daughters who dress oddly/stay out late/never help in the house. It's *normal* for parents and teenage children to have differences, arguments, little tiffs.

The trouble is that you may have had totally unreal expectations of motherhood (just as I had totally unreal expectations of fatherhood). I thought I'd walk through the countryside with my perfect children, pat them on the head when they went to bed, explain Einstein's Theory of Relativity to them over breakfast. I, like you, didn't bargain on being kept awake at night, physical illnesses and too boisterous behaviour. Besides having too high expectations of motherhood (or fatherhood) quite a few of us have too high expectations of children.

'It isn't a bit like I thought it would be,' said one mother to me, of motherhood. 'I'm exhausted, utterly tired out and he,' (pointing to her three-year-old) 'seems to get the better of me every time. I thought being a mum was going to be *romantic.'* What would you say to such a mum? Probably you'd say what I said: 'Don't feel too inadequate about it. Believe me, it's something we've all been through.' It's *normal* that lively infants tire us out; it's *normal* that we wonder whether our child has an overactive brain or just needs a good spanked bottom.

Besides having a totally false picture in our minds of what motherhood (or fatherhood) is going to be like I think the other mistake we make is to *compare* our children with other people's children. Comparisons like this are odious and pointless. Your child may have good powers of observation and excellent manual dexterity. Yet, you worry because your neighbour's child of similar age has better speech, or can read whilst your's cannot. We should, as I've said, look at the whole child and bear in mind that development proceeds by sudden bursts (as on the magical day that your child starts to walk), slow gains and periods when the child doesn't seem to be making too much progress at all. It's wrong to take too much notice of developmental charts – because of the enormous individual differences in ages and stages – and it's wrong to compare your child with your best friend's. They're two very different human beings and you have to make allowances for those differences.

Very few children live in idyllic surroundings: many of them live in one-parent families, more and more live in families where grandparents, aunts, uncles and cousins live a long way away. These days, there is less and less space for children to play, and the increase in road traffic means that 'playing out' (especially for young children) is fraught with danger. It's a wonder, considering the stresses and strains of modern life, that children grow up to be normal, pleasant human beings. But most of them do. I have seen children – brought to see me in the clinic because of some family crisis or other – in later years and have always been impressed how they managed to get over their early difficulties.

So, remember when bringing up children:

There is a tremendously wide variation in the way in which children develop – physically, intellectually and emotionally.

It is normal for a child to go through bad patches of behaviour. The vast majority of symptoms will disappear as the child grows older.

A mother should call in expert advice when she simply cannot cope any more, or when the symptoms persist beyond a time that is acceptable to her.

Most children have some quirk of character, some idiosyncratic part of their personality. Don't expect to have faultless children.

We all lack knowledge of what parenting is about, and what children are really like especially before we have some of our own.

Don't compare. Each child goes through the same sequences of development *but at his own pace.*

Be patient (and a bit more realistic) about your expectations. I'm sure they'll all be fulfilled in the end.

Obedience
See also **Reward and Punishment** *Page* 185, **Rules** *Page* 190

To tackle the subject of obedience I want to give you ten useful tips. If you follow these, you should have no trouble in getting your children to obey you!

Don't over-do obedience. If you do, you'll raise children who are lifeless, repressed and show little initiative of their own. Getting children to do things because they can see the sense in doing them is a much better approach. After all, as we grow older, we have to learn to work alongside other people without being supervised all the time.

When children are young you have to be aware of situations which are dangerous. When your infant goes near the fire, or touches the stove, or plays with the electricity plugs or the TV controls a sharp 'No' will, usually, be sufficient to deter him. If it doesn't, carry him out of the room where the tempting object is out of sight and out of mind. Don't make too much fuss over discipline but when you want something done be brisk about it. Young children want to cooperate so make it clear what you want from your child and *most* of the time (all children get up to mischief sometimes) you'll get it.

Have plenty of 'Do's'. Cut down on the 'Don'ts'. It's a lot more positive to say to a child: 'Play on the grass. Don't go on the flower-beds.' He knows what you want. With older children you might say, for example: 'I don't mind you going to your friend's house on the way back from school but *do* telephone me so that I know where you are.' With teenagers, you shouldn't say: 'Don't stay out late.' That means nothing. Just say: 'I want you back by 11pm.' (Or a time that you decide between you.) Don't just tell children what isn't permitted: tell them what to do and, as they grow older, tell them why. None of us mind obeying instructions if they are clear and we can appreciate the reasons behind them.

As your child gets older let him make decisions for himself or discuss them with you. This gives *him* more responsibility, more opportunity for *self*-discipline. What we're after is sensible rules of living together.

Be fair. Give early warnings about tea-times, about bed-time ('another ten minutes') or about friends having to go home. With teenagers, tell them that tomorrow evening you'll want them to tidy their rooms or that, very imminently, you'll explode with righteous anger if they don't turn the record player down. Don't become angry unless you've told them what to expect, if they don't get around to doing A or B. Don't be afraid of your own anger but use it as the ultimate deterrent. Use it all the time and your children will get used to you and take no notice of your wrath!

Don't ask children daft questions. If you ask your child: 'Would you like to go to the shops?' (and the child *has* to go to the shops) there's no point in getting annoyed when the child, telling the truth, says: 'No.' It's much better to say: 'In ten minutes we're both going to the shops.' Not much chance of confusion, or disobedience, there.

Don't give puzzling instructions, or make enigmatic threats. 'Try to be good today, for my sake,' or, 'Behave yourself this morning, or

162

else ...' are both too vague. You should try to specific. 'Play with John in the garden. Don't touch the lawnmower. Ride your bikes if you want to.' Use a quiet voice, act as though you expect your child to obey you, and he probably will.

Don't nag. Don't play Lady Macbeth (or King Lear) and make a tragedy, a big drama, out of the whole question of obedience. Don't carry on feuds, grudges, quarrels. Avoid scenes, avoid 'going on' about this and that. There'll be days when you rant and rave (it happens to us all) but I doubt whether it really does much to make your children respect, or obey, you.

Have family meetings to discuss plans and bones of contention. This sharing of decisions and of rule-making (so that we get on each other's nerves as little as possible) is, again, good preparation for adult life.

Have a sense of humour about it all. A family is a group of human beings, not a crack regiment. A home is a place where people can learn to share and live together; it's not a prison camp. Children will do as they're told if they like you and if they can see that, behind the rules, there's commonsense. We should, even with young children, emphasize the spirit of doing things together rather than being obedient and bowing to another person's will, whether we agree or not, whether we like it or not. That's dictatorship, not learning to live.

Obsessional Children

I'm a bit obsessional myself – especially about my work. Before I start writing I straighten typewriter, paperclips, biros, liquid paper bottle and diary. Everything's neat. If I find that one of the children has borrowed the stapler and hasn't returned it to it's proper place I become *very* annoyed and can't start until I have it back. Most people have an obsession about something. I knew a man, fairly rich, who used to change his underwear three times a day. I know another chap who can't go to bed without going around the house to make sure every electricity switch is off. Some women have an obsession about keeping the house tidy, others about washing their hair, others that they are too short/tall/thin/fat. Most of the obsessions we come across are benign enough: they don't much get in the way of us leading our lives, coping with day-to-day problems.

It's only when the thoughts, feelings and impulses to do something (so-called compulsive acts) result in anxiety and distress or a much-decreased functioning level that we ought to do something about them. There's no harm in a child, for example, having a spell where he avoids stepping on the cracks between paving stones; if the child has an obsessive fear of dirt, or of infection, or of the house catching fire then that will interfere with his happiness. If he has a compulsion to keep washing his hands, to do everything twice, to count everything that he possesses time and time again that *will* get in the way of him living his life.

My advice is for you to expect your child to be obsessional about *some* things (just as I am obsessional about my desk). If he's a toddler he may like things to be done in a certain order, to be dressed in the same sequence each morning. He may insist on sitting at the same place at table. That's quite normal. If he counts his toy soldiers don't start thinking that he's obsessional in any way that you should fret about: he's probably making sure that nobody's pinched any of them! Teenagers, too, can be obsessional about belongings. A missing hair-brush or (cardinal sin) somebody rootling through their belongings is sufficient to send them into paroxysms of rage and tirades of abuse. We all have our quirks: it's when those quirks interfere radically with our enjoyment of life or seriously affect the lives of those around us that we need to worry.

If you think that your child is too obsessional – too concerned about cleanliness, or over-worried about homework, or having a series of rituals that he simply must do every day – what should you do about it? First, keep your sense of humour; you can talk to your child about his little obsessions but don't forget to say that everybody has them (at least, everybody, adult or child, that I know). Don't be too perfectionist yourself and explain that, in life, we can't get everything right, have everything perfect. Re-assure them with facts, if it's appropriate. If your child, for example, is obsessed about germs you can say that we all come into contact with germs but that the body has its own way of resisting infection.

Don't give your child the mistaken notion that dirty means naughty (for younger children it may well mean fun). Don't say things like: 'What a mess you've made. You *are* wicked.' If you do, you are taking a lot of fun away from the child (see **Messy Play**). Don't say: 'You can have your nice dress on to go out to play but don't mess it up because we're going out later.' If your child does play the chances are that her clothes will get dirty. Don't worry too much if your child has little habits and rituals; all children have them, they come and go.

Just as adult workaholics have to be given insight into how silly it is to live *only* for your work (it's a good idea, with workaholics, to take them out walking, encourage them to have a good holiday, 'get away from it all') so obsessional children should be given some good experiences – going camping, going for a day out, joining a group where they can have some adventure – and given a chance to realize that many of the things we worry about, or things we think are so important, are really very trivial. Take your child out, give him a bit of stimulus, some fresh faces to meet, some new places to see so that he can put his worries into perspective.

If you are anxious about your child's rituals and habits and think that they make him (or you?) unhappy do have a word with your family doctor about it and he will tell you whether you are worrying unnecessarily.

Only Children

There *are* drawbacks to being an only child. I once heard a single child discussing with two friends, who'd come to stay with him for the weekend, how he'd had an erection in the bath. The boy, aged six, was really interested as his two friends told him the same thing had happened to them. Let's face it, an only child doesn't have ready-made companions to share his secrets with and there is a danger that he may be over-protected, given a lot of attention, made the centre of his parents' universe simply because he is the only one and, where the parents can't or don't wish to have more children, he *is* irreplaceable. Some only children are lonely. I saw a girl of nine who lived on a vast country estate: she was very lonely. I saw a boy, aged eight, who lived in a very select road where all the other parents' children had grown up. He was lonely simply because, like that child in the country, there was nobody to play with. However, not all single children are isolated, unhappy and disadvantaged. It all depends on where they live, what other children are around, and how much fun they have with their own parents. It would be a mistake to think that each and every single child is 'lonely'.

There are plenty of only children, living in streets, roads and tower blocks up and down the country who aren't lonely. Their parents *don't* wrap them up in cotton wool, *don't* get too anxious

165

about them. Some of these children, far from being insecure and timid, seem to be very confident in themselves, very friendly and very good at making friends. It's not what you expect. Many single children are more out-going, more self-assured (and, sometimes, more aggressive) than those children with brothers and sisters. About the only generalization we can make with any confidence about only children is that, on average, their language development – at least, their verbal facility – is more advanced than their contemporaries from larger families. This is because they are used to adult conversation and, in many cases, get greater verbal input from the parents.

Often an only child will have a close bond with both parents, or with one of them. I have seen many only children who had, and have, a very close and extremely rewarding relationship with the parent of the opposite sex. This gives the child a marvellous sense of confidence, of optimism, and belonging. The opposite side of this coin is that, where the only child's family runs into family tensions or splits up, the child is affected very deeply. He is in the front line; he has no siblings to act as confidants or to take the strain with him of the emotional upheavals. The lesson is that, as with other families, it is important for parents of only children to work through their problems without making the child the pawn in a game of family rows.

The financial side of things is very important these days. More and more parents are deciding for financial reasons to have just one child or perhaps two. The decision to have only one child does not, in itself, bring major snags and parents must do what they think is right for them. If you *do* decide to have a single child then you should, when your child is old enough, take him to a Mother and Toddler group (this is as much for you to mix with other mums as for your child to have companions for a couple of hours) and you should certainly get him to join a nursery class or playgroup when he reaches the age of three. This will prepare him for big school, give him some practice in sharing with other children and *in* handling feelings of jealousy, annoyance and frustration in a group. He will have practice in making friends and learn, very quickly, that although he may be the centre of attention at home it's a quite different story when he gets out into the wider world!

When you think about it there are plenty of children who, although they have brothers and sisters, do experience isolation in the family. There's the 'little afterthought' and the child who's siblings are too young to play with. There's a boy or girl divided from a sibling by an awkward age gap and lack of mutual interests. So loneliness in the family isn't confined to single children. Often, he only child has compensations – more money, more attention from parents – that some of the isolated children with brothers and sisters lack (see section on **Lonely Children**).

If you are a single parent with an only child you should try to give your child plenty of contact with other adults and children to help make up the gaps in his life. A single child without a father might, for example, be keen to join a swimming club, or the scouts, or a sports club where he can meet a few 'father-figures' and older youngsters. You may consider, if you are a single parent and your child is coming up to secondary school age, whether boarding school would be a good idea for him: giving him opportunities for more recreational pursuits and social contacts. Your local education authority will be quite willing to talk to you about your child's particular needs – and the possibility of financial support – so, if you're interested in this, you should contact your child's present headmaster and have a word with him about it.

My main message about only children is: *don't* assume that your child will be lonely; *don't* assume that he'll be different from other children. What you can do, as a parent of a single child, is to make sure that you give your youngster:

Plenty of conversation, and fun Try not to over-protect him and get him out there, playing with other children. After all, when he goes to school he'll have to adapt to the fact that he isn't the centre of the world, he's one of many.

Lots of love Don't be too strict. Some parents of only children set their standards too high, treat the child as a mini-adult. He isn't, so let him play at his own level and don't force him to grow up too soon.

Social opportunity Don't feel guilty about having an only child. If you give him affection at home, and encourage him to make friends outside of the home, he *isn't* disadvantaged. In fact, he's getting the best of both worlds.

Encouragement at school Many of the only children I have met liked school, and did very well at their lessons. This is because their parents encouraged them, without pushing them. Take an interest in his school work but don't be over-anxious, and go up to the school regularly to determine how he's making out.

Trust Let him make his own decisions, give him support. When he's older he'll bring home girls that you won't like. (Is any girl good enough for the only boy and the apple of his mother's eye. Is any boy good enough for dad's one and only beloved daughter?) Play it cool. You've given him lots of love so let him experiment a little and trust him, in the finish, to come to the right decision. If you leave them alone they usually do.

If you're loving parents your children are lucky, whether they're only children or one of a brood. The number of children is not as important as the amount of love and affection within the family and – here is the point – a loving family can be large or small.

Over-Permissiveness
(For Parents)
See also **Rules** *Page* 190

People, whether adults or children, don't like too much uncertainty, and commonsense tells us that children like *some* rules and to know what's expected of them. If we set no limits on their behaviour we're doing them no favours. It either means we don't care what they do, or else we have a mistaken notion that total freedom is good for children. There are not many situations in life where we can do exactly as we like so the earlier we learn to take into account the needs of others (without losing sight of our own needs and our own special gifts) the better.

Children need to know how far they can go, *they need limits.* The choice of where you put those limits is very much yours. I've met mothers who can put up with all sorts of rowdy play, hilarious games, rough and tumbles, shouting, laughing, screaming from an energetic bunch of youngsters without batting an eyelid. Other mothers (whose emotional elastic doesn't stretch that far) will quickly tell children that they mustn't scream and shout. It all depends on how you're feeling. If you have the Monday morning blues, or a headache, you're going to bring your limits in a bit. At the clinic, when I was feeling fragile, I used to tell the children: 'No noise. Play with the sand or pick a *quiet* toy.' I'm sure that this was breaking all the rules of play therapy but so what? I'm human too.

Naturally, where you set your limits depends upon where you are. If you're in your own house, you make the rules. If you're in somebody else's house you take your cue from them and use commonsense: if visiting an aged aunt, who owns a collection of precious porcelain, it wouldn't be a good idea to have too much rushing about. With my own children, when they were young (and I was looking after them for a day) I would try and get them out to the park, or at least, into the garden. Here, it's less necessary to keep on saying, 'Don't do this,' and, 'Don't do that.' As long as they didn't do anything dangerous or anti-social I let them get on with it. That's the idea of limits: to act as a truce, a bond, between children and adults so that they can get on with their play *within the agreed* rules. And, of course, the thing with rules is to have as few as possible, make sure everyone knows what they are, and stick to them.

There has to be a philosophy about rules. The idea is not to set up a Fascist Regime within your own home. The aim is to let children have *more* fun because they know what it is they are allowed (and not allowed to do). Without some limits, fun becomes chaos, freedom becomes licence and people get hurt. Children aren't silly. They know all this instinctively. If you watch them devising a game to play amongst themselves you'll find they have rules ('No hiding upstairs', 'No going into gardens'). They don't set up rules for their own sake; they have rules because it makes the game more enjoyable. *We* don't let them do as they like for *our* convenience, and their safety and enjoyment. I can't see anything wrong in that.

The way to establish a good atmosphere in the home – one in which people can enjoy themselves without treading on other people's toes – is to follow a few rules yourself:

Be consistent in your discipline. Don't be easygoing one day, lax the next. Children find that *very* confusing.

Agree on what goes, and all stick to it. Don't fall into the trap of saying: 'You wait until your father comes in.' If a child is doing something wrong, tell him. You and your husband (or wife) should decide *together* the 'Do's' and 'Don'ts'.

Don't fuss over detail. Leave your anger and wrath for real transgressions of the rules. With children, when they're enjoying themselves, shirts (and faces) do get dirty, trees get climbed, shoes get scuffed, your kitchen gets a less-than-pristine look. Don't set your standards *too* high and take all the enjoyment out of their life (and yours).

Respect your child's imagination. If he says, 'Today I'd like to blow up the world/gun down the maths teacher,' say something like, 'My, you're feeling destructive.' Only if he behaves in a destructive way, i.e. starts hitting his brother or a chair, need you say, quietly, 'That won't do.' Children do sometimes have aggressive, destructive thoughts, that's nothing to worry about. If they behave destructively, that is. Just say, 'No, I'm not having that.'

Explain that every family has different rules (they're bound to, since each family is unique). If the children go to granny's and she spoils them, or to a neighbour's house where they're allowed to run riot, tell them: 'Glad you enjoyed yourselves. When you're home, *our* rules apply.'

Change, not tighten, your limits as the child gets older. There should be no need to tell a nine-year-old not to break toys (a two-year-old may have to be told). The nine-year-old may talk with his mouth full. If it annoys you, say so. If it drives you desperate make it a rule that he doesn't do it. Stick to what limits you have decided upon but don't forget to discuss them, and to change them where necessary, as your children get older. Most young children are happy to be told to be in by dark. Don't apply the same yardstick to your teenagers. As they change, and become more responsible, so the limits change.

Be reasonable. Don't worry about long words like permissiveness and overpermissiveness. Just decide what you want in the way of behaviour and why you want it. Be prepared to explain (and discuss) the rules with older children, and the reasons for them.

Don't demand the impossible. Give them a chance to have fun. Only intervene when they cross over your own limits and then say, loud and clear, that marvellously useful word, NO.

Parents – Children's Relationship With
See also **Attitudes** *Page* 11

It's as well to remember, when you're bringing up children, that there are no perfect parents. Many's the mum who has said to me: 'My Sarah (or Mark) doesn't seem very happy at times.' I'm not surprised. Very few of us (see section on **Maladjustment**) are perfectly happy all the time so don't blame yourself, and start feeling guilty, just because your child is sometimes confused, or worried, or miserable. It happens to us all and it's part of life, of growing up. Don't make yourself responsible for every little thing that goes wrong in your child's life. Don't think that, somewhere, is the Lovely Mum (or lovely Dad) who never makes mistakes. *The Perfect Parent (despite what you may think) doesn't exist.*

The truth of the matter is that some of us are better with certain ages of children. And some of us, let's be honest, are much better with other people's children than we are with our own. Perhaps the fact that we love our own children so much gets in the way of our being detached, or even sensible, about them. Ages and stages do attract different responses. I know some mothers who are absolutely marvellous with babies. They'd like to have babies all the time. When the children get older they find them less attractive. 'Children are like dogs,' one of these mums said to me. 'They're loveable when they're small but when they're bigger you don't know what to do with them.' I must admit that, when my own children were young, I was mostly interested in infants. Now that my three are older I realize that adolescence is a fascinating stage in growing up (though it *can* be difficult since most adolescents, as well as being extremely large, are very sensitive, moody and awkward).

In my book *On Teenagers* (Elm Tree, 1980) I relate the story about a Perfect Mum (or, at least, *I* thought she was) throwing a pan of porridge at her children. This was at breakfast time when the children were making a row and she had a headache. They stopped their noise and for weeks afterwards, if one of them played her up, the others would whisper: 'Shsh, remember the porridge.' When she told me that tale it cheered me up tremendously. It's *normal* to be angry with, or depressed by, your children sometimes. It's *normal* to lose your temper. It's *normal* to have days when you can't cope, or think you can't. When people ask me what I was like as a parent when my children were young I say: 'Not bad, except I kept losing them, mostly in Woolworth's.' I hope you don't keep losing yours but, no doubt, you'll have your own blind spot: something you don't do very well, or a tendency to get incredibly angry when your children don't do certain things. Don't worry about it. We all have areas of incompetence.

It is important to remember not to over-protect your child and worry about every little detail of his life, from birth onwards. That's rather like opening a Swiss watch every five minutes to see if it's working. Play it cool. Let the child do things for himself, give him space to grow, let him follow his own nose – but don't lose him in the park. Make sure that your child is washed, dressed, fed and loved and let him get on with living. If you're in there, breathing, at the end of the day, you're winning. And again don't try to be too perfect yourself. Do it your way and have a bit of confidence in yourself. If you keep comparing yourself with mythical lovely Mums, or Lovely Dads, you'll have a permanent sense of inadequacy.

Don't forget, in all this, to treat your child as a human being and also – this is particularly vital when he's a teenager – a *friend*. Imagine what it feels like to be in his shoes, consider his feelings. If he says, 'I'm no good at history,' say, 'Well, it's not an easy subject. We can't be good at everything.' (*Not*: 'You're an idiot.') If he says, 'I lost my penknife at school today,' say, 'I'll bet you're annoyed.' (*Not*: 'You get it back tomorrow or there'll be trouble.') The aim is to build up the child's confidence and to suggest to him that we know a little bit about – and sympathize with – what's going on inside his head. Don't try to be a psychiatrist but do try to have some appreciation of *his* inner world and *his* emotions.

The idea is to live alongside your children, not through them, and to have some aims, hopes and ambition of your own, apart from theirs. When they've grown up and left home and come to visit you they'll want to see a warm, interesting, still-active human being rather than a worn-out wreck. Fun is important, too. Bringing up children is hard work but surely we should enjoy their company from time to time?

Play
See sections on **Fantasy** *Page* 76, **Fun** *Page* 91, **Messy Play** *Page* 143, **Under-Fives** *Page* 249

Pocket Money

When I was in the army, doing my National Service, I had a pal who came from a very wealthy family. One day I asked him to lend me some money. He threw across the cheque book, one cheque signed. 'Fill in the amount you want,' he said. It must be nice to have so much money that it means very little to you.

For most of us, money is always in short supply; just as it is for children. I'd like to think that we ran our families like the chairmen of international oil companies: very efficiently, with tight budgets, knowing exactly where the money goes. The truth is most of us muddle through, and money is a fraught subject, often giving rise to arguments, and resentments.

Why give children pocket money? Well, I assume that your children (just like you and me) can't have everything they want. They have to learn to allocate so much for this, so much for that, and to save up for things that they'd really like. *By having a regular 'pay packet' children learn to budget and to come to terms with the reality of cash, or the lack of it.* I don't think it's a good idea for parents to buy everything for the child and to say: 'He doesn't need pocket money.' I don't think it's sound to give a child a lot of

172

money if you're flush and nothing at all if you're hard up. (Though – let's face it – we're bound to be more generous when we have more money ourselves.) Ideally, children should receive an allowance (weekly when younger; monthly when teenagers) so that they can make up their own minds about when, where and on what the money should be spent. After all, that's what they'll have to do when they're adults.

When to start? A child of between three-and-four-years old is quite capable of going to a shop and spending his own money and learning to choose (it usually takes ages!) between A, B or C. An infant can be given a few coppers and a money box so he can acquire a rudimentary idea of 'saving'. Let's say you give your four-year-old 5p and a rise of 5p on each subsequent birthday. (By the time you read this, what with inflation, these figures may well be out of date.) This will give him pocket money of 50p per week at the age of thirteen. (Again, a word of caution. *How much you give is up to you.* It depends on what you earn, where you live, how much the other children receive. My figures may strike you as very stingy, or very generous, so stick to your own decision.) Leave the child to make his – often agonizing – choices; leave him to decide how to make the money go round. Be realistic. You can encourage a child to have a National Savings Bank book and go along to the Post Office to deposit, and draw out, money. You can teach them about interest and even about investments accounts. But the sad truth is it's very hard for children to save up any substantial amount simply because, just like adults, there are more things in life that they want than they have the money to pay for.

Do encourage older children to earn money to pay for the more expensive things they want. If they do jobs for neighbours (sweep up leaves, weed gardens and, for the teenager, baby-sit or take a newspaper round) that's fine.

Don't pay children for routine jobs that they do around the house. Washing the car, the dishes, mowing the lawn or doing the ironing are all part of living together. Once you start paying your children for going shopping or doing household chores they'll demand money for every little task and only do it if there's 10p in it for them!

I think a real appreciation of money comes when children are teenagers. What we have to teach teenagers is that money isn't evil, nor the one reason for existence. It's neutral. *Money is a commodity that we have to learn to acquire and to handle wisely so that we get the most out of it and really enjoy our lives.* Some things cost a lot of money, give little satisfaction. Other things are cheap (e.g. a walk in the countryside, talking to a friend over a cup of coffee) and give us a lot of pleasure. If teenagers want extras and/or things their parents can't afford (new clothes, cosmetics, expensive hair-do's, motor bikes or even cars) I think they should earn the money themselves: there's no better way of learning to appreciate the value of hard cash. Most of the older teenagers I know – those who are still at school or college – don't expect their parents to buy them everything. They have Saturday jobs, or they baby-sit, or do odd jobs, to earn the extra money that they need. This gives them a certain amount of independence, and self-respect.

With teenagers, pocket money (plus a monthly clothes allowance so that they can take responsibility for their dress and personal appearance) is a good idea. Again, I can't give you a prescriptive amount. It depends on you, and how much you think is fair. I'm staggered how much today's teenagers get as pocket money. (I mean both ways: some get enormous amounts, i.e. a thirteen-year-old getting £5 per week! Other children, of the same age, get 30p) What you may decide with your teenagers is that you will give them weekly pocket money, plus a clothes allowance *and* pay for day-to-day necessities (anything from soap, shampoos and toothpaste to bus fares and club subscriptions). Anything beyond this they must pay for by earning the money themselves. If this seems hard then all I can say is that, when it comes to money, life is hard and the sooner that teenagers realize how difficult money is to come by the more careful they'll be when it comes to spending it.

With pocket money the main things to remember are:

Give your child a regular amount. I know, in these days of inflation and unemployment, it's very hard but do try: however little the amount is. It teaches him to manage his own money.

Don't be blackmailed. Children compare ('But Alison Smith gets £2'). Decide what you think is fair and stick to it.

Don't expect little children to save very much. Just like adults, they try like mad but rarely succeed. There are too many things they'd like!

Teach children the idea of saving a little (to buy granny a present, an Action Man, or simply to go to the fair). None of us can have immediate gratification all the time: we have to save up for some of the nice things.

When they're older encourage your children to earn money to buy more expensive items. There's no better way of learning that it (money) doesn't grow on trees.

Discuss money with your child. Tell him about bank accounts,

deposit accounts, HP, and credit cards. Explain that, howe
buy goods, we have to pay for them, and we have to pay m
we overdo hire purchase and borrowing.

Don't be too generous or too stingy. Your child has to learn
to cope with money. When he's young the problem is how to
spend it. When he's older it's how to earn it. Give him enough
pocket money for him to make a few decisions himself and to
prepare him for the reality of life.

Get your teenager to open a bank account. Money in the pocket
goes quicker than Concorde. Anyway, it boosts the ego to go to
your own bank and, later on, have a cheque book of your own
and it's all good practice for the financial rigours of adult life.

Precocious Children
See also **Gifted Children** *Page* 98

Precocious children are ahead of other children in all-round
ability, or in some special area of ability, such as music. They may
also be children who are ahead of their peers in a particular stage
of development: for example, some young children seem to be
'wise beyond their years', others use long words (which, normally,
only adults or much older youngsters would use) and yet other
children may be sexually precocious, taking a great deal of interest
in the opposite sex and seeming to know a lot more than we would
expect from that particular age and stage of development. If your
young child is talented in a particular direction – whether it be
music, maths, mechanical ability – it would do no harm, once the
child has started school, to ask the educational psychologist for
advice on how best to develop your child's particular gifts. What we
don't want is lop-sided development. What we do want is for the
child to mature physically, intellectually, emotionally and socially
'all of a piece' – so that one aspect of his development doesn't
completely outstrip all the others leaving, for example, a child who
is a brilliant pianist but socially, or emotionally, terribly immature
(see section **Gifted Children**). This is particularly important for
extremely bright teenagers who may, because of their social
immaturity, be rejected by their peers and made to feel different
from the other youngsters in the school and outcasts amongst their
own age group.

If you think that your child is precocious in a musical sense, or in
mechanical ability, or in artistic ability *you should go to the school
and tell the teacher what you believe and chat about the best way that*

175

the school can help your child. It doesn't always follow that the young child who says things like: 'This apple pie is infinitely preferable to Mrs Smith's,' is of superior ability. The precocious child may talk like an adult – and give an impression of tremendous intelligence – without actually knowing what the words mean. With those youngsters like this it is important to get a second opinion as to whether your child requires an enriched programme of learning, i.e. more and harder things to do, in school.

With teenagers who are good at sport it is important that the school should know so that they may be aware of training commitments. A young person who is good at swimming may have to train every morning at the local baths; a gymnast may need time off school, say, an afternoon off once a week, if she is of a standard to represent her region or country. Often, if schools don't know about the youngster's special talents, they may unwittingly discourage the pursuit of that special aptitude. Also, young people need to discuss the strains and stresses of competitive sports with a sympathetic adult. I know one young woman who, as a teenager, represented her country at swimming but gave up the sport because she found the whole business so lonely and because nobody she knew really sympathized with the tremendous social sacrifices she had to make to stay in the top rank.

Different outstanding talents seem to appear at different ages. Musical ability can be detected quite early. Children of eleven and twelve can begin to show literary gifts. Mathematical ability sometimes shows through at primary school but is more likely to emerge (or, at least, to be spotted) at the secondary school stage, as is mechanical aptitude, artistic talent and sporting prowess. The best thing is to keep an eye open for any special talents that your child may have, to seek advice from the school, and work closely with the school to ensure that your child has the opportunity to develop his talents but bearing in mind his emotional, social – and in the case of arduous sports or children who are prone to 'swot' too much – his physical well-being.

With youngsters who are sexually precocious don't worry about their talking about it. Don't appear shocked, or treat the mention of sex as something disgusting and underhand. Nobody ever came to harm from knowing a lot about the theory of sex. However, when it comes to actually doing it that's a different story. If you have a young teenager – and some teenage boys and girls of thirteen *are* sexually active – who is having sexual intercourse with a boy friend/girl friend my firm advice is to make sure that your child knows about contraception (see section on **Sex Education**).

Quarrelling
(For Parents)

Quarrels, as part of married life, aren't inevitable: I've met people, married for years, who, they tell me, have never quarrelled. One lady, wed for twenty-five years, claimed that she had never had a cross word with her husband. Then (this is the other side of the coin) there are couples who quarrel regularly, and (by my standards) violently. One friend tells me that, chewing a piece of steak at supper, he was felled by a right hand punch from his wife (he'd made an unflattering remark about the string beans) and woke up, five minutes later, with the largest black eye he'd seen in years. 'Mind you,' he said, 'we quarrel a lot. Chase each other around the house at three-o'clock in the morning. It adds a bit of spice to life.' The odd thing is that the man's wife is a social worker.

I think most of us quarrel with our spouses from time to time and, most of the time, the quarrels are limited to rows, or 'blazing rows' during which we say things to each other that we later regret. After the row, we probably feel guilty and wonder what effect this sort of thing has on the children. It does have an effect since children need and want to give their love to *both* parents; all children are loyal to those they love and so it does worry them if they have to face a conflict and decide which of their two parents is 'right' and which is 'wrong'. (Usually, it's a bit of both; most people argue irrationally and because of a deep frustration within themselves.) Our spouse is often the recipient of our anger merely because he (or she) happens to be the handiest person around whom we can shout at and project all our own frustrations and anger on to.

Children *are* upset when parents shout at each other or treat each other with violence. The parents are the twin pillars of a child's world and, when parental anger erupts, it is as though their whole world has collapsed. Also, children often think that parents mean what they say in quarrels; they don't know that people can say things like, 'I hate you,' but can, later, still love the person who has been the object of their wrath. Another frightening thing for children is that rows tend to erupt, flare up suddenly, before anybody realizes what is happening and before anybody can do anything about it. Personal feelings of anger and resentment are sometimes expressed in what is, at best, an undignified way; at other times feelings may give vent to anger, force and violence which may assume dangerous proportions in that one of the participants (or innocent observers) risks physical injury.

Let's be honest. It would be better if there were no quarrels in your marriage: but there almost always are. So what steps can you take to minimize the harmful effects that rows might have on your children? I think you should:

Realize that we all have angry feelings. They are expressed, and they pass. You can reassure yourself that for children to be brought up in complete peace and harmony would be an inadequate preparation for the hustle and bustle and the give and take of real life.

Postpone (if you can) a really nasty quarrel until the children are out of the way. They'll still know that something is wrong but will be spared the gory details of your row.

Quarrel (if you must), then kiss and make up. Don't let your disagreement go on with nasty, harmful remarks for days on end. Children will be bothered by this just as much as by a short, sharp row that's over in a few minutes.

If caught, unawares, in mid-quarrel say: 'We were having a quarrel.' Don't try to pretend that you weren't. However, you can add: 'We were having an argument about … just as you and your sister argue about bedtimes.' Explain that adults, like children, have quarrels from time to time but they get over them.

Tell your children that people who are married do quarrel. This doesn't mean that they don't love each other, or mean to kill or harm each other. It just means that they get fed up with each other (or with life, or their job) and start to argue.

I doubt whether there is such a thing as 'ideal marriage'. If ideal marriages exist, they must surely be few and far between. Most marriages are rickety bundles of humanity tied up with the strings of kindness and love. If you want an argument, you'll find plenty to argue about in marriage. Every day, something happens that could (potentially) spark off a row.

As with children and *their* quarrels and squabbles (see section on **Disagreements**) what really counts is whether the people squabbling really care about each other: there *are* people who don't feel loved unless they are able to argue and quarrel with their partners. If people care for each other, love each other, there is a better chance that their arguments will be resolved.

Do get into the habit of discussing your grievances together *before* they flare up into an almighty row. In one family I know they have a 'Grudge Board': each member of the family writes up his complaints and these are discussed at a weekly meeting. In another family, at the end of every month, they have a meeting where any resentments can be voiced. This is a bit idealistic, I know, but it is important to discuss problems. You either talk about it, or fight about it. I think it's better to talk.

One last word. Where antagonism goes on for weeks or months, or where one partner is constantly looking for an excuse to have a quarrel, it may be wise for you to seek further help and advice. This can be obtained from your family doctor or from your local marriage guidance centre. The National Marriage Guidance Council (NMGC) provides a service for those wanting useful books and pamphlets on family problems. A comprehensive list of such literature is available from NMGC Book Department, Little Church Street, Rugby.

Reading

When a mother sits a child on her knee and reads him a story she has the right idea: reading should be *enjoyable*, an opportunity to enter a wider world of imagination, stories and facts, rather than a chore. You shouldn't, with a young child, buy a great stack of books (nothing is more liable to put him off reading) but, rather, buy a few favourites and read them over and over again together. One of the most frequent questions I'm asked about the under-fives is: 'Should I teach my child to read?' There's no divine law that says you shouldn't do so (many's the child that has learned to read by reading a simple picture-and-word book with one of his parents) but there are a lot of things that will give your child 'readiness for reading' and will ease his way when he goes to 'big school' at the age of five.

Firstly take the child out and *talk* to him about what you see. Everything is of interest to a youngster – a cow, a dog, a can of beans on a super-market shelf – particularly if mother chats about it.

Secondly have some books in the house that the child can look at containing pictures of things that the child has seen. A picture of a hamster, or a postman is even more interesting if the child has a hamster as a pet, or has seen the local postman delivering a letter. Books (the lesson is) tell us more about the world around us.

179

Thirdly teach the child the colours of objects and simple concepts like 'big', 'little,' 'round', 'square' so that he begins to recognize the similarities and differences between everyday objects. It is vital that you teach your child nursery rhymes and simple songs (the aim here is merely to get the child to take a delight in words and, as a by-product of this, increase his vocabulary).

You could label one or two things in the house – John's room; goldfish bowl – so that the child sees that words relate to things. (Use lower-case letters, not capitals.) You could even teach the child some of the sounds of the letters of the alphabet and how those sounds join up to make simple words.

Teach your child how to do jig-saws and to play games – such as dominoes – where looking and matching are involved. Many games and activities encourage listening and talking: toy telephones; playing shop; cooking; 'Kim's Game' (put a few objects on a tray, cover them up: your child has to try to remember what they were); asking for some of the things you buy at a local shop; buying a stamp at the post office; asking the child (and listening to) what he has been doing during the day.

What do we, as parents, do with older children who cannot read? Perhaps they are now in school and experiencing a deep sense of failure because they have not acquired satisfactory reading skills; in this situation practical help and guidance will work better than nagging or criticism. Success is most important at this stage so you should choose reading materials (flash cards, picture-word dictionaries, and a book) which aren't too difficult so that your child can re-gain some of his lost self-confidence. Praise a lot, don't nag, and try to avoid showing displeasure at the child's progress.

At first, use a *look-say* approach, combined with the *sentence* method. You could make up a book together; your child tells you a story, you write it down (in printed, lower-case letters, using a felt-tip pen) in a large book. Any words that the child has difficulty over write down on cards (flash-cards). You could do two cards for each word, so that the child can match similar words together and use the cards to build up (and to match) sentences. When the child has mastered about fifty words (i.e. words he can recognize on sight) you could teach him by the PHONIC method i.e. show him how each letter, or group of letters, has a sound and that sounds can be joined up together to make (some quite long) words e.g. HIP-PO-POT-AM-US or DEV-EL-OP-MENT. Cut the cards in half and see if your child can pick out the two halves of the word to make up a complete word.

The cards should be large at first, but can be made smaller as the child becomes more skilled at word recognition. Many of the children I have taught to read have carried a collection of cards in a match box; in their spare moments, I told them, they were to take out their cards and do some word-matching, sentence-building or (if they had somebody to play it with) have a game of 'snap' with their cards. Cards, plus encouragement, are the secret of success in the first stages of reading.

After a while you will find that you run into some snags. Here are a few and advice on what you can do about them:

Reversals: Train your child's eyes to go from left to right by using a card (to cover the bottom part of the page) plus finger pointing whilst reading. Tracing, and joining up dots (as in simple puzzle books) are two useful exercises which emphasize direction. At the top of the page, draw an arrow going from left to right and put a small dot over the left-hand word of each line to show your child where to start.

Repitition. Encourage a slower rate of reading and/or read aloud along with your child for a few lines or so.

Additions or Omissions of Words. Flash cards with non-complete sentences. Your child has to pick a word (from, say, four cards) that will complete the meaning. You could also play 'Spot the Mistake': read a sentence and make an error and see if the child can spot where you have gone wrong.

Guessing at Words Wrongly. More practice with sentence flash cards. Use of an easier book (for a day or two) in order to emphasize success and accuracy.

Difficulty in Recall. Show child a word on a flash card; cover it up; ask child to locate the word in a sentence or amongst six other flash cards.

Inability to Read Quickly. Practice in skimming over the page to locate a certain word. The child must point to the word and say it, once it has been found.

Just a word about phonics; letter sounds are often best taught in pairs, and by recognizing them as part of familiar words e.g. mother; father; summer. The words we teach to children when they first learn to read should include as many words as possible from their day-to-day vocabulary (e.g. ice-cream, television, beans-on-toast) and the reading book can be based on a child's particular interest (even if that interest is only food or a programme on television). The rule is: always try to make reading meaningful.

Fantasy (whether it is the child's or whether you find it together in a suitable fairy story or adventure story) is a powerful aid to interest. With some of the children I have taught, the child has been the hero of his own book fighting against dragons, or monsters or (with older children) gangsters. There is no reason on this earth, if you take into account the interests of your child, why learning to read should be dull.

What you do, then, is to elicit the child's own ideas and thoughts, and record them. You can do this using painting, drawing, models, tape-recorder or even a typewriter. Eventually, the child will want to write down what he has been doing or thinking, and to read what he has written. That is when you can start to teach. Remember, the first book for the child is probably one you have made together. After this you can go to the shop and choose together a book (not too difficult!) that your child would like to read. Make it a game; enjoy it; two sessions of twenty minutes are better than one of forty. Never go on too long: so that your child gets bored. Frequent doses of flash cards, and a little phonics, work wonders for the reluctant reader. Don't forget that your local library has a children's section and a variety of books: some of which may well interest your child. Why not go along together and pick something out?

It is vital to liaise with your child's class teacher before starting out on any formal reading scheme. There are a wide variety of good reading schemes (such as the Ladybird titles which cover a range of subjects and reading ages) but you should make sure with the teacher that a particular book is suitable for your child's own level of reading skills. You could ask the head or the teacher to recommend a suitable book; later on, when the child is more 'into' reading, have a word with the children's librarian who'll have a vast fund of knowledge about children's books.

Reluctance to Speak

You should talk to your infant as much as possible. Nothing pleases me more than to see a young mother pushing a pram along talking to her baby. Whether the baby understands or not is beside the point. He's learning sounds (and words); later, he'll learn to imitate those sounds and words and he'll be well on the way to acquiring the vital skill of language.

What happens, though, if your baby is very late in talking? The main thing you do is worry. Is my child dull, or mentally retarded? This is the first question that comes to you. The truth is that the vast majority of late talkers have normal intelligence. The second

182

thing you do is to compare your child with your friend's or neighbour's. I can only reiterate the advice given to Mrs Worthington about putting her daughter on the stage: *don't*. It's silly to compare babies too closely simply because they differ so much in their rates of development; and this is particularly so when it comes to speech.

If your child is a late talker you mustn't jump to the conclusion that he's lacking in intelligence, or stupid. The thing to do is to talk to your child in a relaxed, friendly way, take him out to see interesting things which he might want to talk about, and let him play with other children so that he has to communicate with others of his own age. If your child is very shy, glove or finger puppets are useful toys: the child may find it easier to speak via the puppets rather than directly to adults or other children.

Here are three traps which you mustn't fall into if you want your child to talk readily:

Trap 1 The Grunt A mother came to see me because her daughter, aged two-and-a-half, didn't speak. I took both of them into the playroom; the child played at the sand-tray whilst I chatted to mother. *What I noticed was that every time the little girl wanted something she grunted, pointed, and mum fetched the object to her.* Mother was, without knowing it, teaching the child *not* to learn to speak. When mum relaxed, and encouraged the child to say what she wanted, the child soon learned to speak (and she *was*, I assure you, a very intelligent little girl).

Trap 2 The Shout Getting annoyed with your child will not solve the problem: it may well make the situation worse. The right approach is to talk to him in a friendly manner, encourage him to ask for things (especially at table) by name and, last but not least, try to get over to your child something of the sheer joy of language. You can read your child nursery rhymes, play chanting games, counting games and buy some children's records. Painting pictures, besides being an alternative way of communicating, may also help to stimulate – along with finger-painting, dough, and sand-and-water play (see section on **Messy Play**) – children to talk to others about what they are doing. Don't force it; try to avoid angry demands that your child speak; put him in situations which are so interesting that he wants to communicate his feelings about them to you and which get rid of (rather than add to) his frustrations.

Trap 3 The Anxiety Bug The more impatient you are, the more anxious you become over your child's lack of speech the more you transmit your worries to the child and the less he responds to you.

A mother brought her four-year-old son in to see me. He'd started to talk at the age of one, spoke until he was two, and hadn't spoken since. Mum was a very anxious, talkative person. We met for a few weeks, chatted (whilst the little boy played and I spoke to him from time to time in an unhurried, non-anxious way). One morning mum phoned me up. 'He's spoken, this morning, at breakfast,' she said, excitedly. 'What did he say?' I asked. 'The provision of marmalade in this establishment is quite inadequate,' was the reply. The trouble, I suspect, with that, very intelligent, child was that mother babbled on without listening to what he had to say. It's important to speak to children; it's also very important to *listen* to them.

Sometimes, infants talk very indistinctly and it's hard for a mother to make out what her child is saying. Years ago, there was a little boy on the radio who went about with his sister Winny. When he spoke, it was such a collection of incomprehensible babble that everybody had to ask Winny: 'What did Horace say?' I saw a little girl like this who couldn't (or wouldn't) talk properly. I placed a 'shadow' (i.e. a friend, or interpreter) with her. One day I went in the playground, spoke to the reluctant talker, got an answer, and said to the friend: 'What did Susan say?' The little interpreter looked up and gave me the reply: 'She said clear off.' This story illustrates one thing worth remembering: some children will speak in certain situations, not in others, to other children but not to adults or only to certain children. If this happens the idea is to leave well alone: the child will speak to you (or to his friends in the playgroup, or infant class) when he is ready.

If you are very worried about your child's indistinct speech (or about a lisp or such poor pronunciation that nobody can understand what your child says) it may be wise to *have your child's hearing checked* (this can be arranged by the family doctor) and to *seek an appointment to have your child assessed by the speech therapist* (the local health clinic, or your GP, can arrange an interview). In particular, if your child suffers a lot from colds and catarrh bear in mind that his tubes may be obstructed and that he may suffer from intermittent hearing loss. You should seek an appointment at the local health clinic if you think this might be the case and if your child has reached the age of, say, four or five without any improvement in his speech.

Here are Six Important DO's to help your infant to acquire the language which he needs to communicate:

DO sit your baby on your lap (mums and *dads!) and talk to him.*

Don't use 'baby language'. Just talk about anything at all. By listening to you (and seeing your pleasure in the sounds *he* makes back) your baby is encouraged to make more sounds. Avoid talking to the baby in a crowd (because he hears all the voices as a babble and finds it hard to distinguish particular sounds). Frequent tête-à-têtes are the best idea.

DO use lots of nouns (i.e. names of things) with your toddler. This gives him the labels to stick on his little parcels of experience. 'That's a train.' 'That's a duck and it swims in the water.' Nouns are the bricks in the house of language, so give your child as many as possible.

DO expand your child's language by explaining things to him. If he asks, 'What's that?' (a train) don't just say: 'It's a train.' Go on to say that it carries lots of people, it goes on wheels, it goes to London, where you've been to on trains. Words cost nothing.

DO comment on a child's play and give him some key words. Don't interfere too much but give him some spontaneous natural comments as you go along. 'My, that's a lot of water. That's almost full to the top.' Top, bottom, bigger, smaller, left, right (plus the names of colours, plus numbers) can all be taught as you're playing with your child, as can lots of other important concepts or ideas.

DO arrange situations where a child can learn new words, add to his vocabulary. If you live in the town, visit the country for the day (or vice-versa). If your child and his friends play Mothers and Fathers suggest that, one morning, they play Doctors and Patients. They'll need new words so stand by ready with them!

DO give your child plenty of new experiences and the words to go with them.

Language is a marvellous thing. Don't worry if your child is late in speaking. Go on talking to him and the chances are that he'll talk right back at you.

Reward and Punishment
See also **Motivation** *Page* 149, **Obedience** *Page* 161

You, like me, may have weeks when you wonder what it's all *for*. Your husband (or wife) and children may be doing rewarding things, enjoying themselves, whilst there you are slaving away with very little return for your efforts. Everybody, believe me, needs some kind of rewards; few of us can carry on for long unless we get some recognition, from somebody, for our efforts. The odd thing is that, with both adults and (especially) children, inexpensive rewards usually work better than costly presents: what people are waiting for is a word of praise, a smile, an arm around the shoulder, small tokens of thanks, affection and love. With adults, an expensive dinner, a costly present, *is* a reward; so is a kiss, a kind remark. For a child, an expensive bike, a transistor radio, costly presents, all act as rewards but they are no substitute for love, or for overt affection: doing things together, a sympathetic ear. Rewards are vital to human beings; the best rewards cost nothing.

The second thing that needs to be stressed is that, with both adults and children, reward works better than punishment. The trouble with punishment is that, administered often enough, it soon loses its power as a deterrent. If you feel very annoyed, and smack your child in righteous anger, that's forgivable (and it may make you feel a whole lot better and, more important, save you from bearing a resentment against the child). If you go on smacking your child for misdemeanours the whole thing loses any meaning: it doesn't stop the child behaving badly and it may radically alter the whole relationship for the worse. We can see this in school when a child, bad at maths and punished for being bad at maths, is put off school altogether. The punishment hasn't made him better at his worst subject; it's simply destroyed any affection he may have had for the school. Punishment has to be related to the crime, and swift. Often, children are unsure *why* they are being punished or else they are punished so long after the crime they've forgotten what they did in the first place. My advice as regards punishment is to use it *very* sparingly. Reward, as I've said, works much better.

What most psychologists now agree on is that *behaviour which is rewarded tends to carry on whilst behaviour which isn't rewarded (i.e. ignored) tends to stop.* That sounds a very simple rule but it's one that's hard to put into practice (especially when you consider that it isn't easy to ignore bad behaviour). Where we go wrong is to ignore *good* behaviour. Go down to your local supermarket and you'll see plenty of mums (unwittingly) teaching their children to behave badly. When the child is good, the mother ignores him: the child offers to carry the wire shopping basket, wheel the trolley, help weigh out the tomatoes, and the mother ignores him. As soon as the child starts to whine, complain, or knocks something over, or play about, the mother pays attention (usually, by telling the child off or even, sometimes, by buying a packet of sweets to distract him!). *What the mother is doing, without realizing it, is rewarding bad behaviour.*

It's an easy enough mistake to make. I notice it with teenagers and the media. When teenagers behave well, they are ignored by the media; if they fight, create disturbances, behave abysmally, they find themselves in the newspapers ('Teenagers Run Riot') or on the television news. This, most psychologists would agree, is paying too much attention to bad behaviour and hence reinforcing (or encouraging) that kind of behaviour instead of its opposite. Back to *your* family, *your* children. The moral is clear. By all means, show annoyance if your children are bad but, please, don't forget to reward them (give them a hug, a word of praise, a 'thankyou') when they're good, or do something to help you.

When you are using rewards, don't overdo them. Say your friend is talking to you and you smile at her from time to time, that's a powerful reward. If you smile for hours on end, at every little thing she says, she's liable to think that you've taken leave of your senses. It's the same with children. The Golden Rule is to *reward frequently at first and then reward from time to time once the behaviour (and the relationship) has been established.* This sounds complicated, but isn't. Take an example from your courting days. At first, bunches of flowers, boxes of chocolates, candle-lit dinners are the order of the day. Later (when your partner thinks he's safe) these little rewards may tail off. Providing we get *some* rewards from time to time we're happy (and the wise husband, or wife, will make sure that the dinner, the chocolates, the cup of tea in bed or the flowers still make an intermittent appearance; not so often, perhaps, but often enough to sustain the romantic, and rewarding, element in the partnership).

Reward (rather like punishment!) if it is to succeed *must be given immediately after the behaviour.* If your child washes up for you, or cooks a meal, say: 'Thanks, darling,' and give the child a hug. *Don't* say, a few days later: 'Thanks for doing the tea last Monday.' It doesn't work as well.

Don't overdo the compliments, or any other reward, and try to relate the reward to the behaviour. It's a fact of life that piece-work (i.e. payment by results) makes people try harder than a weekly wage simply because they can see that there is some connection between their efforts (i.e. their behaviour) and the rewards that they receive. If a child *tries* particularly hard (even though he may, from time to time, make a botch of something) don't forget to praise him. If he doesn't try hard *don't* praise him. Why lower the currency value of your word of praise? Don't say that everything that the child does is good (he'll know it isn't) but do praise him when he's done his best (he'll know, like you, that he's tried hard). Be as consistent as you can (within human limits!) with rewards. If your daughter rushes in, hands dirty, without wiping her feet, throwing her coat and school books on the nearest chair, don't give her her tea one day and shout at her the next. *Decide what behaviour you want, insist on it, and then (this is the most important bit) do reward it – if it's only with a smile – when it appears.*

What you should try to remember is:

Rewards work better than punishment.

Smacking (see section on **Corporal Punishment***) get less effective the more you use it.*

Children need rewards as much as adults.

Paying children attention, listening to them, are very effective rewards and a smile, a word of praise, are two of the most potent rewards there are.

If you never reward people – adults or children – for good behaviour they'll try different methods of gaining attention.

Don't forget to reward yourself once in a while. You deserve it.

Rudeness

There are three types of rudeness: firstly, thoughtless or involuntary rudeness; secondly, calculated rudeness; and thirdly, 'testing out' or challenging rudeness – when the child's aim is to discover how much cheek or bad manners you'll take without making some kind of protest. In considering rudeness you have to bear in mind that, very often, adults are extremely rude to children: breaking in on their games, stopping their conversations, shouting at them and, sometimes, having very little regard to their feelings. If we are persistently rude and discourteous to children it's only reasonable to expect them to pick up our lack of courtesy and to be rude back. The aim, really, is not to produce children who are over-deferential to adults (see section **Uriah Heep Complex**). It is to encourage children to behave in such a way that they don't hurt the feelings of other people, or offend the tastes and habits of others (see section on **Swearing**).

I'm never sure, in these days of women's lib, whether we are supposed to give up our seat (on bus or train) to a lady who is standing. I do, but I'm a little old-fashioned. What I am clear about is that it's rude for any of us, young or old, of either sex, not to give up our seat if there's a woman on a bus who is heavily pregnant or to a woman or man who is burdened with large carrier bags. Common courtesies, ordinary politeness, oil the wheels of society and they make the day just that bit more pleasant. Without any politeness at all life becomes extremely brutish and unpleasant.

I don't think we should be too artificial about teaching manners. I don't like to hear: 'Say thanks and I'll give you a sweet,' or, 'Say thankyou and mummy will give you a biscuit.' This smacks, to me, of bribery and corruption. If you say 'thankyou' your children will learn quickly enough that this is the usual way of expressing appreciation. Don't be too strict on young children. A lot of their rudeness is quite involuntary. If a four-year-old excitedly bursts into your conversation (perhaps saying something like, 'Mummy's got no tights on today,' to the vicar or, 'Mummy's tidied the house for you 'specially,' to the lady next door) take it as a sign that the child wants to share something with you (as he certainly does when he interrupts to announce, solemnly: 'I'm four.'). Treat that kind of interlude with friendliness and with good manners on your part: the child will be intelligent enough to note your own consideration for others. Kindness and courtesy are caught, not taught.

Calculated rudeness shouldn't be tolerated. Coming into the house with muddy boots on, insolent remarks and doing things, deliberately, which the child knows will annoy can quickly be stopped by saying: 'I'm not having that kind of behaviour here. Cut it out.' If he doesn't stop, stop his pocket money for a week or tell him that he has to forego a treat. Don't be too savage but, on the other hand, make it manifestly obvious that you're in deadly earnest when you say you don't like being treated rudely. If you are in earnest your child will get the message. Don't make a big issue out of every little act of discourtesy (especially of the forgetful kind). Just make sure that the things which are important to you are done.

There shouldn't be any problem when children test out (as they well might) to see just how much cheek you will take or how much abominable behaviour you will stomach. 'We don't say that here,' is usually enough (or, 'I think that's very rude, if you don't mind me saying so'). Signal your displeasure as soon as the discourtesies arise. If the child 'plays up' and deliberately acts badly just to provoke you just say, 'We don't do that here.' I've heard this said, quietly but firmly, in playgroup after playgroup and it's surprising how a young child – potentially a moving disaster area with no thoughts for anybody but himself – soon gets the idea that other people exist and that he has to toe the line. He likes toeing the line. Too much freedom is as terrifying to children as it is to adults.

Be polite and courteous yourself. Indicate, mainly through your own behaviour, what you think is the best way for people to live together. Children will want to live in that considerate way too. Rudeness is so prevalent amongst adults because they have learned that it pays to be rude. Sadly, in the long run, rudeness doesn't solve anything. It certainly makes life a lot more unpleasant. You can't do anything about rudeness in our society but you can lay down your own standards of behaviour in your own home and live up to them yourself. My guess is that your child will follow suit.

Rules
(For Parents)
See also **Obedience** *Page* 161, **Over-Permissiveness** *Page* 168

Children need a framework, they like to know what the rules are, how far they can go. At the same time they don't want things to be *too* strict; they want to have fun and enjoy their lives. What do I mean by over-strictness? My grandfather was a good example of the strict morality common in Victorian times: in his house children were not allowed to talk at meals, they had to be in bed at a very early hour, there was no answering back, and they were physically punished (boys and girls) with a leather belt if they dared to transgress his laws. I think that's all rather overdone. Children do like to know where they are, but they also like to have a little excitement. Life, after all, is for the living: it shouldn't be lived in a doom-laden, repressive, gloomy atmosphere where everybody is taking the whole thing far too seriously.

OK, then, we can all agree that children need some guidance but where do you put your framework? Where do you draw the line? With young children it is quite easy to show that you are annoyed by the tone of your voice. There is no need to smack them, or to indulge in lengthy explanations. A friend of mine, with two young children under five, never says NO. If they do something naughty she just gives them a look. 'Mummy's got her angry look,' they say, and stop whatever mischief they're up to. My friend's range of looks would qualify her for the National Theatre. (She's particularly proud of her 'sad' look and 'vicious' look – indicating, respectively grievous disappointment, and *great* annoyance.) What's good about this signalling system is that the children understand it perfectly. I did ask my friend what would happen if the children didn't stop when she gave them a look? What would she do next? 'I don't know,' she told me. 'It's never happened yet.' Don't overdo lengthy explanations with young children of why you don't want them to do this or that. *Just make sure they know when you don't approve, and signal your displeasure in the most economical way possible. They'll get the message.*

With young children, too, you may want to save up your NO (and the indication of annoyance or disapproval that go with it) for *safety* purposes: not touching the fire, or electrical equipment, or the hot stove. (The kitchen can be a dangerous place so you'll have to have some rules about the child playing there, maybe *not* playing in there, unless you're present.) Don't use the word NO too often or you devalue it, the child gets used to it, and takes less notice of it. *Don't* spoil him and give him his own way all the time but *don't* inhibit his natural curiosity and need to explore. Most important of all, no verbal battles, no slanging matches, no giving way to tantrums. When you say No you mean it.

Older children, like their younger brothers and sisters, need *some* hard and fast lines to give them security. Maybe father (or mother) no longer know best but they have to act, at least some of the time, as though they know they do. If your teenage boy asks you if he can have a motor-bike, and the idea terrifies the life out of you, say NO. If your teenage daughter asks if she can go to an all-night party and you're really very much against the idea, say NO. If you want to explain why, then do (but don't, for goodness sake, think you have to). Just put on your Sitting Bull, obstinate, face and say: 'Because I say so.' Providing you're just and reasonable in other things, providing you don't say No all the time, youngsters will accept it. What they don't like is parents who waver, are inconsistent and unjust. You could say: 'I'm sorry. I know how much you'd like a motor-bike, but no. I'd never be happy about it.' (Or, 'Sorry, darling, I know how much you want to go to that party but I'd be worried rigid.') It's no more than the truth and, parents, believe it or not, have feelings, and rights, as well.

Your job is to equip your children for life and, as adults, they're not going to find that they can do exactly as they want. Other people, besides themselves, have to be considered and that is one of the reasons why you, like it or not, sometimes have to say NO. It's one of the most useful words in the English language and nobody will respect you if you never use it.

The main points to remember are:

Children can accept a plain and simple NO without becoming permanently alienated from you.
A request, an argument, dealt with swiftly quietly and firmly has less chance of developing into a major battle.
Use your NO as little as possible but when you do use it, mean it.
Be fair. Explain why you say NO if it's appropriate, e.g.: 'No, you can't stay out to play because it's tea time,' or, 'No, you

can't have sweets because you've had an ice-cream' (or 'they'll rot your teeth'). Say yes when you can, e.g.: 'Yes, you can make a cake in the kitchen but I'm trusting you to tidy up afterwards.' (Don't say: 'No, you can't,' because it means they'll make a mess. They have to learn and they can't learn if you keep forbidding them to do things all the time.)

Sometimes, you'll say NO because you're in a bad mood, feeling 'crabby'. This *isn't* justice, but it's human, so don't worry too much about it. It happens to us all.

Set reasonable limits. You won't, I hope, go for Victorian standards of manners and behaviour. On the other hand, don't ever get to the stage where you're afraid to say No to your own children. If you do, take my word for it, they'll make your life a misery.

Have fun with your own children. Relax a bit. Pull a few faces occasionally but don't take it all too seriously. After all, the whole idea of having children is to enjoy them.

Running Away
See section on **Wandering Children** *Page* 264

Scapegoat Children

What always amazes me (and it may amaze you) is how different children are even though they live in the same family and have the same parents. It shouldn't really amaze us, since each child is an individual and totally unique. We *know* each child is different, we *know* we should treat them equally, and avoid favouritism. This is easy enough to do if we're sharing out a chocolate cake or giving out biscuits. When it comes to the emotions, justice is not quite so simple. For one thing, we can (temporarily, I hope) 'go off' a particular child or find one child easier to talk to than another. We may find that a particular child 'gets on our nerves' and irritates us. We'd like to be absolutely fair but it isn't always possible, because we're human. The other thing we do (which I think mitigates against absolute fairness) is to label children, and allocate roles to them within the family. 'John is very clever.' 'Jane always helps me.' 'Mark is a proper little mischief.' If you label children in this way (and it's sometimes hard not to) you can be sure that they will live up to the label. If you keep stressing how badly behaved

192

Angela is, compared with Susan, you merely create a self-fulfilling prophecy and ensure that little Angela tries even harder to capture your attention through mischief. She finds it harder and harder to get rid of the label that you have stuck on her.

It's easy enough to make a scapegoat of one of our own children; when we're frustrated, feeling annoyed, we all need somebody to blame (anybody will do, except ourselves!). That's where the scapegoat comes in. If you're not careful, you find yourself punishing one child where another child gets off scot-free – praising one child, and handing out nothing but criticism to the poor old scapegoat. I always felt sorry for that goat who, in the Old Testament, had the sins of the people symbolically laid on its back by the chief priest and was then sent out, alone, into the desert, to atone for all the things that the members of the tribe had done wrong. I don't think it's fair or just to make any child a scapegoat. We all need somebody to dislike, someone upon whom to project our aggression, somebody to blame, but I don't think it should be one of our children. Believe me, I've heard the cry: 'Why blame me?' often enough. One of my children used to say: 'I get the blame for everything around here.' When I came to think about it, she did. She was quite right: we were being unfair. After that, both my wife and I tried to cope with the stresses and strains of daily living without blaming *her* for our disappointments.

Staying with friends some years ago I was terribly impressed how they never stopped praising *both* their children. 'Isn't he intelligent?' 'Isn't she clever?' 'Aren't *they* lovely?' They were, too. I've never seen such happy confident children. That made me think. Our worst feelings (it should be our best) are often projected on to those we love most – our friends, our family, our children, or one particular child. Parents, I'm sad to say – I know because I've done it myself – *are* quite capable of picking on one child, blaming him for everything, making him feel miserable. This can sometimes happen to a physically- or mentally-handicapped child (which is *very* unjust) but, more often, it happens to a perfectly ordinary, and perfectly innocent, member of the family. *Ask yourself: Do I ever treat my children as a scapegoat?* I think we all do, sometimes. It's unavoidable but that still doesn't make it right. If you're aware of what you're doing (i.e. acting unfairly) you have a better chance of easing off and treating the child with a bit more humour and justice.

Just because it *is* easier to put the blame on somebody who happens to be handy than to search for the real culprit (often, ourselves?) we all, at some time or other, take part in the blame game. There are very few families who can claim that they've never had a time when they made a child a scapegoat. In my own family, it used to be my youngest daughter, Sally. If anything was broken, if anything was missing, if anything went wrong, the cry went up: 'Where's Sally?' She was the naughty, lively, mischievous one, and she got the blame. We stopped this convenient scapegoating after a while; it simply wasn't fair. Once we'd stopped, it was obvious to us that Sally was no naughtier, no more of a mischief, than the other two children. She'd got the label, and it had stuck. Of course it had. Labels do. It's much easier to put them on than take them off. That's why I think we should try to avoid labelling anybody, but particularly our own children.

I think we should try to take the following steps to avoid one of our own children being a scapegoat child:

Avoid saying (even jokingly), 'She's the terror of the family – a right little madam,' or, 'He's an absolute devil.' Do you really want your child to live up to his label?

Be fair (difficult, I know). Don't take it out on one child all the time. Next time things go wrong, have a *good* look round.

Have a good look at your children today. I think you'll find that they're fairly normal, average human beings, like yourself. I doubt whether you're harbouring a super-villain in your midst, so don't act as though you are. Most children are naughty, ill-mannered sometimes. Weren't you?

If you make a scapegoat of a child one day (and scapegoating is fairly common – it's part and parcel of our adaptation to stress) forgive and forget the next. Don't carry it on. Don't make a war of attrition out of it and make your child's life a misery.

School Phobia

Each week, thousands of children run away from or refuse to go to school. Why? Let's have a look at some of the reluctant school attenders. There are:

School rejecters. They have a common dislike (or fear) of school because they never have any success there. They see the classroom as irrelevant to their lives (and to their future prospects of employment). If your child wants to be a motor mechanic, or a hair stylist, he or she may find the school curriculum too academic or boring. Schools have a duty to educate children according to age, aptitude and ability but, often, school subjects bear little relationship to what the child is going to do. Non-attendance is largely a secondary school problem and may involve children who are chronically absent and those who, like Tom Sawyer, take time off to go fishing. In either case, the school is failing in its task of giving the child a sense of belonging, and of achievement.

What you must do, *as soon as your child shows signs of disliking school,* is to have a word with the class teacher and with the headmaster about the child's needs, his strong subjects and his weak, so that the school may provide a timetable which will provide some success for your child.

School phobics underline this need for early liaison between home and school in the interests of the child. The phobic may have a fear of maths (or some other subject); he may be afraid of a particular teacher; he may be worried about a trivial matter (trivial for adults, but not for him) such as undressing for PE; he may have a fear of a school bully (or bullies). This fear of a particular subject, or person, may swiftly change into a dislike of school in general but, with understanding, tact and compassion on the part of the teachers the problem can often be nipped in the bud and solved before it becomes a chronic fear of everything to do with school.

You should try to find out what has been happening to your child to put him off school and go to the school and take steps together to solve the problem and to reassure the child.

School Refusers may refuse, quite adamantly, to go to school. Assuming that you know of nothing at school which is worrying your child, could it be that he is worried about something at home? Have you (the mother or father) been unwell recently, or rather depressed about something? Often, mothers suffer from 'these four walls' feelings and perhaps the child is picking some of your feelings of inadequacy or loneliness. If you do feel miserable, do try to get out of the house; there is nothing worse for any of us than being 'cooped-up' all day (see section on **Working Mothers**). Children go to school much more willingly if they know that mum is busy and active and not too miserable and lonely.

Once a child starts to stay away from school, it becomes more difficult as time goes on, to get the child to attend regularly. So, as soon as you detect any signs of school phobia, take the following steps straight away:

Make an appointment to see your child's class teacher to have a chat about the child's progress in school. If this produces little result go to see the headmaster and ask if the *education welfare officer* (who acts as a link between home and school) can see you and your child to discuss the problem. If you wish, you can make an appointment to see the E.W.O. by ringing up the local education offices.

The educational psychologist is qualified to deal with the emotional and educational problems of children who are non-attenders. He or she can be contacted via your family doctor or at the child guidance clinic.

Remember, *do act quickly* if your child begins to stay away from school. No child likes to be labelled a failure and I'm sure that you, with the help of the school, can find an area where your child can find what he needs most: a little bit of prestige and some success.

School Reports

School reports, in themselves, tell us very little. They're written for the most part in a curious jargon which is very difficult to interpret. In my time I've had to put up with school reports which stated, of my own children: 'tries hard' (What does *that* mean? Is she hopeless? Can't she keep up with the others?); 'working reasonably well' (I don't like the sound of that 'reasonably'); 'acedemically sound' (more than can be said for the teacher. That should be 'academically'); 'friendly, sociable boy' (of my son who never says a word at home!). School reports tell parents very little about the *teacher*, about what he or she is aiming at and what he or she proposes to do. *Without further explanation and without an opportunity for further discussion between parents and teacher, school reports can be uninformative, misleading (and sometimes downright rude).*

In many cases, the report on the child is discouraging and worrying for the parent who receives it. The report doesn't tell the parent how best to help the child and it can often stir up parents' anxieties rather than tell them what is happening to their own child in school.

What would you like to be told about your child? Obviously, you'd like to be told how he's getting on with the work, what his strengths and weaknesses are, how he gets on with the other children (and the teacher), whether there is anything you could be doing to help him in his school work. Some schools have a homework record book which the parent must sign at the end of the week to say that the work has been done. This gives parents some idea of what is going on. Other schools, instead of 'works steadily' and 'good progress,' have lengthier reports which say in which areas the child has improved and what he needs to do to achieve more. These reports are *signed* by the teacher rather than being accompanied by scrawled, illegible initials. A few schools send a letter, at the end of each term, giving a clear indication of the child's progress during that term. Most schools, however, stick to the time honoured formula of the cryptic comment and leave you and I to puzzle it all out as best we may. What should we do about it all?

What you must do is to regard your child's school report, whatever form it takes, as a basis for further discussion. 'That's fine,' or, 'That's terrible,' you can say, as the case may be. Then, you must telephone the school and arrange to see the headmaster and the class teacher to discuss what steps both the school and the home need to take to help the child, especially where he isn't working up to his potential (see section on **Under-Achievement in School**). In many schools, these days, there are regular parent-teacher meetings at which the child's progress is discussed over a cup of tea: these are very useful as misunderstandings between home and school can be cleared up and practical steps taken to ensure that the child's work improves (or, more cheerfully, both teacher and parents can congratulate each other that the child is doing well). If your school does not have these regular meetings it is up to you, the parent, to arrange to see the teacher. If you get a report which says that your child is 'lazy' or 'doesn't try' you should at least take the trouble to see whether the teacher is simply failing to interest the child, or is taking an approach that irritates your child.

This discussion is vital. With one of my own children (described as 'not trying' and 'lacking concentration') I found that the teacher was very critical of her, very strict, and very sparing in her praise. I went to see the teacher and suggested, as diplomatically as I could, that she was taking totally the wrong kind of approach with this particular child. Flattery, praise, telling how good she was would, I hinted, work like a charm. It did. The next term her work was 'extremely good'. I knew that this particular daughter was sensitive and could be easily discouraged (aren't we all?) by constant criticism. We *shouldn't* think that teachers are perfect, that they are founts of perfect wisdom just pouring knowledge into the child's head. Their relationship with the child (and we can help to get that right if we meet the teacher and tell him or her what we think the child is like) is essential to the child producing maximum effort.

When I see the remark 'not trying' on a report I'm afraid I wonder whether it is the child or the teacher who is being lazy. If we don't take an interest, don't go to the school regularly, don't take the trouble to discuss anything we don't understand on our child's school report, the process of learning is incomplete and misunderstandings crop up.

What abouts marks, exam results? Surely (you ask) these are objective? Not so. If you're told that your son has scored eighty-two per cent for geography and fifty-three per cent for chemistry you might conclude that he was better at geography than chemistry. The snag is that, even here, the facts, terse statements of 'truth' can let us down. It is quite possible that the geography paper was easier or that the teacher marks higher. It's the same with grades. Some teachers never award on A (or its equivalent); other teachers are more generous.

The moral of all this is quite clear. You should:

> *Treat school reports as only one part of the communication between home and school.* Reports cannot replace a well-written letter (to or from the school). They cannot replace the need for regular face-to-face contact between teacher and parents.
> *If in doubt about anything on the report, ask for an appointment to see the class teacher.*
> *Look out for phrases such as 'lazy', 'lacks concentration', 'not interested'.* These could be signals that your child has a poor relationship with his teacher and/or that he is not being motivated to do his best for some reason.
> *Treat your child as an individual.* Most schools want to carry on a dialogue with parents. You can help by taking an interest, going to meetings at school, getting to know the teacher.

Most of the parents I know see school reports as 'useless'. They needn't be, if they act as a basis for regular discussion between home and school.

Sex Discrimination

I don't think it matters that baby girls are dressed in pink, boys in blue. I *do* think it matters if we think of *boys* as future bus conductors, engineers, doctors, lawyers, engineers and *girls* as future shop assistants, nurses, factory workers and secretaries. In the future, there will be many more women doctors, engineers, lawyers (and bus drivers). More women will be out there, in the world, tackling jobs hitherto reserved for men, so I don't really consider it is good advice to say to a daughter: 'The best career for a girl is to get married.'

If you think about it carefully (and I hope you will) you'll quickly spot the flaw in this remark. More and more women will want to marry *and* have a career to return to when their children are older, and when they (the women) still have years of life ahead of them. A woman with a skilled job, or a profession, is more likely to have self-respect and social approval. She can pass this self-respect on to her children. Anyway, these days, in most families both parents go out to work when the children are older – it makes the partnership more economically viable (and more democratic) when a woman has an interesting and well-paid job to go to. There are some families where the woman is the sole bread-winner: her earning power is vital to the welfare of her children. So, if we give our children the idea that dad is the one who 'works' whilst mother 'stays home' (I'd call looking after children and cooking and keeping the house clean *very* hard work) we are giving them a totally unreal picture of the world as most of our children will experience it.

You should avoid teaching your child that men must work and women must be chambermaids. You'll know you've gone wrong if your child says something like: 'Mum, you're not as clever as dad, but you're better at mopping up dirt.' Boys as well as girls should help with the housework (including nasty jobs like washing, painting, washing dishes, ironing); boys should learn to cook; girls should help with the gardening, mowing the lawn, and putting out the garbage. Boys should be taught to mend (and make) clothes and to use a sewing machine. Girls should be asked to help with cleaning (and repairing) the machines around the house, including the car. The watchword for the families of the future will be *sharing* and that means greater flexibility of role and *both* partners having a go at the dirty jobs.

You shouldn't say things to your children like: 'Only boys play with toy soldiers/bricks/engines.' (Or, 'only girls play with dolls.') The reading books you buy for your children should not depict dad in the garden digging (or sitting down) whilst mother is in the kitchen cooking. Story books, from fairy stories to adventure stories, should be bought for both girls and boys. Girls like adventure; they like to do things. Boys like romance; they like relationships. Girls are tough, boys can cry, if they want to. The *attitude* that your children have towards the opposite sex is very much up to you. If you can provide a variety of stimulus for your children of *both* sexes, if you can avoid pushing them into stereotyped roles as boys and girls you'll give them a better chance for the future when the roles of men and women are going to be far less rigid than they have been in the past. If you want to prepare your children for the real world, the world of tomorrow, take the following ten steps to end sex discrimination:

Show both boys and girls lots of affection. (Some babies, I know, don't seem to want to be cuddled as much as others. This, in my experience, is nothing to do with whether they're boys or girls.)

Don't set up as a Martyr of the Kitchen Sink, or Earth Mother, when your baby is born. Give your husband jobs to do.

Be flexible about toys. If your girl wants to play with the dumper truck, your boy to push the pram, let them. Have a wide variety of toys for either sex to play with, including toy furniture, lorries, a doll's house, art and craft materials, sewing sets, sports equipment and model-making sets.

Don't have books in the house which show dad as doing all the exciting things, and going out, whilst mum stays home and does the cooking.

Don't let your children watch television programmes that portray patriarchal, male chavinist attitudes.

Dress your girl up in girls' clothes, if you enjoy it (and if *she* does). Dress your boy as a boy. But, if your girl wants to wear jeans, T-shirt and sneakers, and your boy a flowered shirt, do let them wear what they want. *Don't be rigid and old-fashioned about clothes.*

Don't make your son's room into a macho, sporting-type den whilst your girl has a 'pink-icing' bedroom. The kind of play materials they have in the room, the sort of posters they have, are an acid test of your attitude towards the role of the sexes.

In the house, allocate jobs fairly. Everybody, regardless of sex, should help with the dirty jobs.

Accept that girls can play football, and other games and enjoy them. Boys can cook, or knit and sew, and enjoy these activities. When your children are teenagers, make sure that the girls go out and explore, do adventurous things, go to camp, join clubs. Make sure the boys do some of the cooking and cleaning to be done at home.

I hope (and I hope you hope) that we have heard the last of remarks like: 'One good thing about girls – at least, you can dress them up.' I hope we've seen the last of fathers who force shy, sensitive or simply uninterested sons into all sorts of aggressive, competitive games because they (the fathers) like that sort of thing, just as they sneer at men who can crochet a tie, cook a decent meal, sew on a button. In future, a man will be lucky to find a woman who will act as a life-long skivvy to him. Even if he did, the marriage would fail because lack of respect for, and understanding of, the needs of his partner. I know it's not easy but I hope you'll prepare your children for tomorrow, not yesterday.

Sex Education
See also **Awkward Questions Children Ask** *Page* 12

Probably, there's more nonsense written about sex than about any other subject. You, like me, may think that we live in a sex-obsessed society but one in which, ironically enough, there's very little emphasis on those things that matter to human beings: such as touch, tenderness, consideration, friendship, loving and being loved. Sex should take place within a caring relationship; it's the whole relationship that counts, not just the sex. How do we put *that* across to our children? How do we make them understand that sex isn't something 'dirty' to be whispered and sniggered about but is, like birth and death, part of life itself and not something to be degraded or used to degrade other people, not something nasty, not something that anybody need feel shame about?

I think we should start by answering children's questions openly, honestly, without prevarication, as they arise. Be blunt. Use words like 'penis', 'sperm' and 'vagina'. Better to hear them used naturally when you're young than to first come across them when you're an adult. Don't go into too much detail and baffle them with science but tell them, without embarrassment or anxiety, what they want to know. Your attitude, your frankness, is something that will reassure them just as much as the information you give them.

Where should the facts come from? What should they be? I think parents *should* play a part in a child's sex education. *Many children, now, have sex education in schools but it is what goes on in the home that makes the deepest impression.* If parents can establish a climate within the family whereby a child can ask questions, discuss things that puzzle or worry them (including, when they are older, relationships and right and wrong) then they'll avoid the mistake of treating sex as a dirty subject and separating it off from the rest of their lives.

What do children want to know? Young children want to know where babies come from. 'They grow in mummy's tummy,' they can be told. No more. Not too much all at once. Then, next: 'How do babies get there?' Tell them, but keep it simple. Later on, you can give them a more detailed description or read a book together which will give them the facts in stories and pictures. 'How does daddy's penis get inside the vagina?' 'Why do boys have willies?' 'Mummy, there's blood on your knickers.' At first, these questions and statements may embarrass you but you'll soon get into the habit of answering their questions honestly and taking the opportunity to teach them about sex in a natural, continuous and spontaneous way.

No girl should reach menstruation without having been told about periods. *Don't* say: 'There's a booklet on the mantelpiece I'd like you to read.' Discuss it, well before the age of menstruation, and remember that some girls can have their first period at the age of ten or eleven. If it is unexpected, unprepared for, it can be an alarming experience for a young girl. Boys, before reaching teenage, can be told about responsible relationships and acting kindly and courteously towards others. At teenage, they'll need to know about contraception, about venereal disease, about how a woman becomes pregnant. Sex education isn't (as some headmasters of boys' secondary schools seem to think) only to do with girls. It's to do with boys as well, and it's just as important to them. You may feel that, when the children are older, it's better for you to talk to the girls and dad to talk to the boys. Many parents prefer this but I think it's better (if you can manage it) not to divide the sexes up like this but to answer questions, from boy or girl, as they crop up. An open attitude towards sex, and honesty, from both mum and dad, is the best cure for promiscuity or the sheer misery and confusion over the topic of sex that I know.

If you feel confused, doubtful, uncertain about sex yourself (who isn't? We're bombarded from all sides with the subject) do admit it. It doesn't matter that our own sex education was appalling; it does matter that we don't pretend to know everything. We have to teach our youngsters to make moral judgements for themselves and to teach them that they don't have to have sex because their friends do. *If your teenager is having sex make sure that she (or he) knows about and is using contraceptives no matter what your thoughts may be on the rights and wrongs of it.* In today's confused world, believe me, sex education isn't an optional extra: it's a young person's vital need to have frank and open discussion with his or her parents on such a central part of life. Don't forget, though, to teach your children something of the beauty of sex; its symbolic nature; its role in communication with another loving, caring person.

Fortunately, these days, there are a number of good books which will help parents in discussing this vital topic with their own children. These include:

Where Do Babies Come From? Jill Kenner National Marriage Guidance Council Publications, NMGC, Little Church St., Rugby. (The NMGC has a list of books and booklets on sex and relationships which is available to parents on request.)

Girls and Sex. Wardell B. Pomeroy. (Penguin Books)

Boys and Sex. Wardell B. Pomeroy. (Penguin Books)

Learning to Live with Sex: A Handbook of Sex Education for Teenagers. A Family Planning Association Publication, Bateman Buildings, Soho Square, London W1 (Tel: 1-734 9351)

Both the *Family Planning Association* (FPA – address as above) and the *Brook Advisory Centres* (Registered Office: 233, Tottenham Court Road, London W1P 9AE. Tel: 01-323 1522) provide advice to parents and/or teenagers on birth control and sexual relationships.

There is a very useful booklet published by the Youth Libraries Group, Central Children's Library, Paradise, Birmingham B3 3HQ. It is called *Sex Education* and gives a very full list of books and materials, suitable to different ages and stages of children, available to parents, teachers and counsellors. A copy of this book can be obtained from your local library.

Sex Games

When my daughter was six-years-old she had a birthday party. I remember great squeals of delight coming from the front room. She and her friends were playing 'The Cat's Got The Measles' – a stripping game in which an item of clothing is taken off if you're caught with your legs crossed when the rhyme ends! Most of the children, by the end of the game, are naked. Does that shock you? What about this? A friend of mine, a mother with two young children, went into their bedroom and found her daughter, aged five, lying in the nude with her legs up in the air whilst her son, aged seven, examined his sister with a couple of 'medical instruments' (a large spoon and a pan scouring brush). 'She's having a baby,' announced the boy, solemnly. The mother told me that she was surprised at her reactions. She felt *extremely* annoyed and embarrassed. She told the two children to get dressed immediately and never let her see them doing that sort of thing again.

Perhaps she was making too much of the incident. But how

would you react if you, say, found your infant examining another child's bottom? What would you do if your daughter, aged five, came in and said that Mark, aged four, had taken out his willy and asked to put it in her 'hole'? Would you let two infant boys play with each other's genitals if they were having a bath together or would you stop that kind of thing without further ado? If young children go up to the bedroom together and strip off and play with each other (possibly touching each others genitals as part of the play) what steps would you take? Parents, when their children are babies, often imagine that they would not mind at all the kind of sex games that children play. When it comes to it, however, and their own children are involved, they are often upset, embarrassed and led to say angry things to the children which they often later regret.

You may well (like thousands of us) have hang-ups about sex, and about the human body. Few of *us* had parents with an enlightened attitude towards this important (and unavoidable) part of life. What we have to do is to avoid passing on our own doubts and anxieties on to our children (see section on **Sex Education**). *It is quite normal for children between the ages of three and twelve to take part in some form of sex games.* 'Mothers and Fathers', 'Doctors and Nurses' are games in which children can explore sex roles and satisfy their own curiosity about the human body and its functions. When your young children are curious about sex differences, when they want to explore their interests in each other's bodies, they may do it in ways that strike you as being 'rude'. Two boys may go down to the bottom of the garden and pass urine together. That isn't rude, or dirty. It is part of the pride, and the natural curiosity, that they have concerning their own bodily functions. Two young infants may go off to the bedroom and tickle each others' genitals. If you over-react in this sort of situation and imply that there's something deeply shameful about this sort of thing, you may cause the child to look upon that part of his body as dirty, rude and something to be ashamed of. The best approach to sex games is to keep calm and realize that such games are extremely common amongst young children.

You may want to discourage certain sex games, especially if one or more of the children (or their parents!) are likely to be worried upset by what is going on. Some sex games (e.g. a boy being told to dress as a girl by other children; a boy trying to put a pencil inside his sister's vagina) *should* be stopped but here, again, it's your attitude and the way you set about it that is vital. You should tell the children, in a matter-of-fact way, that it really upsets John to be dressed like a girl; if they force him to do something he doesn't want to do, it is bullying him, and not allowed. To push something into the vagina is dangerous and shouldn't be done at any time. With your own children you can use the opportunity to explain why you don't like them doing certain things but don't mind others.

Sometimes, the discovery of sex games can lead to valuable communication between parent and child in which the parent can indicate that they accept the child's sex interests as normal and are prepared to answer any questions that the child may have. This, however, has to be done later and in a natural manner. Often, children feel guilty, secretive and slightly ashamed about their sex games (whether they have been told off about them or not) and to be discovered *is* embarrassing for them. (So much so that, sometimes, parents suspect the worst and imagine that the children have been up to all sorts of terrible things.) Go by your own instincts when you discover your children playing sex games. (Some of them can be quite an eye-opener: children have marvellous powers of mimicry and very powerful imaginations!) Say what is allowed and what isn't but do have a sense of humour about the whole thing (think of what you got up to when you were a child!) and use the occasion to teach the child something and, at the same time, take some of the anxiety out of sex (rather than add to it).

When you come across your child playing sex games you should try to remember:

Sex games are not perversions but a normal (and almost universal) way for young children to find out more about the human body. It is part of their thirst for knowledge and it reassures them that, despite the differences in anatomy between boys and girls, there is nothing wrong with them.

Don't imagine that you're breeding sex maniacs at the bottom of the garden but if you want a sex game to stop, say so (but say it calmly).

Give the children words to help them to describe experiences. 'You wanted to see John's penis.' 'You wanted to know how Joan urinated.' *Realize that what children want more than anything else, is to understand.* It is when children don't understand that they become more and more curious, explore even further.

If you discover children indulging in sex play don't say daft things like: 'What are you doing?' It's quite obvious, most of the time, what they're doing. Just say: 'Get dressed. Play something else.' Discuss the whole thing later, when you've calmed down.

You could tell the chileren that, when you were a child, you played sex games (if you did!) Then, you could say: 'You mustn't touch Wendy's vagina. That's not allowed.' If you think that games involving undressing aren't allowed, say so. *You* set the limits, say what goes. If you do it calmly, reasonably, you won't make your child afraid of sex, or of love.

Shyness
See also **Daydreaming** *Page* 42, **Introversion** *Page* 123, **Walter Mitty Complex** *Page* 261

We live in a noisy, competitive society – one to which the sociable, outgoing individual is better adapted than the shy, retiring person. Nevertheless, I'm against trying to change introverts into extraverts. If children are shy and happy, my advice is: *leave them alone.*

You should ask yourself two questions about your shy youngster: can he join in with other children when the occasion demands? and, is the child contented when alone? If the answer to both questions is Yes, I don't think you ought to fret too much about his shyness. On the other hand, if your child is withdrawn, isolated and suffering from loneliness I think that you should do something about it. After all, the natural context of most human beings is some sort of group; very few children seek to be by themselves for prolonged periods.

Most children of school age seek companionship – they like to have a best friend with whom they can share experiences. Excessive seclusion, or persistent lack of sociability – with a complete absence of friends – is usually something that is forced upon a child, and not chosen. We, as parents, have to be on the look-out for those occasions when a child, up till then friendly and sociable, suddenly becomes withdrawn and/or starts to live in a world of his own.

Has your child run into trouble at school? Is he being bullied or rejected by other children? Has he failed in something (either at home or at school) which would lead to a loss of confidence in himself? Faced with stress we mustn't be surprised when some children, instead of fighting back, turn inwards and withdraw from a world which has hurt them. One thing is for sure: the child who suffers in silence puts up with just as much pain as those noisier children who 'act out' their problems. Though the noisy child is easier to spot, the shy child may need an equal amount of sympathy and practical help.

What can you do, in practical terms, to help your shy child? There are, in my view, two main goals. The first is to build up the child's confidence by enhancing his skills and giving him a sense of achievement. We have to find jobs for the child to do at which he can succeed, and from which he can gain prestige.

Secondly, to help the child to a better acceptance of himself we ought to tell him that we like him, and appreciate him for what he *is* (as well as the little things he *does* for us). You shouldn't, ever, forget to tell your child that you love him, even though (as often happens to all of us) you may be going through some period of stress and worry in your own life.

The three things to bear in mind are *prestige, praise and something to do*. Children gain prestige out of knowledge, and or being able to do things: your shy child may be 'the one who knows about stamps' (or cars, or space exploration) and it may well be worth a visit to his teacher (the mother's or father's presence there works like magic providing you haven't gone there to criticize). Think up a role for the boy in the school which will give him some status – even if it's only being in charge of opening windows or ringing the bell for the mid-morning break. A shy boy who joins the cub-scouts, a shy teenager who is persuaded to go along to the local youth club, a youngster who learns to swim, or to ride a bike, are being encouraged to mix with others and to gain the prestige they so badly need.

Praise and *something to do* can be linked together. Your child may like to help you by making the Saturday lunch (or Sunday tea) for the whole family. Some children like to budget, shop and cook (even if it's only to bake a chocolate cake) and many are quite capable of laying the table and serving up a nice meal. If your child does this, don't forget to say thankyou, and to praise (in moderation). Your child may like to go out walking with you, or throw a ball around in the local park, or just sit and talk. Ten minutes, at the end of the day, *listening* to the child is a great confidence booster for him. I know time is precious but you'll find that the minutes invested just talking together pay out, emotionally speaking, big dividends. *Appreciation* is what makes shy people blossom. Encourage your child to talk, make him feel that he really has something worthwhile to say and you'll soon find that you can't stop him talking!

Many people (including some famous actors and actresses and, perhaps, including yourself) are basically very shy but we have to learn to overcome it. Man is a social animal and we all have to learn to mix with others. With your child you may have to go along to the cub-scouts the first couple of times, and stay there during the evening to give him confidence. Perhaps you yourself are tied to four walls and find it difficult to get out of the house? If you can give a hand at a local playgroup or even take a part-time job it may cheer you up, put you in touch with other people and give your child (hopefully) a brighter and more cheerful parent.

In my time I've resorted to all sorts of ruses to help shy children: persuaded them to take part in the school play, be the art mistress's 'special helper', persuaded them to join various clubs. 'Please leave shy children alone,' one mother wrote to me. Honestly, I do, when they want to be alone but no child has ever done other than thank me for persuading him to join in an activity that he enjoyed, in the company of other children.

Here are a few tips:

Don't send your child to school in formal clothes if all the other children are wearing jeans (or vice-versa). Shy children can be excruciatingly embarrassed about clothes.

Don't spend time talking about your child's problem. You may have a teenager who is worried about his spots/shoes/hair (not to mention another dozen possibilities!). One youth organization joined, one activity entered into, is worth to the youngster concerned a thousand words about his loneliness.

Do converse with your child and, especially, *listen*: to what he has been doing, his interests, his aims.

Do stay with your child an hour or two if it is his first day at playgroup or school, or if he goes to join a different school. I'm sure that the playgroup leader/teacher will understand: they are (or should be) well aware how terrifying new situations can be for shy and sensitive children.

Do praise your child, where praise is due.

Finally, a story. There was a shy child in an infants school. The school had a simulated wedding (one of the children's older sisters had married and everybody was into weddings). The shy girl was picked to be the 'bride'. Wedding cars (real ones) were loaned and a 'reception' held in the school hall. Both bride and groom (a handsome boy) looked marvellous. So great was the prestige that Susan gained from her starring role that all the children, including the groom, wanted to be her friend! I'm not suggesting that you have simulated weddings at home but you get the idea: try to build up the child's self-esteem, and status, make your child feel good and this will enable them to face the busy, bustling world outside.

Sibling Rivalry
See also **Differences Between Children in the Same Family** *Page* 55, **Jealousy** *Page* 125

A certain amount of rivalry between brothers and sisters seems inevitable. A brother (or sister) may be better looking than we are, or more intelligent, or luckier. We're bound to go through stages when we strongly dislike (or even hate) a sibling for something or other; usually, we get over it and, by the time we're adult, may be extremely friendly towards the person who was once the object of some of our worst feelings. I think sibling rivalry does most harm when it's too intense, it lasts a long time and it carries over into relationships with other people so that we see each and every situation as a competitive one.

The psychologist, Alfred Adler, considered sibling rivalry was an important factor in the child's development. He also thought that position in the family was vital: a second child will try to out-do the first and be more pushy and aggressive; a third child will try to out-do the second. The last child may be the 'baby' of the family; rather spoilt and immune from feelings of rivalry.

It doesn't really matter whether you subscribe to Adler's ideas. I subscribe to some and, certainly, I've noticed that a second child is often, though not always, more outgoing and belligerent than a first born. What really matters is that you recognize that there is bound to be *some* rivalry between your children (see section on **Jealousy**). It may not be a bad thing, it may spur them on. The main thing is that you should, as you go along, get across to your children two important lessons: firstly that we can't always win in life and secondly, that we get a lot more fun out of living when we learn to share, and to work in a friendly way, with other people. Don't stop your child from competing (if he wants to); don't stop him from trying to excel. Do show him, though, how to accept defeat sportingly and without too much stress and shame. This is a crucial lesson and prepares us for situations, later on, where we do fail. The best response is to get up, smile and try again. The worst response is to sulk, feel sorry for ourselves, or (even worse) give up, simply because we're not winning.

The awful thing about wanting to win at everything is that it takes a lot of pleasure out of activities that can be enjoyed for themselves. There are people who don't enjoy a game of chess, or tennis, unless they win. They can't drive on the road without overtaking every car in sight. They feel quite ill if their favourite football team loses. For them, everything is competitive; every trifling little encounter is a situation which they must come out on top. I think this is very sad. There *are* people who are our rivals (at work, perhaps) and we want to do better than them, but to treat everybody as a rival is to miss out on a great deal of love, affection and friendship as we go about our daily business.

That's fine but what do we do, in practical terms, if we want our children to grow up with a healthy sense of competition but without a win-at-all-costs mentality which may make the rest of their lives miserable? I suggest the following as the Ten Golden Rules:

Give everybody a role in the family.

Get the children to do some jobs together. There'll be some squabbles but the earlier they learn to cooperate, work together the better.

Don't let your children manipulate you and don't give all your attention to one, very demanding, child.

Accept each child for himself. Don't make odious comparisons.

Don't try to treat each child exactly the same but try to give, during the week, each child your undivided, unsolicited attention, even if it's only for five minutes.

When you play games try to point out that it doesn't really matter who wins; what matters is that you enjoy the game, whether it's tennis, Monopoly or football. Your *attitude* is important. A sense of cooperation is caught, not taught.

Encourage your children to join clubs and take part in activities outside of the home. This will help them to learn the rules of living, and playing, together.

If war breaks out between your children don't take sides and don't become involved in their every little squabble. Merely tell them to stop arguing and (unless there's been some blatant transgression of justice) refuse to get caught up in their arguments. Insist on a truce, or peace. Let them work the Peace Treaty out for themselves.

Say to them: 'Brothers and/or sisters do fight and argue, sometimes.' This is the truth, and they'll be glad to hear it, especially when you add: 'But they have to learn to share things.' Cooperation *can* be learnt in the home.

For Adler, the antidote to a lot of neuroses and human misery was social interest. Fellowship, a feeling for others, taking part in joint endeavours are very important. There's very little we can do in this world by ourselves. We *don't* have to be rivals. We *do* have to help each other. Those vital lessons are best taught in the home, amongst brothers and sisters – our own children.

Sick Strangers

When I was a boy of, say, seven or eight I would wander about with my pals without a lot of parental supervision, or anxiety. There wasn't much traffic about, many of the adults were familiar faces, it was a smaller community than the towns and cities in which most children now live and there weren't so many strangers about the place. Now, for nearly all of us, the tally of people we don't know as we walk down the street far outnumbers those that we do. The vast majority of strangers are kind, ordinary, worried people – just like me and you. A tiny number of them *may* do harm to children: physically assault them, sexually assault them, or try to entice them away. The fact that the possibility of assault and physical or psychological harm exists puts parents in a very difficult spot. Children have to be told that sick strangers – adults who harm children – exist. At the same time we run the risk of frightening the child, making him confused, over-cautious and lacking in spontaneity and trust when he meets new people who wouldn't dream of doing him harm. We don't want the child to be nervous, full of unnamed dreads; we do want him to be courageous and optimistic in his view of the world; we don't want to cast a shadow over all of his relationships with adults outside of the family – yet, we do want him to know that sick adults may have to be contended with. It's hard to tell the child; it's unfair, or dangerous, not to tell him. What on earth should we do?

My view is that, as in so many other aspects of our relationships with children, honesty is the best policy. If your child goes to school – and especially if he goes to school by himself – he should be told not to talk to people he doesn't know, never to accept sweets or other gifts from them and never to accept a ride in a car with a stranger however nice that stranger may seem and even though the stranger only wants the child to show him the way to somewhere. The child shouldn't talk to strangers in the park, or any other place. If the child finds that the stranger keeps on talking to him, or follows him, he should walk to the nearest group of adults and tell them what is happening, or go to the nearest house and ring the bell and stay put or, with older children, go to a telephone kiosk and ring 999 and ask to speak to the police. Children of three- or four-years-old should be told, quite clearly, that they should not leave the company of the other children when they are playing and must *never* go off with a grown-up whom they don't know. The main points are: no talking to grown-ups he hasn't seen before; no sweets, or other presents, from strangers; head towards other children, or other adults, if a stranger speaks to him, and never go in a car or a lorry with somebody whom he hasn't seen before.

Those are the rules but it is important to tell your children *why* it is necessary to make those particular rules. Explain sensibly and clearly, keeping any emotion or anxiety out of it, that there are some grown-ups who are sick. They don't have mumps, or measles, or chickenpox. They're sick because they want to hurt children who have done them no harm and whom they don't even know. The best thing is to keep away from them just like we'd keep away from somebody who had chickenpox. Somebody, some grown-up, may be able to cure the sick person one day so it's best to tell you, the parent, if you are spoken to by a strange person so that he can be found and given the help he needs. This makes sense to a child. No gory pictures out of the newspaper, no frightening stories, no calling sick strangers 'monsters' or 'dreadful people'. They're sick. Your child will have sufficient compassion to understand that and, with your help, will have sufficient sense to avoid the sick stranger should he come across one.

If your child is offered a lift by a perfectly innocent acquaintance of the family and turns down the lift (say, home from school) I think this is one of the prices we have to pay. We live in a world in which there are a lot of strangers about and in which, for a child, the discrimination between who is potentially harmful and who is a caring, decent adult isn't always an easy judgment to make. Better to err on the side of saying no than saying yes. Sometimes, you will find that your child moves about, especially in the school holidays, from house to house, playing in one friend's house, then in another's. It is important for the child just to let you know where he's going, and who with. The sad fact is that, sometimes, children are assaulted by adults who aren't strangers but who are known to them. It's silly to make too much of this or the child's whole world is going to be peopled by potentially dangerous adults. That idea would be a most regrettable one to encourage. On the other hand, get into the habit of saying where he's going, and for how long. Get to know the parents of the children your child plays with; don't let him visit houses where you hardly know the parents at all. It's a great shame that we can't always send children out in the morning, leaving them to their own devices, knowing that they're safe. We shouldn't get too anxious about sick strangers but we should take reasonable precautions.

Sleeplessness
See also **Disturbing Dreams** *Page* 60

We've all had our share of being kept awake at night by a baby teething, or a child who is ill: it's part and parcel of being a parent, though, if you're anything like me, after a few nights of missed sleep you will begin to feel somewhat groggy and frayed around the edges. What I want to talk about here is the older child who won't go to sleep: the Late Night Bedgoer ('Just another five minutes, Mum'), the Nocturnal Prowler ('Can't I have a biscuit?') or the Small Hours Socialite ('I'm not tired'). Lots of children, these days, are over-stimulated (usually by television) before bedtime, and find it difficult to go to sleep when their head eventually touches the pillow.

What to do? *Routine* is important. A goodnight kiss, a little chat with mum before going up to bed, is likely to make the child fall asleep in a happier state of mind than if he has been allowed to stay up, with older brother and sisters, to watch the Late Horror Movie. A child who has a bath, or a wash, cleans his teeth and is then allowed to read in bed (after going upstairs at a prescribed time) is more likely to go to sleep than the child who pleases himself. *Children who have a fixed bedtime find it easier to go to sleep;* those who decide for themselves, or who doze off on the settee whilst watching television, are going to find it harder to sleep.

When should children go to bed? Obviously, it depends on their age and (sometimes) how long you are able to put up with their company in the evening. Whatever time you decide *do stick to it, and make sure that the child knows what the time of going to bed is* (though you'll probably think it's OK for your child to stay up a little bit later on Fridays and Saturdays since there's no school the next day).

Some children have trouble falling asleep and an over-excited mind may have something to do with it: this is where a bedtime routine is useful. *Fear*, or loss of confidence, especially in a child who sleeps alone, may be due to some simple reason: an exciting story told to the child at school (or, with infants, other children telling them about ghosts, bogey men and witches), a lurid comic, a violent, frightening TV programme may be the source of the trouble. You could have a quiet chat with your child about what is worrying him. There's enough savagery in the world and I don't think it's a good idea to burden children with too much horror beyond their years. When young children tell me the television programmes that they are allowed to watch I'm not surprised they can't sleep!

If your child's sleep is disturbed by restlessness perhaps he may be worried about something. Is he being pushed too hard in (and so worried about) his school work? Often, if you go to school and have a word about the child's worries, the class teacher will take the pressure off a little and the restlessness will cease.

The child who wakes up in the night and calls out for mum or dad, or makes his way to the parents' bedroom, may have some real fears (which he should talk about) *or* he may be manipulating you into giving him attention at night as well as in the day. If you think he *is* playing on your good nature tell him, firmly, to sleep in his own bed (but leave the landing light on for reassurance). You can chat about his problems for one night but, after this, explain that he must sleep in his own room. Otherwise, you are going to regret it when his strategem of waking you up, or getting into your bed, becomes a habit.

Some children are hyperactive, always on the go even at night and I won't try to deny that they're difficult to deal with. Solutions to the problem vary from trying to tire the child out during the day – the snag is that this is more likely to tire out you than the child – to elaborate bedtime rituals (e.g. a drink, then half-hour's play, followed by toilet, wash, story in bed, final kiss and cuddle, lights out). One mother told me that her bedtime ritual finishes with the last chimes of a musical box placed on top of the wardrobe. By the time the music ends her child is fast asleep (and so, on many a night, is she).

A pre-bedtime (and bedroom routine) is vital. *It's very reassuring to young children if mother takes them up to bed, has a little chat, and then kisses them goodnight.* (I know you're tired at this end of the day but, believe me, a little bit of affection here saves family rows in the long run.) Children like to have a pattern, a routine, and a recognizable bedtime pattern is a great comfort to them in time of stress and tribulation. There are, after all, few adults (never mind children) who can face the slings and arrows of life without a good night's sleep so you owe it to your children that *you* (and not they) decide the right time for them to go to bed.

I'll admit that children's need for sleep seems to vary enormously: some children seem to need very little. At the same time, I've seen so many tired-out children in the classroom (who look as though they could do with a week's rest) that I must stress that, in order to be alert, bright-eyed and bushy-tailed, children, like us, need their sleep. You must work out your own routine and stick to it. You have nothing to lose but the bags under your eyes.

Smoking

I remember the first time my brother smoked a cigarette. It was in a cinema; he was twelve at the time. I recall him standing up, a few minutes after his first fag, to rush off to the toilet to be sick. That didn't stop him, though. He smoked for the next thirty years, then gave up. 'Bad for your health,' he told me. He's right. Cigarettes are linked with a number of diseases: lung cancer, emphysema, bronchitis, chest infections and a 'smoker's cough'. Over 7000 people die each year on the roads; over 100,000 people die annually from cigarette-induced diseases. Smoking is a messy, costly habit. Since there are so many drawbacks to the whole business of smoking why do people do it? Well, once you've started (as you may well know) it's not easy to give up: there's the physical dependence on the drug, nicotine, and there's a very strong psychological dependence: cigarettes as a source of comfort in times of stress. Then, there's sheer habit. We all know people who can't answer the telephone without lighting up a cigarette. I once knew a man with two telephones in his office; if one rang, he'd light up; when the other one rang, he'd cross the room to answer it, light up a different cigarette, and leave the first smouldering, unsmoked, in the ash-tray.

Don't worry. I'm not going to regale you with the nastier side-effects of smoking. This is about children smoking. All I want you to do is agree with me – whether you smoke or not – that it would be a good idea to present your child with the facts and to say, quite clearly, that smoking is a stupid way to spend your time and your money. How do you best set about discouraging your child from smoking? (And I aim my remarks, I say again, to parents who don't smoke and those who smoke sixty a day providing you agree with me that it's a silly habit and you would prefer your child *not* to smoke.)

I'm not for saying to children, in a bossy kind of way: 'Don't smoke. I forbid it.' The forbidden might gain a spurious kind of attraction and (like my brother) your child will smoke to 'look big' in front of his pals and to defy his parents. After all, you can't keep your eye on him every minute of the day. I once saw a group of children – they were all of them no more than eight or nine years old – sitting on the pavement smoking away. They were smoking because it was wrong, it was something grown ups did and, most of all, it was something they weren't supposed to be doing. They knew it was 'wrong' to smoke but they didn't know why.

A much better approach is to include smoking in the kind of things you talk about in your family. Keep it as part of the aspects of life you discuss with your own children. As with sex, and love and other topics be open and frank about the subject. 'I smoke,' you could say. 'It was the worst thing I ever started. It costs me a fiver a week; that's £260 a year; I could go on a good holiday for that, or do lots of other things I want to do.' (Only say it if you mean it.) It *is* a daft habit and, if you're honest about it, your children will see the point. 'The thing to do,' you could say, 'is never to start smoking. Once you've started it's very hard to get out of the habit.' This, said naturally and without any bossiness, to children of about nine or ten (and keep talking about it, from time to time, throughout their later years) will impress them much more than the 'Don't smoke, that's an order' approach.

These days, in junior and middle schools children have excellent health education lessons which include the dangers of smoking. This is the right time (between the ages of eight and thirteen) to impress upon children that it's a mug's game. It's no good showing them a withered lung in a glass jar at the secondary school stage – it may be too late, some of them will have already started. If you want to prevent your girl smoking (and smoking has increased amongst school girls in the last twenty years) you could talk about the glamorous advertisements for cigarettes and then discuss the fact that cigarette smoking, amongst pregnant women, can lead to the baby being born dead or deformed. It certainly, in all cases of a pregnant woman who smokes, doesn't do the unborn baby any good. The time, again, to talk about all this is when your child is between the ages of, say, ten and thirteen. Don't leave it too late: two-thirds of the adult smokers in Great Britain became regular smokers before the age of sixteen.

Keep your channels of communication, and opinion, open. Discuss it, chew the fat over it. Fortunately, now, there are signs that smoking is becoming less fashionable and many people are giving it up. We are more aware of how it pollutes the atmosphere, damages health, *and* offends non-smokers. A colleague of mine went to a dinner party. 'Do you mind if I smoke?' he asked the hostess. 'Yes, I do,' she said. He was the only smoker there; he went to sit at the bottom of the stairs to have his cigarette, quite alone.

The more social sanctions we have against cigarette smoking the better (and I notice an increasing number of 'No Smoking' signs in restaurants, on trains, in cinemas). It is, nevertheless, the attitude of parents which can make all the difference to whether children become smokers or not. It's still a battle. The government spends ten times as much on road safety education than on health education about smoking.

What you should remember, as a parent, is that the earlier in life smoking begins the bigger the risk, later on, of dying of lung cancer. But school children who smoke *also* suffer more chest infections and from coughs and bronchial disorders. Be aware of this but don't rely on the horrific aspects of smoking ('Your Uncle George has lungs like a string bag. Aunty Doris died at forty-two because she smoked.') Just be matter-of-fact and tell the truth. The truth is that the human lung can only take so much cigarette smoke; sooner or later it will damage your health, or kill you. Show you don't approve (many teenagers give up because a person that they like, a boy friend or girl friend, doesn't approve). It isn't manly or glamorous to smoke. Don't say: 'I forbid it.' Say: 'Anybody who begins the habit must be an absolute idiot.' I think most of us, whether smokers or not, would agree with that. Your children won't rebel against you and smoke if what you're saying is said often, calmly, in a lot of different ways and with conviction. Children have a lot of commonsense. They recognize good sense when they hear it. If their friends smoke, even if you smoke yourself, they will be less likely to smoke if you talk about it and, from the heart, tell them what an awful, dangerous habit it is. If you're a smoker, your words will carry only slightly less weight. They'll be able to see for themselves how hard it is, once you've started, to get off the hook!

Spelling

Does spelling matter? I think it does: it holds a child up if he can't spell, it mars his written work and, later on, it means that he is unlikely to make a good impression on teachers, examiners or prospective employers. We won't spoil a child's enthusiasm for written work if we get the child (whether infant or teenager) to learn a few words each day, and get them to realize that many words belong in families (see that useful little book by Fred Schonell, *The Essential Word Spelling List* (Macmillan) available from W. H. Smith). Words like *lamp, camp* and *damp* belong together: they have the same endings. So do longer words such as posi*tion*, igni*tion*, remis*sion*. Your child should learn to look for *patterns* of letters in words (e.g. words beginning with kn such as *kn*ots, *kn*ocks, *kn*its) and learn words with similar beginnings, middles or ends.

What about the exceptions? Irregularly-spelt words with the same sounds (e.g. although, sew, so) *have to be learned by heart* and (just as important) your child should be given an opportunity to use the words he has learned in a piece of written work. Certain 'rules of thumb' have to be memorized: the magic e (makes the vowel in the middle of the word say its own name e.g. *bike, bake, coke);* 'i before e except after c' (as in *received, receipt)* – a rough guide, but useful; 'We must accommodate two cc's and two mm's in accommodation.' Awkward words (like *occurred*) have to be learned by heart. This sounds like hard work but it can be fun. Spelling bees with mum and dad, a weekly word bingo, little spelling tests, the use of a children's dictionary to look words up, a book in which to jot down (alphabetically) difficult words, can all make the task of proper spelling enjoyable. Children don't mind learning to spell, especially when it's fun, and six words a day keeps illiteracy away.

Many adults I know can't spell. I have some difficulty with spelling myself and there are some words I always have trouble spelling (e.g. *nursery, recurring*). I keep a dictionary on my desk and *I look them up.* There is no shame in looking up a word and, let's face it, it's not much more trouble to spell a word right as spell it wrong. Build up your child's image of himself as a good speller and remember that plenty of enthusiasm is worth more than criticism, or lack of interest.

If your child has severe spelling problems you should liaise with the child's class teacher and work out, together, a plan of campaign for tackling the problem. You could give the child a short dictation – very simple at first – and let him go through it and correct his errors so that he can see, week by week, how his spelling improves. Collect any words that belong together and make a note of them at the back of the child's word book (*ex*hibition; *ex*treme; *ex*ercise) and encourage the child to use these words in sentences and to learn them by heart. This sounds a chore but no child I know minds hard work providing it brings him success.

Elizabeth I couldn't spell but, in her day, most people couldn't read or write. Besides, she didn't have to apply for jobs. Spelling matters. It can be fun.

Stammering

Stammering (called 'stuttering' in the USA) is an age-old problem and there have always been a number of 'cures' for it. Demosthenes, the Greek orator, who lived about 350 years B.C., used to stammer. He was advised to put a pebble in his mouth, and wave his arms about, when he gave a speech. Apparently, this worked: presumably because it took his mind off what he was saying. These days, we have rather more modern therapies. These include: (a) *Shadowing.* A cassette-recording is made of somebody else's speech and the child listens to it through ear-phones and repeats what he hears, using a quiet voice, as the tape goes along. The child is listening and talking at the same time and concentrating so much on listening that he sometimes totally forgets his speech problem and talks with complete fluency. The problem then is to transfer the fluency he's gained to day-to-day situations where the child is more aware (over-aware?) of his own voice. Some success *has* been achieved with this method. (b) *Delayed Auditory Feedback (Daf).* Using a tape-recorder it is possible, with a special appliance, to 'feed back' the child's speech into his ears (through ear-phones) with a delay of about a fifth of a second. This sometimes dramatically reduces stammering (presumably, because there is less over-anxious 'monitoring' by the child of his own speech). Again, this is a useful technique and one likely to give confidence to the child since it shows that he *can* speak without a stammer in certain situations. The task then is to carry over this confidence into normal, everyday situations. (c) *Group Therapy.* This is particularly useful with teenagers and young adults. In a group, with other stammerers, the youngsters are encouraged to say, 'Hello, what do you do for a living?' i.e. ask questions of others, and to chat to them. The point of the group is that, since the other members have a similar affliction, the embarrassment, guilt and sense of failure associated with the stammer is lessened. The speech therapist encourages each member of the group to act out social situations which are normally anxiety-laden (e.g. meeting strangers, going to a party, going into a shop). With plenty of practice, in a non-anxious, non-critical environment, a lot of confidence is built up and the stammerer is taught that he can manage to handle social encounters which he would normally shy away from.

219

It is clearly silly to make too many glib generalizations about stammerers. What we have is a (large) number of individual *children* who stammer. With some of them it's a slight, hardly-noticeable impediment; with others it's a severe difficulty which greatly hampers their communication with others. Some children stammer over certain words; others stammer over certain letters. With some children stammering has become a habit; with quite a few the anxiety and embarrassment associated with the stammering makes them stammer even more. What we have to do is to act normally towards the child and make sure that, through impatience or embarrassment on our own part, we don't make things worse rather than better.

Stammering may have something to do with the brain. One theory is that the brain mistimes its impulses so that the child wants to speak, then goes wrong in saying what he wants to say, then (knowing he has gone wrong) becomes tense and makes more mistakes. The impulses that control the speech muscles then get into a 'log jam' and, however hard the child tries, he continues to stammer. There is, however, a learning aspect to it. The child experiences anxiety in saying what he wants to say and then becomes generally anxious about saying anything at all. With quite a few children certain situations (especially meeting strangers or people in authority) will spark off his stammer and he becomes so afraid that normal speech becomes impossible. The child who stammers has to learn how to relax and take his time over trying to say something and how to stammer openly with as little embarrassment as possible until he has learned to overcome the stammer.

How can you help your child if he suffers from a stammer? I suggest that you:

Relax yourself and don't over-react. Don't criticize, or tell the child off. If the people around him accept the stammer that will take the pressure off him and he will be less tense about the whole thing.

Be patient, don't interrupt. Give him time to get his words out.

Avoid situations which are bound to make him feel anxious and cause him stress. Encourage him to talk to you but don't force him to talk to unfamiliar people unless he wants to.

Build up his confidence in other things: anything from football to pony riding to looking after pigeons. The more things he is good at, the better.

Tell the teacher before he starts school. It is better for her to know so that she doesn't put the child to unnecessary embarrassment.

Go to the family doctor and get an appointment to see a speech therapist when the child is starting school. Speech therapists are specially trained to deal with children who stammer and they can both help your child *and* give you a lot of reassurance.

Get your child to join a choir, if he's interested in singing. Some children don't stammer when they sing (or whisper). You can't have him whispering the whole time. You can give him the opportunity to sing.

Buy a copy of *Stammering – Practical Help for All Ages* by Ann Irwin (Penguin Handbooks; £1.35p) This contains a great deal of practical advice and lists some 'Easy-Stammering' exercises as well as providing references for further study.

Finally, praise your child and don't forget to congratulate him when he has a run of success in getting his words out. With children, criticism and pessimism make them worse. Words of praise, a little success, work like magic.

Stealing
See also **Kleptomania** *Page* 128

There are a number of reasons why children steal. They may be encouraged by their peer group, or by their parents. Children may steal to 'look big' or, in some cases, because their parents steal. In a few cases, a parent may take her own child(ren) to the shops with her on a stealing expedition. They may steal for personal gain. This group includes children who steal cosmetics, transistor radios, records or other items from local shops, or for comfort when stolen items are often hoarded as though the youngster wanted to prove to himself that, because he has status possessions, he is a worthwhile person. Some children steal because it gives them excitement. Here, the escapade is usually more important to the child than the stolen goods. The danger is that, as the thrill of stealing diminishes, so the child becomes more daring and ambitious in his thefts.

Stealing by 'finding' is another form of the vice. Many adults, on finding a £5 note in the street, would pocket it. Legally-speaking, this is stealing by finding. With children, for whom the boundaries between 'mine' and 'not mine' are more blurred, small items such as pencils, pens and even purses may be appropriated. When the child is taxed with the theft he'll say: 'I found it.' Infants can't be expected always to make the distinction as to what belongs to them and what doesn't.

Further motives for stealing can include stealing out of revenge, or spite. A child, treated unfairly at school, may steal something 'on principle', as a tacit protest against some real or imaginary injustice. A child may also steal to 'buy love'; giving other children (stolen) presents in order to win popularity. This is usually condemned to failure as the other children may accept the presents but still refuse their real friendship. Sometimes, also, the stealing may be symbolic in which the items stolen represent some (usually unconscious) emotional need. A boy may steal clothing from a boutique because of conflicts over his sex-appeal or a girl may steal cosmetics because she has had an argument with her boyfriend.

In a sense, all stealing is symbolic: of either protest, resentment, or a yearning for love or a feeling of worth. Even thieves who are greedy can be seen to be insecure, lacking in self-esteem and it is the need to be thought of as powerful, wanted, worth knowing, that forces them into theft.

What can you do as a parent to stop your child becoming a thief? What can you do if you suddenly find that your own child has been stealing? I think there are several rules which parents must stick to. They are:

Lay down your own system of 'right' and 'wrong'. If your young child has taken a toy which does not belong to him it should be quite sufficient to say: 'Take that back.' Similarly, if he has taken money from your purse, you should say: 'Put it back.' *Don't* over-react to petty theft but, at the same time, make quite sure your child knows what the rules are.

Trust your child. Send him on little errands, giving him some responsibility with money, perhaps give older children a clothes allowance which they must manage themselves, all of which build up an attitude of trust.

Love your child and, if he steals something, condemn the act but make it clear that you still love him.

Explain to your child why he shouldn't steal. Say that it creates an atmosphere in which nobody can relax or trust anybody else. Say that, if somebody stole something from *him*, he'd be unhappy about it. Stress that, when people care about each other, they don't steal.

Set a good example. If somebody gives you too much change at the supermarket, and you walk off with it, you can hardly expect your child not to be influenced by your own dishonest outlook.

Tell your child that he is really wanted, and loved. I have a theory that children (and adults) who feel really cherished don't steal. Why should they?

Experimental psychology is, in my view, a poor substitute for love, discipline and a few rules within the family. We live in an alarmingly dishonest society in which quite a few adults are unwilling, in return for a fair day's pay, to do a fair day's work. The high incidence of children who steal is part of this easygoing morality. Most children, I maintain, *will* respond to example, to care and to rules; they don't really like moral laxity. What concerns them, above all, is justice.

If you have a child who steals persistently it may be that this is a cry for help, in which case you would be wise to seek professional advice. This can be obtained from your child guidance clinic (an appointment can be arranged via the family doctor or through the headmaster at the child's school). If confidentiality is important, you should go along to the clinic and arrange an appointment with the clinic secretary to see the psychologist.

Sulking

Different children react to frustration or chastisement in different ways. One child, having been told off, will rant and rave, make a terrible fuss. Then, a few minutes later, he'll bounce back, all smiles, and the whole incident's forgotten and done with. Another child, of a different temperament or different philosophy of life, will simmer and brood over some, real or imagined, injustice for hours or even days. What we usually do is to ignore this sort of sulking behaviour and, if we do ignore it, in most cases it goes away. There's no point in being a superb sulker if nobody is taking the slightest notice of you.

However, there is something more you can do for your sulky child besides ignoring his sulks. The child may need help in seeing things in perspective so put into words – simple words – what you think he's feeling. 'You're in a mood because Sally's gone to a party and you weren't asked.' 'You're feeling very angry about John going off to the cinema without you.' 'You think I've been very mean to you.' If you have been unfair, admit it. If you think that your child's been hard done by, say so. What gives children the sulks more than anything else is a sense of cosmic injustice – that no matter what happens they're going to get the worst of the deal.

If your child is going through a fit of the sulks allow him time (a short cooling-off period) to get back to normal and then make a friendly overture. Don't be put off if you are rejected – perhaps he isn't ready yet to re-join the human race – and don't call attention to his sulking other than saying: 'You're still in a mood.' Don't, ever, start sulking at a child, or bear a grudge against him because he is sulking over something you've done or something that's happened to him. Life's too short for that. Children, or adults, who sulk are wasting a lot of precious psychic energy and the sooner they're helped to cope (by you being matter of fact and down-to-earth) the better.

Some of the champion sulkers I have met had good reason to sulk. It wasn't that injustices had happened to them (injustices happen to us all). It was the fact that none of the adults surrounding them seemed to understand *why* they were sulking, or to care very much. I think the least we can do for sulkers is to say: 'You feel hard done by. You feel you haven't been treated fairly.' At least that shows we understand how they feel without suggesting that life is always fair. It isn't and sulking, by isolating the child, makes it even worse. So do be brisk with your sulking child, and don't get angry or over-react. Do, on the other hand, show a bit of commonsense sympathy. That's the only cure I know for the sulks.

Superiority Complex
See also **Inferiority Complex** *Page* 113

Feelings of superiority (i.e. of being 'above' other people) are closely related to feelings of inferiority (i.e. being 'below'). They are two sides of the same coin. Both sets of feelings spring from the notion that if you take, say, six people they would have to be arranged in order of precedence, with somebody the 'best' and somebody the 'worst'. Though in fact there is no reason why you couldn't arrange them around in a circle, with everybody equal, and each one contributing something, according to what he's good at and his own stage of development. In a family, for instance, it's a good idea to get everybody to contribute. Running a family is like sailing a boat: it works better if everybody does something, some little job or other. It's wrong to have one person slaving away and other people lazing about. We have to teach our children coopera-tion (see section on **Inferiority Complex**) as well as competition.

Nobody would deny that we live in a highly competitive society and that we do tend to rank people in 'order of merit' whether it be for looks, wealth, or brains. Erich Fromm in his book *The Art of Loving* (Unwin) claims that we live in a world which is 'production-centred, commodity-greedy'. In other words, we spend so much time getting and spending, trying to out-do each other, that love (and especially brotherly love) gets a very poor look-in. We're all very conscious of our 'status' and how other people see us. Sometimes, we're so obsessed with the impression that we're creating that we forget to take into account the lives and, especially, the feelings of others.

You, like me, have met people who were so intent on impressing you, on coming out 'on top' that you can't help wondering whether they don't suffer from an *inferiority* complex? Surely, a person with any real self-confidence doesn't have to go to so much trouble to impress us? I once met a famous scientist. My job was to meet him at the railway station, take him to the university (where he was giving a talk) and then take him out to dinner. I expected him to be smart, well-dressed. He had on an old pair of baggy trousers, a well-worn sports jacket (leather patches on the elbows) and over his left shoulder he carried a raggedy macintosh. It makes sense. When you know you're good, you don't have to impress. The other eminent people I've met were the same: natural, charming, relaxed. They related to other people as (real) people. They didn't pretend, they didn't try to 'pull rank', to make sure you knew how important they were.

It's harder for you and me, I admit. We have to make some kind of impression; we are more aware of status because most of us don't have very much. Fine, but that *doesn't* mean that we have to see life as the 100 metres dash, with other people as deadly rivals. *We have to learn to be more loving, more cooperative or we miss so much fun in life.*

The need to be 'superior' grows out of feelings of being inferior. It's possible, however, to be superior without beating other people, putting them down. What you do is set a standard for yourself, and battle against yourself, to beat your own standard. In *this* battle, you can enlist the cooperation of friends (since we rarely achieve anything alone; we need other people to reach our goals). This is a different kettle of fish from trying to score off others all the time. Set your own aims, your own goals and cooperate with other people to achieve them.

All right, let's get down to practicalities and ask: how does all this affect you in your own family? I believe that you should take the following steps if you want your children to have fun in life and not be *too* swayed by notions of inferiority and superiority:

Ensure that each of your children contributes towards family life.

225

Start them off, by doing little tasks for you, and by helping each other, *as early as possible.*

Don't allow one child to dominate, or manipulate other children. Grown-ups don't like dominators or manipulators, so it's bad practice for adult life.

Show, by gentle guidance, and lots of encouragement that each child can achieve something for himself. Build up his self-respect, don't put him down, and (of course) treat each child as a unique individual.

Don't let any child have his own way all the time (see section on **Rules**). He won't get his own way in adult life.

Don't let your child hurt others to achieve what he wants. That's no way to learn cooperation and cooperation is the only way we ever achieve anything.

Instil the spirit of helping, doing things together, when the child is young i.e. during the first five years of life. These are the important years when we learn many lessons about how to relate to other people.

The main thing to remember is that I'm not better than you nor are you better than me, we're different. It's those differences that make life so interesting and rewarding – providing that we learn to live together. If you put on airs and graces my suspicion is that, deep down, you're feeling inadequate. Let's forget about 'superiority' and 'inferiority'. Let's get together and help each other, and teach our children to do the same.

Swearing

Let's imagine a mother turns up, really angry, on your doorstep. 'Your seven-year-old,' she says, 'has been teaching my child to swear.' When you ask her which word or words have annoyed her, she's too embarrassed to tell you. You apologize, and beat a hasty retreat, to ponder further the problems of swearing and individual standards.

For many parents the use of swear words by children *is* very upsetting. It's no use saying to your irate neighbour: 'Don't worry about it.' She *will* worry and all you can say, in your child's defence, is that many children use words that they have picked up in school (or at home) that they don't fully understand but which can certainly cause offence to the adults who hear them. Also, you could point out, there's a lot of swearing on television, in public places, as well as school playgrounds. Children are great imitators.

Is it any wonder that they, from time to time, pick up some forbidden expressions?

One way to deal with that angry neighbour is to say: 'O.K. I'll have a talk to my child about swearing.' Keep your promise. Explain to your youngster that there are adults for whom the use of certain words is deeply distressing and, therefore, in order to protect their feelings, he must stop using those words. Take the word 'spastic' (to describe a child who is clumsy or inept). I find that particular epithet in very bad taste and I'd certainly discourage any child I heard using it. Swear words have a purpose (as anybody who has dropped a sledge hammer on his toes will know): they can be used to express anger, pain, shock or disappointment. The snag is that they can often offend other people's sensibilities.

Swear words (as you'll have gathered, as a parent) can be used to impress or emphasize what is being said. That's fine, for a while. After a short time swearing becomes boring, repetitive, redundant: it doesn't really add anything to what the person is saying. Much of it is mindless, or unnecessary exaggeration. Your child comes home. 'It was ....great in school today', he says. What does the adjective add to the information he's giving you? I heard a mother in a supermarket say to her five-year-old: 'If you do that again, I'll break every bone in your body.' (This was for some trivial offence.) This kind of language shows a law of diminishing returns: when you want to impress, or shock, or chide your own child you can't because he's heard it all, and worse (from you, or others) before.

There are parents who swear a great deal, and it would be foolish to expect their children not to follow suit and to curse without realizing that there is anything unusual about it. I heard a four-year-old, in a playgroup, building an airport with wooden bricks, say (when he dropped one): 'Oh, sod it.' Where did he get that expression from? My guess is that he picked it up in the home.

What can parents do about their own children swearing? Here are Six Golden Rules:

Lay down the law in your own home. Tell your child(ren) what's acceptable and what isn't, for you. We have to accept that standards vary from family to family and that what's thought of as quite shocking in one home is acceptable in another. Stick to *your* standards.

Accept that most children use swear words at some time or another. Certain words (e.g. knickers, pantie girdle) have a nice, rhythmic quality about them. They can (like a four-year-old's fascination by the word 'bum') be safely ignored, unless they particularly offend you (in which case, put your foot down). These are all part of the 'naughty words' stage and, as the prophet said, these things shall pass away.

Don't over-react. Teenagers may swear to look big; young children may swear to gain attention. If you rise to the bait and show too much disgust or horror, the child will have succeeded in his aim of provoking you. Dealt with by a minimum of fuss ('That's a boring word,' or, 'Not that word in front of me, thank you') these attempts at shocking you will soon lose momentum.

Set a good example of polite and considerate language. If we swear ourselves we can't object when our children do the same.

If you feel strongly about swearing, have a swear box. The fine for swearing could be, say, 2p in the box and the proceeds to go to charity.

If you must swear, use substitute swear words, or phrases. In my own family we use the word 'sugar' for frustrating occasions. The word 'shit' is not allowed, neither is the word 'Christ' simply because the first offends my sensibilities and the second may well offend the religious sensibilities of others.

When you think about it most swear words are sexual in origin and refer to sex in a debasing way; or the words are blasphemous and refer to things or people which, down through the centuries, have been set aside as holy. Our own views on swearing, whether traditional or 'modern', must be set alongside the feelings of others, and the possibility that *they* may be deeply offended.

Why not, with your own children, use the simplest method of all to stop swearing? Say to the child, calmly and without any fuss: 'I don't want you to use that word.' As with a lot of things, it isn't what you say but the way that you say it. My guess is that the child *will* stop. There's no point in swearing when nobody's impressed.

Talking – Slowness in
See also **Reluctance to Speak** Page 182

Tantrums
See also **Defiance** Page 45

Let's start off with the Terrible Two's – since having tantrums is *not* unusual with children of this age. What exactly is going on inside your child's head when he blows a fuse, gets into a blind rage, throws one of those awful tantrums? The answer is he's utterly over-excited, totally exhausted, agonizingly frustrated or terribly, terribly angry. You might, in the face of a tantrum, take a very cool approach. 'Calm down, darling,' you'll coo. That could make him even more furious, quite despairing that adults will understand his feelings. Here is he, at the age of two, just beginning to be a real person, just beginning to be separate from mum, just beginning to master the world when he suddenly finds that, no, he can't ride that tricycle (he keeps falling off), he can't put the screw into the hole, he's just broken his best toy or (worse) he's doing something incredibly exciting – and getting the hang of it – when that silly mother, or father, calls out: 'Come in now, darling, it's time for tea.' It's like every evening, just when he's getting something going with the building blocks, the same silly adult says: 'Time for bed.' He feels misunderstood, he feels annoyed, he can't see your priorities, he can't see why you don't understand. Then, his frustration turns to anger, builds up to sheer, uncontrollable rage and he throws an almighty tantrum, kicks, screams, shouts, cries, even bites. He's mad because you ask him to *wash his hands* just when he's finishing off the all-time great, wooden brick version of London airport. You can see, I hope, something of his point of view.

That's fine, I can hear you say, but what do I do if my child throws a tantrum in the supermarket? What you do is pick him up, carry him out bodily (possibly pretending he's somebody else's little wretch and you're just returning him to his mother!) and, leaving your wire basket of goodies inside the store, sit him down outside until he's got over it. Don't fuss or say anything. Just wait until he's calmed down – with you standing there like the Statue of Liberty welcoming all well-behaved children to your shores – and then say: 'Let's go back in now.' It's your child's feelings you're concerned with so ignore other people. They're not important; your child is.

It's exactly the same if your child throws a tantrum in the house of your lovely, immaculate neighbour. Out into the hall with him to let him 'cool off'. If you must bodily handle your child then do so. Let's say your child is out with you and insists on pushing the push chair but *you* want to get on. Don't moan, grumble, grouse. No words. Into the push chair with him and away. The child may, and often does, try it on. If you give in all the time you are laying up not riches in heaven but a lot of trouble when he's older.

Some children are really adept at trying it on. Your child may yell, 'I hate you,' or, 'You're a horrible, nasty mother.' Allow him to express his feelings verbally, move him out of the room if there's anything he can hurt himself with, but don't shout back. He has to learn to control those outbursts, those feelings of hate. If you're firm, if you say, 'We're not having this,' you're helping him to control his rage. If you fly off the handle, you're adding to his sense of isolation, bewilderment and powerlessness. Don't fall for his threats or attempts at blackmail ('I won't love you any more') or you'll be paying off the instalments for a very long time. He doesn't really want to win every time: if he does he has no brake on his own, extremely powerful, emotions.

It's only commonsense to keep an eye open for tantrums and to try to prevent them happening. If you watch your child playing be aware when he runs into difficulties or becomes very tired. I saw a little girl at a fair-ground; she was thoroughly tired and over-excited. 'You want a ride on the bobby-horses, don't you, my sweet?' said mum. My sweet didn't. She burst into tears and started to hit out at mother. What she really wanted was for mum to have the sense to say: 'Enough is enough. Let's all go home,' and go. It's the same with toys. If you can see that your child is attempting something he can't do, then help him, or divert him to something else. This is better than watching him getting more and more annoyed with himself and then being surprised that he, in despair, throws a tantrum. You might see a pattern to tantrums. He may throw a beauty when asked to wash his hands, come in from play, go to bed. If there is a pattern you can alter it. Give him an early warning call or two ('ten more minutes') and explain to him why it's important that he goes to bed, for example, at the right time. Make out a routine, make sure he knows what it is: this lessens the chance of frustration and anger.

The main things to remember are:

Try not to over-react to tantrums. They're normal with young children. There's no point in throwing a tantrum if it has no effect – even young infants cotton on to this.

Expect a few tantrums with an infant who is presented with a new baby brother or sister. If you ask your child to help you with the baby, include him in (rather than unwittingly push him out) he won't have to throw a tantrum to get your attention.

Be aclm. Have a sense of humour. That's the best way to cope with disappointment. Your child will get the message.

Show that you don't like tantrums but, after one of them, you still love your child. 'My, you *were* annoyed yesterday.' That shows that you understand a little of what he felt and indicates that he can still, despite those tantrums, feel safe with you.

Teasing

Please, don't tease. It's surprising how many adults tease children in fun when, often, there's nothing very funny about it. One adult I know held out a £10 note to his nephew. 'Buy yourself some sweets,' he said, teasing. The boy, aged four, grabbed it and ran off down the road towards the shop. Serve that man right! Why tease children, since it only makes them think that it's an acceptable thing to do? I don't think it is, particularly when you're on the receiving end. Usually, it's older children who tease younger: taking their toys away from them, stopping them doing what they want to do. Sometimes an older sibling will torment a younger: pinching him, breaking his favourite toy, making cruel remarks, snatching a prized possession and making off with it, and generally making his life a misery. If the younger child runs to mother, cries, or complains, this can make the older child, rewarded by this easily-provoked display of distress, turn to even more devious ways of annoying his brother or sister.

It isn't always bigger, or older, children who tease. Sometimes, a younger child can taunt, make sarcastic remarks or refuse to leave alone an older (and bigger) child. Having found a chink in the victim's armour the tease exploits it for all it is worth. What is interesting is that some children seem to be the victim type: they annoy other children and when (inevitably) they are teased and annoyed in return they come to adults for protection and sympathy. Having received it they run back to the group, annoy the other children, and the whole thing starts all over again. From time to time, though, a timid child is teased by a bully (the age-old story of the stronger child taking something that belongs to the weaker child and refusing to give it back until the tears start). Some children, in order to protect themselves, meet other children with a mixture of suspicion and fear (which shows on their faces); the group detects this, and the child is teased simply because of his wary attitude and lack of confidence. Some children, equally cruelly, are teased because they look different, speak differently or are wearing the 'wrong' clothes. Poor children may tease a child who is better off than themselves; well-off children may tease a child who comes from a poorer home and hasn't got the same possessions as themselves. It's all very unjust but what can you, as a parent, do about it?

In the family it's a good thing to make clear that you are not willing to put up with teasing. If you intervene at an early stage and say: 'I'm not having that,' and tell the child that it is cruel to tease, your child should at least have to weigh up the satisfaction he gets from teasing against your annoyance and anger. Later, when you've cooled down, you could take the child aside and say that teasing makes the person who is teased very unhappy and it's one of your rules that you just won't tolerate it. Cinderella was teased by her older, ugly, sisters and *they* weren't very nice people, were they? You should watch what leads up to teasing. It's possible that a younger child follows an older child around all day, getting in his way, spoiling his play and 'asking for trouble'. Obviously, here, the child has to be encouraged to play with some interesting toys by himself, or play with children of his own age group, so that the older child can get on with his own play. Usually, if you ask the older child, he will give the younger one some undivided attention for a while, be his 'teacher,' so that he can get on with his own play the rest of the time. If two children provoke each other it's worth a lot of trouble to separate them, to let them have friends they can each play with, so that one is not 'shadowed' (and annoyed) by a younger sibling.

Obviously, the less you tease your own children the better. Not all children enjoy being thrown up in the air, tickled, their toys held out of reach, being called a 'crybaby' or generally poked fun at. Think back to your own childhood when adults (or other children) teased you. There's very little fun in it; nobody likes to be made to look silly and it *is* so easy to ridicule a child who loses his temper or cries. Teasing between parents is not a good idea: children can't understand the difference between friendly teasing and cruel remarks so why make teasing remarks (and set a bad example) in the first place? If parents are easy-going, affectionate and self confident it gives the children that confidence and self assurance to deal with the bully, and the tease.

Some practical steps to take about teasing are:

Don't tease within the family. If you do you can't complain when when your children tease other children, or are teased themselves.

Explain to your child, if he is teased, that everybody gets teased at some time. The best way to react, you should say, is to take no notice. The teaser will soon become bored if his nastiness doesn't evoke any response.

If your child does have a blemish (like a long nose or ears that stick out) don't call attention to it yourself but talk to your child about it, if he wants to talk. Say: 'Everybody's different' (which is true) and point out you love him for who he is including the long nose, or whatever.

Watch young children, from time to time, whilst they play and put a stop to teasing as soon as it starts to happen. Then, give the victim something to do, something he's good at, something he's interested in. Teach him something, build up his confidence.

As the child gets older encourage him to stick up for himself. Don't try to overprotect him from bullies and teasers. The best shield you can give him is lots of love at home and the knowledge that he can tell you any of his troubles – openly, honestly and without embarrassment – whenever he wants to.

If your teenager is worried about a blemish on his skin (or about protruding teeth) do go with him to see the doctor (or dentist) about it. Adolescents do worry terribly about these things and a word from an expert (and some practical steps being taken, where necessary) can be very reassuring to them.

Look upon teasing as part of life. We've all suffered it. The children who get over it without any trouble are those who pick up from their parents those two handy parcels to carry through life: self-respect and self-confidence. Don't tease your own children, praise them and tell them how marvellous they are. Then, when somebody does tease them, they won't rise to the bait. They'll know that those nasty words are untrue anyway, that sticks and stones may break their bones but words will never hurt them. When somebody steals their school lunch, and holds it tauntingly aloft, they'll know how to give the teaser the look that withers. Teasers look awfully silly when the child who's teased is too self-assured to react.

Teenagers
See also **Youth Clubs** *Page* 273

In 1661, Moliere, the French playwright, wrote: 'Young people hereabouts, unbridled, now, just *want*.' Adults have been complaining about teenagers ever since. A good friend tells me: 'I love my son dearly but I find it hard to like him. All he does is grunt at me.' People are always telling me that their teenagers talk too much/ don't talk enough/are untidy/treat the home like a hotel/are only interested in pop music. I agree. Teenagers can be utterly appalling. They can also be great fun, providing that we can find a way of living together.

I think that we have to try to be pals with our teenage sons and

233

daughters. When children are infants they need love; when they're older they need love *and* friendship. There'll be quarrels and disagreements but real friends work things out together, give each other space in which to lead their own lives. We have to live alongside our teenage children and we have to get them, fairly often in my view, out of our hair.

We have to have some sympathy with teenagers. They have more freedom, money and educational opportunity than we ever had. Yet, too much freedom can be frightening and it's not an easy world in which our youngsters live. In some ways it is more puzzling and more demanding, than the one we grew up in. What should you do if you really want to help your teenage son or daughter? Here is my ten point plan of action. You should:

> *Listen to them.* Most of us can talk; it's harder to listen. Often, young people have ideas and opinions which are worth listening to.
> *Praise them,* where praise is due. Don't hark on the bad but tell them how pleased you are when they do something for you.
> *Be honest.* Don't try to be Sigmund Freud, or Florence Nightingale. Be you, and say what you think, but be prepared to discuss your views with them.
> *Negotiate, don't dominate.* You'll find, oddly enough, that teenagers have a need to be misunderstood and most of them like to be allowed to make *some* mistakes. If you step on them at every turn, crush the individuality out of them, you'll have animosity, or blatant rebellion, to contend with.
> *Love them, and leave them be.* They look a lot more sophisticated than they are. Underneath they have a desperate need to love, and be loved and to belong. Don't overestimate their maturity, and don't let that gloss of maturity fool you.
> *Give them some responsibility.* In our house we have an institution known as Day of Hell. On his or her day, one person does the cooking, washing up and cleaning. Everybody does a day (three children, two parents); nobody is excused; at weekends we do our own thing. I'm not suggesting you follow this plan; I *am* suggesting that your children do something in the home. If you set up as general maid and pastry cook (or butler/chauffeur) and ask for nothing in return you can't be surprised if they take advantage of their luck. As a matter of fact, it isn't luck. To do everything for them is no way to prepare them for adult life.
> *Have some rules.* Take parties, a common need (it seems) of

teenagers. In our house, when the teenagers have a party my wife and I go out, return after 11pm, say hello to everybody, and then go to bed. We do not allow parties if we're not there; we insist that any glasses, crockery (or anything else) that's broken is paid for. That's all. We've had no trouble (touch wood) so far and no damage, either to the house or our souls. Do discuss matters with teenagers, and work it out together. Parents have rights as well and your teenagers will understand that they cannot always have things exactly as they would like them.

Trust your teenagers, especially with regard to sex. If they are absolutely determined to get up to mischief, they will. If you're a friend to them, who answers their questions straight, and who doesn't pry too much into their lives, they won't let you down.

Live your own life. It's their spring, not ours, but it can be our Indian summer. Keep growing and developing as a person yourself, and allow your teenagers to do the same.

Don't ape teenagers. If you're a square, stay a square. They'll love you more for it. They want a real person for a mum or dad, not somebody who is trying to be 'with it'. This doesn't mean you have to be dull, but don't imitate their behaviour and dress.

Years ago, on television, I saw a film 'starlette' being interviewed. She was a beautiful young woman, about twenty-one years of age. The interviewer asked her what she did at weekends: did she go out to night-clubs, fly to Paris, go out for expensive meals. 'No,' said the girl. 'I go to see my parents.' The interviewer was puzzled. 'I just like my parents' company, that's all,' the young woman explained. 'I find them very interesting company.' What an incredible compliment that is!

Let's hope that, when you and I are older and our teenagers have flown the nest (whatever else you say, it's going to be *terribly* quiet without them) our teenagers will come back to see us not because we're old and doddery but because we're interesting human beings. And friends.

Thumb-Sucking

Thumb-sucking is very common in young children and should be regarded as part of your child's normal development. It's Mother Nature's cheaper version of a dummy. Your child sucks his thumb for comfort, for sensuous gratification, for amusement. With babies it helps them to learn to suck hard (a useful skill!) and it often acts as a prelude to, or substitute for, feeding. Since thumbs are often sucked for solace the thing to do is to give your child lots of affection and plenty of cuddles. The more comfort the child gets from you the less likely he is to suck his thumb.

If, therefore, you're feeding a young baby, don't hurry. If you're breast feeding your child will want to linger, so let him. Satisfy your baby's sucking instincts – he'll let you know when he's had enough – and give him lots of love and physical contact. If you're bottle feeding, similarly, don't rush. Don't put the child down as soon as the bottle is empty. The more comfort and solace you can give your baby the less likely he is to resort to his thumb. Adequate nourishment and lots of affection are the answer to thumb-sucking in babies. If you wish, gently remove your baby's thumb from his mouth whilst he's sleeping so that it doesn't become a habit associated with the pram, cot or wherever else he sleeps.

Why do older children suck their thumbs? Mainly because it's pleasurable and, like a comfort blanket, it gives them reassurance and emotional gratification. Since most children up to the age of three suck their thumbs from time to time and since it cannot harm their teeth (after the age of six it *may* do harm to second teeth) I'm inclined to say don't make too much fuss about it. Don't reprimand your child, call attention to the habit, buy him a dummy or (worst of all) smack him. I don't think the habit warrants nasty-tasting chemical preparations being put on the thumb especially since, as soon as they wear off, back goes the thumb into the mouth. I hope that nobody would do such a cruel thing as to tie a child's hand behind his back or put his arm in a splint so that he cannot reach his thumb. He wants comfort: if he gets lots from you he's less likely to carry on sucking his thumb.

Thumb-sucking is to be expected in a child under three years of age. The amount will vary but most young children under three resort to the habit. Between three and six years it will appear, along with his well-worn comfort blanket, from time to time; and especially in times of stress or when your child is feeling unsettled. Don't panic. Don't fuss. It will peter out, slowly. The practical things you can do are to make sure that your infant isn't bored, that he has enough toys and other children to play with. Some older children suck their thumbs, I suspect, merely for something to do. If you are in a new place, or your child is worried about something, do cuddle him, comfort him, sit him on your knee and stroke his hair, let him talk to you. You are his main source of solace in moments of trouble. You have, or should have, a great deal more to offer than his thumb!

Many adults when they are tired, bored, worried or fed up smoke, or drink or over-eat. Then, they get into the habit of smoking or drinking or over-eating. It's exactly the same with thumb-sucking. The answer isn't abuse, teasing or nagging. The answer is to give the child the Good Treatment: take him out, give him lots of physical contact, build up his confidence by praising him and giving him little jobs to do at which he can succeed. Soothe his feelings rather than scold him; give him something interesting and absorbing to do instead of watching him wondering why he is sucking his thumb. My guess is that if adults were shown a great deal more appreciation, and given a lot more contact comfort, then they wouldn't need to smoke so much. After all, cigarettes are a dummy-substitute; drinking and eating are basically oral gratification. It's sad that we adults seem to be unable to get it elsewhere!

Tidiness
(For Parents)
See also **Messy Play** *Page* 143

When I talk to groups of mums there is one topic that crops up again and again: tidiness. 'I'm not at all bothered about tidiness,' more than one young mum has told me. 'The trouble is my husband's a *terribly* tidy person. Every night there's a mad scramble to get the place straight before he comes in.' That's one problem: *everybody has a different tolerance level for untidiness.* One person's tidy house is another person's Steptoe's Yard. I've had mothers apologize to me about 'the state of the house' when, compared to our house when the children were young, I was entering a veritable palace.

Most mums (and dads) know that it is wrong to interfere with a child's play too much. If you go round picking up toys as the child is playing (or saying to him: 'Don't put that there,' or, 'Be careful with that paint') you're likely to make the child anxious *and* make his play times less enjoyable. So, what *can* you do?

First there is the question of storage: where to keep things when the child isn't playing with them (and where to put everything when you don't want to be treading on it). The following suggestions might help.

Large cardboard boxes covered with wallpaper – as decoration – to be kept in a special place to 'house' all the larger toys. When you're tidying up at the end of the day make a game of it. 'Let's pick up all the animals and put them in the box,' or, 'Let's pick up all the red toys.' If you have a tidying up time your child will make it *not a nasty chore but a habit.* Be brisk, make it fun, and it will all become part of the pattern of the day's play.

Square plastic washing-up bowls in an attractive colour are very useful. Smaller toys can be kept in them and they can be stacked on top of each other in the corner of the room.

Transparent plastic sweet jars can hold all those things which are always getting lost like beads, blocks, little animals and dolls clothes. In some shops you can get them free, in others they sell them for 5p (still inexpensive if you think of all the child's bits and bobs which you might otherwise lose).

With older children it's still better to tidy up together than to shout at them to do it or do it yourself. Tidiness is a matter of convenience and commonsense. You shouldn't turn it into a discipline issue. ('Tidy your bedroom or else …') When my children were older (i.e. aged between eight and twelve) we would have a weekly blitz on the house in which they were required to help and to do their own specific jobs. Tidiness is really a family matter: you have to decide, together, what level of tidiness you want and when you should tidy up. If you are a working mum it's even more important to get across the lesson that *tidiness in the home is one way of showing consideration for others.* It's unfair for children (or adults) to make a mess and expect others to tidy up after them. It's unfair for a mum (or dad) to be very untidy and ask children to be orderly. Parents have to set a good example. Everybody has to help. It can be a chore but it's one that has to be faced and it's better if everyone sets to and helps.

Don't overdo tidiness. Too much order in the home does stifle children's imagination and creativity. You can make things easier for everybody by a bit of intelligent thinking – putting newspaper on the table or floor (especially under the paint-pots), having aprons (or easily washable clothing) for the children if they're doing something messy. Ask them to keep their mess in one corner (or, if you're lucky) one room. Set some boundaries, tell them what you want and don't want (i.e. paint on the carpet) and this will save you getting annoyed after the event. With older children encourage them to decorate (or help to decorate) their own rooms and to take a pride in them. If your children are untidy tell them that they have to limit their play to a certain part of the house. After all, tidiness is like other aspects of living: it's an agreement between people as to what's acceptable, and what isn't.

The thing is to make quite certain who you are being tidy *for*. It should be for you and the rest of the family. It shouldn't be for the neighbours (I'm sure that we do a great social service in our house by being so relaxed about tidiness. When neighbours see the chaos *we* live in it makes them feel a whole lot better). If you are a naturally tidy, orderly person, well and good. *If you spend your time worrying what the neighbours might think you're being tidy for the wrong reasons.* Most people know that it's very difficult to be tidy when there are young children in the home so get your priorities straight: enjoy your children first, think of tidiness second.

With teenagers, a little bit of cunning works wonders. I encourage my teenagers to invite friends around to the house. I've found this is a marvellous way to make them tidy up. It's no good nagging teenagers about the state of their bedrooms, or their general appearance. Give them the money for paint and posters for their bedrooms; give them a clothes allowance and compliment them on their appearance. Many teenagers use untidiness as a weapon to annoy their parents. Don't rise to the bait. Let *them* be responsible for their bedrooms, and their clothes. Treat them as adults, as equal partners in making the house an attractive place for friends to come to – and themselves as attractive people to be with – and they'll see the sense of it.

Here are a few points to help you:

Early in your marriage arrange for your husband to look after the children for a day or two while you're away (even it it's only at your mother's). He'll quickly learn that it's hard to interest youngsters *and* be tidy.

Let your children play. Then, have a 'tidy time'. Don't pester them whilst they're playing. Do the job together, when they've finished.

Have a few rules in the home (e.g.: cups returned to kitchen, not left in bedrooms; pick things up; put things away in drawers; if you eat a meal by yourself, wash up and don't expect others to do it for you). Tidiness is a family enterprise.

Give everybody specific jobs to do. Have them written up on the wall where everyone can see them. Don't shout: 'Tidy up.' That's too vague. Simply ensure that everybody does his or her job and change the jobs around so that nobody gets bored.

Set a standard of tidiness that's acceptable to the family. Be brisk, make tidiness into a routine, and don't worry about it if your neighbour's tidier than you are. Any friend that is worthwhile will judge us by who and what we are – not by the toys, or teenagers' jackets, all over the living room carpet.

Toilet Training

From what my own mother has told me I gather that a great many mums in the 'thirties stood around, pot in hand, waiting for the baby to move his bowels and hoping to 'catch it'. The average age for starting potty training, in those days, was six months! My mother says that she knew one woman whose baby was potty-trained at two months. I can only comment that this is far too early and reflects great anxiety and impatience concerning the whole notion of toilet training. Training has to be given (no young child wants the inconvenience of wetting and soiling himself for, say, three or four years) but it has to be given in a friendly, non-anxious way. If you make too much fuss you run the same danger as making too much of a fuss over feeding (see section on **Eating Fads**). The child can soil himself, or refuse to move his bowels, just because he's fed up of the anxiety you're showing about the whole business. As I understand children, you can't actually force a child to eat if he doesn't want to – just as you can't force a child to move his bowels unless he wants to. Potty training, in short, should be fun.

When should you start training? I think the summer nearest to the child's second birthday is a good time, since the child can play out in the garden or wander about in terry towelling trainer pants and you don't have to have all the bother of nappies. Let me explain that until, roughly, fifteen months your child will pass water or move his bowels quite automatically: the bladder, or bowels, are filled, pressure is put on the 'release valves' and, hey presto, the child fulfils his natural functions. The child can't control the operation but he's interested in what's happening. By about eighteen months he'll be interested in telling you what's happened but not able to tell you when it's going to happen. This is the time to introduce him to the pot, tell him what it's for, let him get used to it. No anxiety. He may like sitting on his pot or pot chair so much, and learn so quickly, that you won't have to wait for those summer months. The vital things to remember are: think yourself lucky if you do train your child before his second birthday; *never* chastise a child for accidents – expect them; expect some regression i.e. going back to soiling and/or wetting himself if your infant is poorly or has had some emotional upset; don't be in too much of a hurry to start and don't really expect your child to be entirely toilet trained before his *third* birthday.

Parents have to cooperate with nature on this one. The fact of the matter is that, as your infant grows older, he gets more and more control over his bowels and his bladder. This is a neurological business – to do with the maturation of nerves going from the working parts in question to the brain. There isn't anything that you can do to hurry it up. What you can do is to introduce the potty in the second half of the second year, tell the child what it's for and give him a bit of practice in sitting on it. If he gives you a signal, say after breakfast, that he's ready to sit on the pot then let him do so without any show of fuss or worry. The cooler you play it at this stage the better: you may find that you're one of those lucky mums who, without doing very much at all, has trained the child by the age of two (barring little accidents!).

Here are Ten Tips for Good Toilet Training:

Ignore stories about babies being fully potty trained at six months. Perhaps they were but how silly!

Your baby should be toilet trained when he can control his bladder and bowels voluntarily – this is usually during the latter part of the second year.

If you introduce the pot before this time think of it as 'bonus' if you have some successes. The danger in introducing the pot too early is that your infant may rebel against it later – thus upsetting you and making it harder to train him in a relaxed way.

Never think of potty training as something to do with being 'clean' or being 'dirty'. These functions are quite natural to all human beings – they *aren't* dirty. Infants are often very proud of their productions. You should be too. You're training your child because it's more convenient, during his third year – both for him and you – to be toilet trained than not. You're not training him, I hope, because you find something disgusting about these perfectly natural bodily functions.

A pot chair is a good idea. It's a little piece of furniture that the child will like; it has a back support and a little shield in front for boys (to prevent 'spraying' and other mishaps!).

Let your child train himself. Never push, never hover anxiously, never get worked up about it. After all, there is only one person who can make sure that what you do will work and that's your child. Left to their own free will, and started off at the right time, the vast majority of infants will be delighted to cooperate.

If you are worried about any aspect of toilet training do have a word with your family doctor about it. He will put you in touch with a health visitor who will be able to give you practical advice.

The philosophy of toilet training is Don't Rush Things. As in other aspects of life the more we rush the less we get anywhere, fast.

Toys

Play comes first, then come toys. Toys are the hook on which your child hangs his desire to observe, explore, create, use his body, play a role, act protectively or simply show off. Certain toys are most appropriate to various ages and stages, and you needn't (especially when your child is young) pay out a lot of money for expensive ones. The baby's best toy, for example, is the mother: he can look at her, explore her mouth, her fingers, her face, listen to her talking. In turn, she (and/or father) can just hold the baby, cuddle him, rock him, bounce him on both knees. This gives an opportunity for play *and* contact comfort: both essential human needs.

With toddlers, a tin, a cardboard box, some wooden bricks may be all that is necessary to act as a spur to his imagination. Young children like to make things happen (that's why an infant will drop a rattle from a pram a hundred times providing mum or dad plays the game and returns it). Dropping something into a box, shaking it, making a noise, is a 'happening' as is putting one block on another, then knocking both down. Most of the materials required for happenings (e.g. a piece of cloth, a newspaper, with which to play 'peek-a-boo') are already in the home. Cotton reels, cigarette packets, old cardboard tubes can be handled, pushed, pulled, looked through. With the young baby in a pram, a mobile (made from string and milk bottle tops) can be hung from the canopy to give your baby something to look at. When baby is young, a tin with a few beans in it (safely encased in Sellotape) is just as effective as a rattle bought in the shops. Home-made toys, I repeat, are great fun for a child if they open out new avenues for his imagination. For a toddler, a cardboard box, plus a piece of string attached to it, becomes a lorry. Why go to the shop and buy an expensive version of the same thing?

The young infant wants toys that he can shake or bang or push along. He wants objects such as wooden bricks that develop his hand-eye coordination. As the child gets older he likes toys which can be used for more than one play activity – a wooden box, maybe, which can become a table, or a stool, or a doll's crib or a collection of chairs, blankets and cushions which can be turned into a Wendy house, a tent or a fortress. A pile of wooden bricks can be made into a house, a railway station, an airport. *I strongly advise you, if your child is between two-and-a-half years and five years to get together with other mothers so that your children can play together.* This is good social training: it teaches your child to share, and to take into account the demands of others. If you have a local playgroup, do take advantage of it. They have a larger variety of toys there, and you will get plenty of ideas on toys and play by just watching and talking to the other mums.

If you want ideas for toys you could write to The Toy Libraries Association, Seabrook House, Wyllyots Manor, Darkes Lane, Potters Bar, Herts. EN6 2HL. This organization produces many useful pamphlets including *ABC of Toys,* and *Choosing Toys and Activities for Handicapped Children.* There may be a branch of the Toy Libraries Association in your area which will be glad to give you advice, especially if you have a handicapped child. For the most part, however, we can get plenty of ideas for toys from toy shops and from toy catalogues. We don't *have* to buy their toys; we can make cheaper versions of the same thing ourselves.

Children between the ages of four and eight usually like to play games (games are merely play, with rules). Dominoes, card games (including snap), snakes and ladders, ludo and blow football are all examples of traditional games enjoyed by youngsters in this age group. They also like to play outdoor games such as 'tick', What's the Time, Mr Wolf? and Grandmother's Footsteps. (Do join in whenever you have the time or the energy: it's all great fun. When they're teenagers, alas, you'll find it harder to share their enthusiasm for hit records so participate while you can!) Children love dressing up, so don't throw away your old clothes. They also love painting and collage, so don't throw away those egg boxes, old newspapers (they'll make, with a bit of wallpaper paste, excellent papier-mâché) and sweet wrappings. When my children were this age they were very imaginative; we kept everything for them to make into *something*; our house began to look like Steptoe's Yard!

The kind of toys you buy for older children (say, between eight and fourteen) will depend upon where you live. Youngsters living in the country have plenty of toys – trees to climb, hills to roll down, woods to explore. The town child needs to develop his coordination, the mastery of his body, via scooters, bicycles, trolleys, skateboards and stilts. He wants to go to places where there are swings, ropes, climbing apparatus, or to a field where he can play football, or a sports centre where various games are available. The performance of some motor skill (or an acrobatic skill, in some cases) is very important to most youngsters. They want to be able to do something well whether it be make models, play table tennis, or chess, or swim, or run, or play cricket or hockey. The aim of ball games is to develop a sense of mastery of one's own body just as, with younger children, toys are used to explore the limits of their world, and their intense curiosity about how they fit into it. Even adults enjoy mastering situations, playing with model trains and toy soldiers. It gives them a sense of power. Toys give (or should give) children a sense of competence.

Here are a few tips about toys:

Encourage your child's curiosity. Start early when the baby is in the pram. String a few toys in front of him. This will give him something to look at and (later) something to reach out and feel.

Simple toys are best. A pan, a wooden spoon, and (if you can manage it) a sandpit, plus spade and bucket. Children have lots of imagination. It's marvellous what they'll do with a few boxes, or two chairs and a blanket.

Try to play with your young child and (as often as you can) with older children. A toy, or a game, shared with one of the parents is much more fun.

Don't worry too much about order (see section on **Tidiness**). Don't tidy up *as* the child plays; let him play and tidy up in the evening (a big box in the corner of the room is very useful). When your children have left home you can have the graceful, immaculate house you've always aspired to.

If in doubt about which toys your child would benefit from (especially if your child is physically or mentally handicapped) *have a word with your local midwife, playgroup leader, class teacher or write to The Toy Libraries Association for advice.*

Finally, keep alive your own sense of discovery and exploration. Men and women are most human when they play. Buy toys for your child (or, better, make toys) and enjoy them with him. Why miss out on all the fun?

Truancy
See section on **School Phobia** *Page* 194

244

Uncooperativeness
See also **Defiance** *Page* 45

How many times have you said: 'He's such a demanding child. He always does what he wants to do, not what I want him to do.'? When you think about it, though, is it surprising that children occasionally want to do their own thing? We, parents, make a great many demands on them and give them sufficient orders in one day to run a regiment. Come here. Stop that. Wash your hands. Clear the table. Stop sulking. Do your homework. Go to bed. Any child, faced with an incessant stream of orders like this, is likely to keep out of mother's or father's way as much as possible.

A good rule is never to ask a young child anything that can be answered with the word 'No'. A wise parent avoids the Shall we? approach: *Mother* (eagerly): 'Shall we go for a little walk and then go and buy a loaf and call in to see your little friend Jason on the way back?' *Child* (firmly): 'No.' It's much better to say: 'Come on, let's go for a walk,' and put the child's coat on before he has too much time to sort out his philosophical approach to physical exercise. The verbally-brisk mother avoids uncooperativeness simply because she is willing to be firm and give her child much less of a chance to say no on those occasions when mother has made up her mind what is going to happen anyway.

All children face the problem of Dependence versus Independence. This can be observed in a toddler clutching at mother's skirts or dad's trousers in the kitchen and then going off to 'explore' – to play in another room in the house, away from the parent and, no doubt, after some time returning into the parent's orbit. The conflict of dependence/independence can also be observed with teenagers. *They* like to feel that they are very independent and, yet, if you forget to buy them a birthday card, or forget to give them a Christmas present, they don't much like it. They want to be free, to rely as little on the parents as possible; at the same time they want to be loved and cherished.

With older children it is important that they see that *their* cooperation is needed as part of an overall plan for the running of the home, of which they are an essential part. Children, certainly from the age of eight onwards, should be given some jobs to do (share them out – don't give the same child, or yourself, all the dirty jobs) in the home. This makes for a better atmosphere and, if you start early enough, it develops cooperativeness rather than the feeling, which some children undoubtedly have, that the world owes them a living and 'the family' owes them bed and board, free, with several extras thrown in. If you are about to require your child's cooperation don't forget to give prior warning: clear up in ten minutes; start winding up your game; lunch in quarter of an hour. If we cooperate as much as possible with our children's needs, then they are much more likely to be responsive to *our* needs as parents. If we make too many demands – or, worse, no demands at all – then we are encouraging that very atmosphere of resentment and uncooperativeness that *can* make family life very unpleasant. A family is a joint enterprise. Everybody has to contribute something in order to make it work.

A final word. Do avoid being too bossy. If something is important to you insist that it's done and use a brisk, matter-of-fact tone of voice. Don't go on and on about it. Nothing is more likely to put children's backs up. If you expect to be obeyed and your attitude is one of concern for your children (but insistence that what you want doing gets done) the odds are you'll get plenty of cooperation. Children by and large know what's good for them. They can spot the ranters and shouters of this world (I admit that we all rant and rave *sometimes)* at fifty paces and cooperation is the last thing that's in their minds.

Under-Achievement in School
See also **School-Phobia** *Page* 194

Imagine you're doing a job yourself. To do your best at it you have to be interested and working in a situation where you can get on with it. Also, the job mustn't be too hard and quite beyond your capabilities, or you'll soon give up in despair. Just as important, it mustn't be too easy, or you won't get any sense of challenge or any sense of achievement when you've finished. If you think of it like this there are a number of reasons why your child may not be doing his best in school. He may be bored (see section on **Boredom**). He may find the work too hard or too easy. He may find that he's in a class, or in a particular lesson, where he doesn't like the teacher or where the other children 'mess around' so that he can't concentrate on his work. Or, he may find the lessons badly taught so that he doesn't know what's going on or simply isn't inspired to do his best. I must admit that I'm always a bit suspicious when I read a school report (see section on **School Reports**) and a child is described as 'lazy'. There's always a chance, I think, that the teacher hasn't given work that stimulates and interests the child and gives the child some chance of success. *The work being done, and the methods used to teach it, must always appear to be sensible, purposeful and interesting to the child who is expected to do it.*

If your child is just not interested in what is going on in the classroom there are a number of 'tricks of the trade' that the teacher can use to motivate him. A child can be given a project to do, based on one of his interests. What *are* your child's areas of interest? What are his strong points? It is better to start from these, and to ensure some success, rather than to cram knowledge, willy-nilly, into the child's head (which he'll soon forget since he isn't motivated to retain it).

I saw a little girl of nine who was marvellous at painting and drawing. Unfortunately, in school, the approach was very formal, with a heavy emphasis on maths and written work. The girl had an IQ of 130 and yet was failing in her school work and miserable about it. What I did was to suggest that she should have a chance to do more art, to illustrate her essays, and have less maths (just for the time being). The change in her school work was dramatic. She perceived that the school saw (at last!) that she was good at something. Her success at art spilled over into writing and other subjects (why be surprised? Success breeds success). Last but not least, the teacher was taking a real interest in her, treating her as a real individual. In other cases, I've seen children who, given more scope for drama, puppetry, poetry or even describing and demon- strating their skills at model-making or mending motor-bike engines, suddenly begin to like school and to achieve markedly improved standards of work. A teacher should know the special interests of the children in his or her class and capitalize on them. A child interested in butterflies, or cars, or football, or hair styling, could give a talk to the rest of the group on the subject or could do a term's (or a year's) project based on her interests. It's remarkable, in my experience, what positive changes in the child's attitude to school this individually-orientated approach can achieve. Please, don't look for more complicated reasons why your child is failing in school if the simple truth is that he isn't interested in the work. Boredom is Public Enemy No 1 in the classroom.

Obviously, there may be other reasons why your child is under-achieving. These will include *illness* (and a subsequent long period of absence from school); *recurrent absences* (due to ill-health or frequent minor ailments); *changes of school; changes of teacher; intense dislike of a particular subject – or a particular teacher – in the school.* (School failure is often due to an adverse *emotional* attitude: to a subject, to a teacher, or even to having to take a shower every week after games.) *Whatever the reason, if you suspect that your child isn't doing his best in school, you should arrange to see the class teacher and the headmaster/headmistress and to explain your views and tell the school something of the child's interests and strong points.* The best antidote to school failure is close liaison between parents and the school. You should go along to parent-teacher meetings, to any functions held at the school, and ensure that you attend any evenings in which you have an opportunity to meet the teachers or hear what the school's policy is towards some particular issue (such as choice of examination subjects) that concerns your child. There is less chance of your child failing in school if you know what's going on and show an active interest in your child's progress. Never say: 'It's the school's business.' It isn't. Not solely. It's yours as well. After all, it's your child.

The necessity of close liaison between school and home becomes quickly apparent if you consider the case of bullying in school. Some children's lives are made a misery because of bullying and *because their parents don't know what's happening.* The child is isolated, without any sympathetic adult with whom he can discuss his very real fears. This should never happen. A child cannot be expected to concentrate on his school work if he is being bullied, or lonely and friendless in school or has worries at home which preoccupy his mind. Children can cope with all sorts of stresses and strains providing they know that somebody knows, and has sympathy with, what they have to put up with. Never leave your child to cope alone. *Work with the school, take an interest, and between the adults concerned it should be possible to work out a plan or campaign that will be of real help to the child.*

Here are some points I think you should remember if you want your child to do his very best in the classroom:

Teachers aren't, or shouldn't be, afraid of explaining what they are doing in the classroom. If you have any doubts, worries, ask them.
If your child strikes you as bright, talks intelligently and does lots of things intelligently at home, but does badly in school, ask for him to be seen by the school psychologist. An appointment can be arranged via the headmaster or the family doctor. The cause of failure, e.g. an eyesight problem or a hearing difficulty, may not be apparent to you. I have known children who failed at school because they couldn't see what was on the blackboard, or couldn't hear what was going on so, in a case of persistent failure, get some expert advice.
Don't impose your interests, and expectations, on the child. Don't

'pressurize' him to be the best and don't do his homework for him. (Though there's no reason why you shouldn't discuss it with him or even help him from time to time, if you can!) Often, pressure on children will make them do worse, rather than better.

If you have just moved into an area, or if you have a period of stress and strain in the family, go to the school and tell them about your circumstances, and something of how the children are reacting. This will help the school to understand your child better and help him more effectively.

Be enthusiastic about learning yourself. Take your child out to new places, talk with him, have a few books in the house. If you show enthusiasm about reading, acquiring new knowledge, seeing and understanding the world about you, so will your child.

Don't side with your child against the school, or see the school as a remote place. Work together, with the school, for the good of the child.

Bear in mind that teachers are human too. When you do meet them treat them, not with subservience, but with a certain amount of sympathy and courtesy. Ask, but don't lay down the law. Discuss practical points, what to do about maths, writing, reading etc. Ask what facilities there are in the school for remedial help. Don't get the teacher's back up. *That* does him, you, and your child, no good at all.

If your child is undergoing a period of failure in school, stand by him. He needs your love and support more, not less, during this time. Nobody likes to fail.

Under-Fives
See also **Fantasy** *Page* 76, **Fun** *Page* 91, **Messy Play** *Page* 143

If anybody asked me what you need to bring up a lively infant I'd answer: 'Physical fitness.' Bringing up young children is hard work and it can be a lonely business. At one time young mothers had granny near at hand to give advice and to act as unpaid baby sitter; now, parents have to make sure that they use whatever resources there are in the neighbourhood (playgroup, toy library, 'cuppa club', mother and toddler group) to build up some human support for themselves in the daunting (but never boring) task of giving children social and intellectual stimulation.

Play is essential to young children: for them, it is learning to live.

Through play, children build up a model of the world: they learn how things work, what goes with what. They also, through play, learn about human emotions and such vital matters as sharing and taking into account the needs of others. There are five stages of play: the *solitary play* of very young children; *looking-on play* – of infants of about eighteen months; *parallel play* – children playing side by side but not really cooperating and working together; *associative play* – children lend and borrow toys from each other; *cooperative play* – where the children aim at certain results together such as 'building a boat' from wooden bricks or playing in the Wendy House together and each taking a part.

Playgroups (and nursery classes) play a vital role in helping a child to play (and learn) alongside other infants (very useful this, since it is what the child is expected to do when he or she goes to school). However, you, the child's mother, are still the most important person in his life and you can teach him many things. What does your child need from you? He needs love and security, new experiences, praise and recognition, some responsibility i.e. to be given some little jobs to do, and lots of new words so that he can put labels on his experiences and the things he sees. Do talk to your child as you walk through a field (or around the local supermarket) together: words are the bricks of learning, and the more conversations you and your infant have, the better.

When you take your child along to the playgroup (or nursery class) be on the look-out for any new ideas you see there. Many playgroups offer to parents the company of other mothers and an opportunity to learn how to provide the right sort of learning situations for their own children. Don't try to bring up your child by yourself. Talking with other mothers in a commonsense, matter-of-fact way about the problems associated with bringing up lively under-fives *can* be a great help to a mother who may think that she is the only person in the world with that particular problem.

The best way for you to think of the ways in which you can help your child is to think of the word PIES – it stands for the child's physical, intellectual, emotional and social development. Let's take them one by one.

Physical Playing with your baby doesn't cost money and the baby's best toy is yourself. Making faces, offering a finger to be gripped, playing 'This Little Piggy Went to Market', and talking (and cuddling) the infant are all very exciting, and cheap. Later, an old saucepan or a cardboard box to put things in, large wooden blocks, simple jig-saws, a large ball to push a box to pull, scribbling with crayons, painting, playing with sand (or water) help the child's motor coordination. Your child will want space (either in the garden or in the local park) where he can run, hop, skip, climb, jump and perhaps learn to ride a tricycle and learn to throw and catch a ball. Digging in sand, being able to skip, to fasten buttons and undo them (you need lots of patience for this, and you have to resist the temptation to save time by doing the job yourself!) are very big steps in the young child's journey towards maturity. The child who can tie his own laces (or can swim) is gaining a tremendous amount of confidence, by the sheer enhancement of physical skills. Tiring for parents, I know; your one consolation is the excitement of the child in mastering his body and his environment.

Intellectual A young child has to learn about many things: size, shape, colour, weight, quantity, volume, time and distance. These ideas, or concepts, can best be learned through play. When the child is playing with beads he is learning about 'sameness' and 'difference', about sequence (what comes after what) and he is acquiring a rudimentary knowledge of number, and perhaps colour. The mother says: 'That's a red bead and here's another red bead.' The child learns that certain things belong together. 'There's a butterfly,' a mother might say as she turns over the pages of a picture book with the child. The infant learns to differentiate between cats, dogs, butterflies, trees, flowers and learns, through placing things in categories, to scaffold his understanding of the world.

What is your main contribution, as a mother, to all this? The most useful mum is the mum who talks with her child and encourages his innate curiosity. She can give him language and it is through language that the child classifies his ideas ('pins the concept') and communicates those ideas to others. So, do make sure that your child has plenty of opportunity to play with as large a variety of play materials as possible and set aside a 'quiet time' each day – I know this is difficult – when you can talk or look at a book together. If you do both, and take the child on walks to see things and talk about them you can be sure that the child will learn. After all, at this stage, the best teacher is the child's mother.

Emotional A distinguished American paediatrician says that to flourish in mind and body a child needs *one person to love him beyond reason*. Certainly the benefits of lots of love during the first five years are life-long: if we're loved we look upon ourselves as loveable, but a child who isn't loved feels an empty space where his self-esteem ought to be. The mother is the child's safe base: the platform from which he launches himself into a largely hostile or uncaring world. Please, mothers and fathers with young children, *show* affection to your child with lots of kisses and cuddles and visible demonstrations of love. If you love the child, make it obvious. Why be embarrassed about it? Time spent on a mother's knee, whilst we are young, is money in the bank as far as our subsequent emotional security is concerned. Eschew the British, stiff-upper-lip attitude towards the emotions and give the child (by hugs, cuddles and other displays of affection) an abiding sense of his own loveableness.

The second thing you can do to help the child's emotional growth is to provide sand, water (and soapy bubbles), clay, dough, papier-mâché and finger-paints for the child to play with. These are what I call the 'comfort materials' and most children find them soothing and satisfying to work with. They make a mess, so put an old piece of carpet down on the floor before you start. You might join in yourself from time to time: these kind of activities are very rewarding and they are one of the most effective cures I know for frayed nerves.

Social Children learn by watching others, by playing with others and being helped by those who are older and more skilled than themselves.

Community playgroups give children a chance to play roles: to imagine themselves as a mother or father going out to work, a nurse or doctor, or even a fantasy figure like Batman or Wonder Woman. Children learn group dynamics: what you have to do, or not do, to be accepted by the rest of the group. They afford a chance (as do mother and toddler groups and nursery classes) to relate to another adult beside the mother and how to obey the 'house rules' in places other than the child's own home. Finally, in a group setting children learn to make friends and how to take into account the wishes of others; both invaluable lessons for life in 'the big school', and the older years.

Besides this, mothers have an opportunity to mix with other mothers and to share experiences and learn from each other. In my estimation, the pre-school playgroup movement is the best 'grass roots' movement of the last twenty-odd years. If you are a mother with young children do take advantage of it.

A useful address is Pre-School Playgroup Association, Alford House, Aveline Street, London SE11 5DH. The PPA are a good source of leaflets and various information to do with the under-fives.

Two relevant books are *This Little Puffin* (Penguin) full of rhymes and songs for young children and *Baby & Child* by Penelope Leach (Penguin) a sound guide to bringing up the pre-school child.

Uriah Heep Complex
See also **Inferiority Complex** *Page* 113

Uriah Heep is a character in Charles Dickens' novel *David Copperfield.* Uriah is a fawning, grovelling, self-effacing individual who, in modern parlance, would be known as a 'creep' or a 'crawler'. Some children find it difficult to express their real feelings towards others but, in face of this difficulty, they *don't* become over-aggressive, or withdrawn. They defend themselves by being over-civil, over-polite, 'oily'. We expect this kind of behaviour, sometimes, from waiters in restaurants, or from shop assistants. It is less attractive when it's part of a child's strategy of survival, since it implies that the child hasn't yet found the confidence to be himself. Against the slings and arrows of life, a child has three main types of defence: fight, flight or imitation. Fawning, over-polite (or downright grovelling) behaviour is a form of imitation – pretending to be something that we are not. It assumes that the world is a hostile, nasty place and that everybody is a possible aggressor. So, a child may bring a teacher flowers simply because he likes her; the Uriah Heep child takes flowers to his teacher because he wants to keep on the right side of her.

I call this need not to offend anybody the Uriah Heep complex. If we are desperate that everybody should like us we stand a good chance that nobody will like us since we never give others a chance to meet a real person. The person we let others meet is too good to be true.

You may have met a too-good-to-be-true child. I'm not talking about children who are naturally charming, polite, well-mannered. The too-good-to-be-true, Uriah Heep child *always* says the right thing, *always* enquires about Granny's health, is *always* orderly, neat, tidy. The child may spend a great deal of time, not playing with his own age group, but trying to please his parents, other adults and older children. His manner, his speech, are ingratiating: both more appropriate to a grown-up rather than a youngster. The goody-goody behaviour carries over into school where the child may try to become teacher's pet, bringing her presents, going to her desk to tell her of this and that. The Uriah Heep child will try to placate the strong-minded, natural leaders children in his class (which is understandable enough) but will also placate (and speak to in the same ingratiating manner) the timid, the shy, and even children he does not know. The 'smooth-talking' approach, the over-politness, may indicate that the child imagines everybody to be a possible aggressor and/or has a lot of hostile, aggressive feelings within himself that he's never had a chance to give expression to.

A little boy of seven that I saw in the clinic was a typical Uriah Heep child. He shook hands with me, spoke in a curiously old-fashioned, stilted, over-polite fashion and didn't seem to mean anything he was saying: he gave me the answers he thought I wanted to hear. He was very neat and tidy, never looked me in the eye, and even had a habit of wringing his hands together as he spoke! He wasn't doing at all well in school although he had an IQ of 130 and was obviously very intelligent. His mother had had a baby a year previously and the seven-year-old professed to love her. He went out of his way to help his parents look after his little sister. After coming to the clinic for about six months, and gradually relaxing and learning to be himself, he confided to me one day whilst playing with some toy soldiers: 'I hate that little brat!' It was the first real, heart-felt, thing he'd said. After that, he opened up, spoke more naturally (and was a little more untidy) and seemed to have a lot more energy. His work in school improved beyond all recognition.

Why? My own theory is the boy was taking up so much energy keeping up his 'perfect child' mask (and keeping down his own aggressive feelings, especially towards the baby) that he simply had nothing left over to put into play, or into his school work. When we wear a mask, we're always afraid of it slipping. Keeping up a facade can be very tiring. Often, Uriah Heep children look exhausted, weary; some tell you that they often feel tired. I'm not surprised since it's hard work to stifle normal assertiveness; it takes a lot of energy to smother all natural, spontaneous impulses. The price of maintaining the constant facade is eternal vigilance – a never-ending self-scrutiny to make sure that one is making the 'right' impression on others. It's too high a price to pay. If the child can, instead, recognize his *own* needs, get to know his *own* feelings, establish his *own* identity, be himself (including the good bits and the bad bits) the chances are that other people will like him anyway. None of us is perfect.

What can you do to encourage your child to be natural and confident, to avoid the Uriah Heep, self-effacing attitude to life? My suggestions are:

254

Be natural, spontaneous and honest yourself. If you're angry, be angry (and say why you're angry). The same thing applies to other emotions like sadness and happiness. Don't feel something, and say something else. This is very confusing to children.

Don't adopt a cringing, subservient, obsequious manner to 'important visitors' (and then talk about them in a less flattering way when they've gone). Children are astute observers.

Don't say you don't care about something that happens to you, when you do. Tell the truth. Why mask your real feelings? If you do, you'll teach your children to be emotionally dishonest.

Accept your child's (occasional) anger and/or hostile thoughts (just as you accept your own). It's better for your child to get into a rage occasionally than to spend the rest of his life afraid of hostility, and afraid of losing his own temper. People do get annoyed. It's part of life.

Be yourself. Why bother to be anybody else? Life's too short for pretence. Pass on that message to your children: give *them* the confidence to be themselves.

Values

(For Parents)
See also **Morality** Page 145

I sometimes start a lecture on children by asking the members of the audience to call out to me what *they* think children need. It's surprising how often the same words crop up: love, a sense of belonging, stimulation and new experiences, discipline, security, praise and recognition, responsibility and opportunities for achievement. Values are rarely mentioned. If they are they seem to come well down on the list.

This is strange when you think about it since none of us can live without some sense of values. In homes which are positive Fagin's kitchens, and children are taught to steal, there is still a moral (or immoral) code. Members of the Mafia, criminals, rogues, thieves and hooligans all have values. They may, for example, be very kind to their parents and children. There are many things which they would not do. It is only a few areas of conduct that their ideas of what is right and wrong do not coincide with the morality of the general community. It is possible for a mother or father to give a child love, a sense of responsibility, plenty of security and all the other vital needs and yet fail to instil in the child a sense of values. The child may turn out to be 'a likeable rogue', a gangster, a burglar, a safe-cracker or just a lazy person who is always looking for the easy way out.

How do you make sure that your child grows up with a sense of values which is going to carry him through life and be accepted, and admired, by the rest of us? What sort of values would these be? It's no use saying, for example, that children should be polite and tidy. Perhaps they should, but politeness and tidiness, in themselves, aren't enough. You'll remember that Hamlet noted down in his little book that, 'one may smile and smile and be a villain.' Some of the most anti-social children can be extremely polite; some criminals are extremely tidy and fastidious.

What's needed are values which, as moral imperatives, can be accepted by the general community. *Kindness,* for instance, might be a key value. If we all acted towards each other kindly it would result in the greatest good of the greatest number. *Respect for others* is another imperative. Without respect for others nobody within the community can go about his daily round in safety. Life, liberty, the freedom to pursue one's own goals are all endangered. You can make up your own list of those values which you think that people living in a community should adhere to. We seem, by and large, to have scrapped the Ten Commandments (a rough-and-ready, but very useful and wise guide to human conduct) and we have to re-think the whole business of how to behave towards each other. It's very important that we do, since the consequences of not loving our neighbour, not acting responsibly towards each other, could be quite appalling in this nuclear age.

What you'll want to know, as a parent, is where children get their values from. The answer is that they, mostly, get them from *you*, the parent. However, and this is where a lot of parents go wrong, values are caught, not taught. They can't be taught directly. Values are absorbed into the child's personality only through his identification with, and imitation of, those people whom he loves and respects. We can threaten a child, punish him, physically beat him but that won't make him change his values. Nor do we absorb values which are thrust upon us by somebody whom we neither like nor respect. With children, we first gain their love and respect; then, they identify with us and accept our values and copy our behaviour. It does no good to tell them to do one thing, and to do something quite opposite ourselves. (For example tell them to 'be honest' when we cheat the milkman, or the check-out girl at the supermarket or the tax inspector.) We can't tell them to respect other people if we clearly have little respect for them ourselves.

Children are great imitators. If parents cheat, the child will cheat. If parents steal the child will steal. If parents lie the child will lie. The attitudes and the *practices* – not the words – are picked up by the children. The moral is plain. If you want your children to be kind, to respect others, or to behave in any other way, the simplest approach is to be kind, respect others and behave with decency and responsibility yourself. If you don't – and, let's face it, thousands upon thousands of parents don't – it is quite silly to expect children to do anything else than follow your uninspiring – and, sometimes, appalling – example.

Act, said Kant, the German philosopher, as though you would like the thing that you do to become a universal law. Do we want dishonesty, lying, mugging and robbery to become universal laws? Or is it better to have such things as kindness and loving one's neighbour as oneself? In the home, at least, *you* have the choice. If you behave kindly and respectfully towards others, so will your child. If you're dishonest, he will be too. He'll get his sense of values from you.

Violence
See also **Aggression** *Page* 3, **Destructiveness** *Page* 53

It's often thought that there are violent people (others) and peaceful people (me and you): quite separate, like the two humps on a camel's back. I doubt whether that is true. I suspect that, deep down, violence lurks in most human beings. Given extreme frustration (see section on **Aggression**), given certain circumstances, we might all resort to violence. That's what makes it so alarming: it's something that could happen to, or be perpetrated by, any of us. A man kicks a car when it won't start; shouts at his wife after a bad day at work, or kicks the cat; a mother, out of sheer frustration, hits her child; a man, half-mad with jealousy or rage, batters his wife; a child, frustrated and angry, smashes a toy to tiny pieces. There is a darker side to the human personality and it *can* express itself in violence. What can we do to prevent it?

Take babies, and baby battering. Babies vary. Some cry a lot, feed poorly, sleep badly; a few do all the wrong things in succession. There are super-babies who do all the right things all the time. It is when a mum who is depressed has to deal with a difficult baby that trouble can occur. Some mothers take time to 'fall in love' with a particular child (see section on **Intense Dislike of Children**). A mother wants a girl, and gets a boy; she wants a blue-eyed, blonde-haired infant and the child is dark. Most mothers get over their disappointment but some don't. The early bonding that should take place between mother and child doesn't happen. When the mother becomes exhausted, desperate, angry, depressed or just totally fed up she may take out her frustrations on the baby: a face is bruised, an arm is broken, a limb is shattered and (twice every week, in this country) a death occurs. This is tragic; we must seek to prevent it.

If you feel that you simply cannot cope with your young baby you should call in professional help. A health visitor from the local clinic will be able to advise you and perhaps put you in touch with a social worker who will visit from time to time and have a chat. *When you're feeling utterly desperate don't try to cope alone.* Tell somebody; go to the local social services department and say what your problem is and they'll put you in touch with somebody who can help. They're used to helping isolated mothers; it's part of the job; it's what they're paid for. Your enemy is isolation, not the baby, so do talk about your problem to somebody *before* you reach the stage where you simply cannot cope.

It's exactly the same with marital difficulties. If you and your partner are always arguing (remember that most couples do quarrel from time to time) and those arguments are leading more and more to a breakdown in your relationship, and to violence, then you should seek outside help. This is essential since you may have reached the stage where you can no longer see the problem clearly: all you know is that, every time you see your partner, you have feelings of hostility, anger or hate. It's unlikely that you'll be able to deal with your own strong feelings of frustration and resentment. What I suggest is that you call the local branch of the Samaritans (the number is in the telephone book) and/or contact your local branch of the National Marriage Guidance Council (the address can be found at the local library or given to you, in confidence, at your Citizen's Advice Bureau). No marriage guidance counsellor would claim that he can solve your problem; all he would claim is that *talking about it to somebody helps.* If you're caught up in the centre of a living hell you need somebody who is out of the eye of the storm, who can calm you down, and help you to realize that what is happening to you has happened, and is happening, to many thousands of couples all over the country. You'll be treated as a real person, with a real problem. What we need, when we're in deep trouble, is understanding of our plight.

258

So you must get help rather than let the problem go on for years and years.

A word about teenagers. I feel sorry for them. They are exploited by television, magazines and record company: given a diet of violence, unreal romance and pop records to feed their souls. They are encouraged to have high expectations but there is no way in which the vast majority of them are going to lead a glamorous, rich, successful life. The reality is harshly different to the picture of life that has been built up for them by the all-pervasive media. No wonder some of them resort to vandalism, to violence and to making a name for themselves at the Saturday afternoon match (see **Football Hooliganism**). What they suffer from is merely an exaggeration of what we all suffer from: unreal expectations, a constant feeling that somebody else is doing better, feelings of powerlessness and anger that the majority of us can have so little impact on the world which surrounds us. That's where the violence comes in. It's better to be a vandal, a hooligan or a thief than to be a nobody.

What can you do, as a parent, if you see your teenager getting in with a bad crowd, heading towards delinquency and, possibly, violence? I think you should keep the channels of communication open. Don't say: 'I can't do anything with him/her.' Keep talking, show that you care. Be honest about your own frustrations and anger, tell it how it is. Say that this is a ruthless, hard world and it isn't easy for teenagers these days. Treat your youngster as a human being and discuss things with him. If he hasn't got a job tell him how rotten he must feel about that; look out for any project in the community that he could help with. The antidote to violence *is* caring; it's an appalling thing that we don't care enough about our youth; the only thing you can do is to try to make up for the callousness of society in your own home.

A final point. Words can be violent too. In some homes, where the parents are perhaps better educated, neither parent would resort to physical violence. Instead, though, verbal violence takes place: constant cruel remarks, sarcasm, deeply hurtful comments, coldly-angry taunts and/or explosive, furious expressions of hatred, contempt and frustration. If you have this sort of chronic verbal warfare do, again, seek help. To the victim of this kind of verbal onslaught the pain is just as sharp (and lasts a great deal longer) than a kick on the shin. Phone up the Samaritans (or go to see the family doctor) and ask to see a marriage guidance counsellor.

We live in a violent, greedy society. Our need to belong, though, can be fulfilled in the family group. It is possibly the only safe base the child has in this otherwise confusing world so it's important for you to work out your own problems, and provide a safe base for your child.

Visits

Why visits? I suppose visits have three main purposes: *to widen a youngster's view of the world* (this can apply equally to a toddler going to the local supermarket or to a teenager going to a foreign country or an 'exchange visit'); *to make the mother-child (or father-child) relationship less fraught and cloistered by giving both parent and child something interesting to do; to give the child insight into how life is lived, how things are made, and how things work, so that he builds up a more comprehensive picture of the world about him.*

With young children your slogan with regard to visits should be 'Think Ordinary'. Please don't think of a visit as being synonymous with taking your toddler to the zoo. (This can be a waste of time; my own youngest child, when she was one-and-a-half, described every animal she saw at the zoo as 'Doggy'.) To a young child a visit to a local shop can be very exciting. You could with a (pre-school) child visit your local bakery, or the fish yard, or the garage when the tanker lorry comes. You could visit the local church when they are doing their bell ringing practice or take your child to the water works, or around the back of the supermarket. Or take him to the local bus or railway station. There's plenty for him to see and visits *don't* have to be places that are far away and/or charge an admission fee. The world is a fascinating place to a young child so, as far as visits are concerned, your own town, your own neighbourhood – anywhere from the duck pond to the pet shop – is your oyster.

With teenagers, it's a good idea if they can stay for a week or so with relatives or friends: this encourages independence and gives you a break from them, and vice versa. Younger children enjoy over-night stays (even if it's only sleeping in the house next door) but a certain amount of care is needed if a young child wants to stay with a friend for a week or longer. A week is a long time and, if the child isn't used to the place, you may find that your youngster is ringing you up saying that he's very homesick. The best strategy, as regards staying away from home, is to start off with over-night stays and build up to longer visits. Even then I don't think it's a good idea to send a city youngster to the quieter parts of Norway for six weeks as part of an exchange visit. It's probably better to go for a week or a fortnight and find out what it's like before committing your youngster to what could be six weeks of bliss – or purgatory.

When visiting the homes of friends or relatives the rule for your children should be: When in Rome do as the Romans do. I know one or two 'trendy', progressive couples whose children, once they are in other people's homes, run riot: rummaging through drawers, leaving toys all over the place, making a mess wherever they go. I think that's rude. After all, good manners is consideration for other people; what your children do in your own home is your business but I don't think any of us can assume that our views are held by everybody. The children I have in mind are seldom asked anywhere twice. 'I just can't afford to pay for the breakages,' one fraught mum told me. She also told me that this was a first and final visit.

As regards visitors to your home, you may or may not want them. One day you'll be in need of company, the next you'll want a bit of peace. It's exactly the same with children. The visitors that they like best – and it's probably the same with us adults – are those that we know fairly well and don't have to make too much fuss over. I think that it's good for children to have a constant stream of visitors (providing mum or dad is in the mood) because they see new faces, hear new voices, get used to meeting new people. I don't think it's a good idea for visitors to direct too much of their attention to the children present: this will result in showing off, in shyness, or confusion. You talk with the visitors; let your children get on with what they are doing. It's rather like a visitor going into a good classroom. If it is a good classroom, the children will take some notice of the visitor, perhaps want to be introduced to him or her and then, if they have interesting things to do, they'll want to get on with their work. So don't make visitors an occasion for making your child the sole focus of attention. If you enjoy your visitors, whether they be frequent or sporadic, I'm sure that your child will pick up the fact that you are enjoying the visit and the odds are that he'll have a nice time too.

Walter Mitty Complex
See also **Daydreaming** *Page* 42, **Fantasy** *Page* 76, **Shyness** *Page* 206

Walter Mitty is a character in a story by James Thurber. Mitty is a brilliant surgeon, a pilot, a falsely-accused defendant in a murder trial, and (last but not least) a man who faces a firing squad, 'erect and motionless, proud and disdainful, Walter Mitty the Undefeated, inscrutable to the last.' It's important to tell you that he is all these things only in his head: in reality, he's a hen-pecked husband, incompetent and forgetful.

It is quite normal for children to fantasize (see section on **Fantasy**) and for adults too. We have all been to an interview, made a mess of it, and imagined that we'd been superb and that we'd been offered the job. We've all dreamed of being left a huge legacy by a relative, or of winning a lottery with a large money prize. Adults day-dream and so do children: you might be out for a walk with your son and realize that in his imagination, as he strolls along, he's a pirate, or a soldier, or a great explorer walking through unknown and dangerous terrain. It is this ability to fantasize that makes men and women different from other animals; it is their readiness to use their imagination that makes life so much more exciting for children.

Where does it go wrong and when does it become a complex? It is when we have a chronic need to impress others, accompanied by a lack of any confidence in ourselves, that we fall into the trap of acting a part (or we take more and more refuge in dreams as a compensation for what we see as a hostile world).

I remember seeing a boy, aged ten, in the clinic. 'My dad's got a Rolls Royce,' he told me, 'and my uncle's a helicopter pilot.' Both statements were untrue. When I got to know him a little better he stopped lying but he still insisted on how many costly foreign stamps he owned, that he'd done well in an examination at school, that he was a good runner. What he didn't realize was that I liked him anyway, for himself, and not for his achievements. Another patient, a man of twenty-five, came to see me. He'd been to Oxford and had a distinguished academic career. He had a good job, yet he felt depressed, ill-at-ease with himself and pessimistic about the future. I'm not surprised. He'd spent his life, until then, trying to impress others with his ability. He didn't realize that, yes, we admired him for what he'd achieved; we liked him even more for who he was (and he was a very kind, attractive person who'd totally lost himself in his search for achievements).

The moral is that you may be thrilled at some of the things your child has done, and very proud; you may be disappointed at some of the things he's done. *The message to get across is that, whether he fails or succeeds, comes first or last, you still love him.* You can tell him as much. 'I love you because you're you. If things don't always go right with you, if you don't succeed, I'll still love you.' That takes

262

a great weight off his shoulders: he knows he's loved *quite* apart from his achievements (though you can still be proud, and tell him so, when he does something special).

I was quite straight with that ten-year-old in the clinic when I'd got to know him. 'Look,' I told him, 'you don't have to be good at everything to make me like you. I like you anyway.' In fact, he was a very likeable lad: he simply didn't believe in himself as a loveable person.

Don't, with your children, set up a situation in which the one who gets high marks, or wins races, or always comes first, gets most love and attention from you. That's unfair. What people want (and especially children) is to be loved for themselves, without strings. Mrs Mitty was unfair to Walter; she didn't accept him for who he was; he had to compensate, in his imagination, for the deficiencies within himself that she relentlessly pointed out. (Let's face it, it's quite easy to find fault with others if you try hard enough.)

Here is what you must do to build up your child's inner-confidence:

Be honest. If he's done something, and he's made a mess of it, say: 'That's not up to your usual standard.' (If he's done well, tell him: 'You've made a good job of that.') Children respect us more if we tell the truth.

Don't over-flatter. It's better to say: 'Your ears may stick out but I still love you,' (and laugh) rather than tell him he's perfect.

Show appreciation of his efforts. 'Thanks for cleaning those windows,' you could say. 'They look really sparkling.' This builds up his image of himself as a competent, helpful person.

Love your child for himself and don't always compare him with brighter (or duller) or more handsome (or less handsome) children. Comparisons are, in this particular, nonsense: he's a unique individual and has his own strengths and weaknesses, his own qualities.

When your child is a teenager make sure that he does what he wants to do, for himself, and because he enjoys it. The message to get across is that he doesn't have to be something eminent to win your love, just so long as he's himself, working hard at what he's chosen to do, and reasonably content, then you are there, in the background, to re-fuel him with love on his journey through life.

Accept your child for who he is, and his strengths will emerge; make him something he isn't and he builds his house of personality on a false foundation. This acceptance of the child is beautifully illustrated in Virginia Axline's book, *Dibs: In Search of Self*

(Penguin). As Dibs is accepted for who he is so he emerges as a very attractive child indeed; one who, for five years, was considered as being educationally subnormal but who is found (after therapy) to have an IQ of 168!

The Secret Life of Walter Mitty is a very funny story but it's also rather sad. None of us find a secure refuge in being somebody we are not. One of the best lessons you can teach your child is to be himself and, as himself, he is loved.

Wandering Children

Most young children are born under a wandering star. Watch, for example, a three-year-old at the seaside with his mother. He'll wander off, quite happily, to the water's edge and play quite contentedly *providing that he can see his mother, can locate her when he wants her.* If the mother gets up, moves away, he is totally confused. If, and this is more likely, the beach becomes more crowded and he can't see his mother he's likely to become panicky or end up, in his bewilderment, in the lost children's office. In the park, children lag behind or wander off; if the mother stays where she is a child has a good chance of finding her; if she's walking along, and other children get in between her and the youngster, then the re-location mechanisms get jammed and panic sets in. Frankly, the only way to prevent young children from wandering and getting lost is to keep as static as possible and to keep an eye on them.

With older children it sometimes happens that the child stays out longer than he should and is then afraid of coming in because he will be shouted at or in some other way punished. Similarly, children in school who have committed some misdemeanour, or simply don't like school, wander off around the shops, or go off into another town on the bus rather than face up to the demands of the classroom. The thing to do here is to act quickly – make some concessions to the needs of the child, discuss the problem with him, forgive and forget – or else the child will associate wandering off with freedom, adventure and having a good time and will find it hard to accept the discipline imposed by the parents at home, or the demands made by teachers at school. Often, chronic school truancy starts off with some quite trivial matter which, with a bit of commonsense, could have been cleared up quickly and with little fuss. Don't escalate 'staying out' or 'staying off' offences. If your child's migratory impulses lead him to come in late have a word about it and say you worry about him when he's out. Then forget the whole business. If he stays off school (and you learn about this from the class teacher) don't panic. Ask your child why. If you react sympathetically there is more chance of his going back. If you can't elicit any reason why he stays off school do go to the headmaster and ask for an appointment to see the educational psychologist. He can probably find out what it is that is putting your child off the classroom.

With teenagers, you must expect a bit of wandering. Teenagers like to go off and 'mess about' somewhere (and they don't want you to know where that somewhere is). The more adventurous of them may go off youth hostelling, on long cycle rides or even, these days, to distant towns to watch a favourite football team. If your youngster comes back happy and pleased with himself I don't think you should damp down his spirit of adventure. With football addicts, I would certainly stop the youngster from going to away matches if there is any sign that he is becoming mixed up, in any way, with football hooliganism.

The safer the base the further the youngster feels free to wander from it. These are the stirrings of independence and they should, wherever possible, be encouraged, whether it's a couple of nights' camping or a trip to a foreign country, or long cycle rides. They are all part of the process of young people weaning themselves from parents.

If, on the other hand, your child constantly threatens to run away from home (or actually runs away from home on a number of occasions) you must face up to the fact that there may be a fraught, anxious or unpleasant atmosphere which drives him to seek escape. Do talk to your child honestly and if you are going through a marital crisis do seek help from your local branch of your National Marriage Guidance Council, from your family doctor or, if it's a critical matter, from the Samaritans. All these sources of help will completely respect your privacy and talking to somebody about your problems may be the first step on the way to solving them and so helping your youngster.

Working Mothers
(For Parents)

I'll be quite straight with you. When a young mother asks me in the clinic whether she should take a part-time job, I am prone to suggest that she should, if it would get her out of the house, brighten her up a bit, and meet a few people outside of the family circle. *Children, even quite young children, would rather have a mother who is bright and cheerful when she is with them than have one who is depressed the whole time.* You may have doubts about leaving your child. Some of these doubts will stem from things you have read or from what other people have told you. The truth is that there's no evidence to show that children with working mothers differ from those whose mothers stay at home. *What children want, above all else, is that their mothers should be reasonably happy.*

The other thing is that we all need a rest from each other: we can still love our child without being with him for twenty-four hours a day. If a baby, toddler, or pre-school child constantly gets on a mother's nerves, makes her feel tired and miserable, it may be better for both of them if they have a break from each other during the day. The younger the child is, the more care has to be taken in finding a suitable child-minder or part-time mother substitute. Once a suitable person has been found, the baby or toddler seem to settle down *providing that mother isn't too anxious about the whole business.* It is better, probably, for the mother to stay with the child at home during the first two-and-a-half years but, even here, a baby-sitter, a friendly neighbour, or a infant and toddlers group run by the local mums can give mother a chance to get her hair done, go shopping or (and this isn't a bad idea from time to time) put her feet up. A short break from a child is essential to keeping up our morale, our confidence in our abilities as mothers, or fathers.

That said, it is a fact that many mothers of young children go to work not because they want to but because they have to. Their income is essential to the family. It is these mothers who are often guilty about leaving their children to go to work. Will their children suffer by their absence? The answer seems to be no. In a survey of several thousand children (all born in 1958 and 'followed up' until they were adults) The National Children's Bureau found that:

The physical health of children with working mothers was as good as those whose mothers stayed at home.
At the age of seven those children whose mothers took jobs once the children started school were *less* well adjusted than those whose mothers took jobs before!
On average, there is no difference in school attainments between children with mothers who stayed at home and those who worked.

Children of working mothers are no more likely to become delinquent than those with non-working mothers.

I suspect our misconceptions about working mothers arise from two sources. One is that mothers who want nothing more than being with their own child, at home, find it difficult to understand the feelings of mothers who get fraught, tense and run-down at being cooped-up with a child all day. The other is the misunderstanding of the notion of 'maternal deprivation'. Over the last twenty years a number of distinguished psychologists have stressed how important to the child is the constant, unremitting care of the mother – a warm, intimate, continuous relationship in which *both* find satisfaction. *I do not think that such a relationship depends upon the mother being with the child all the time, day-in, day-out. Providing that the mother is consistent, providing that she is loving, not rejecting, providing that the child can discern a pattern to the day, it is possible that mother and child will love each other more, not less, as a result of having a break from each other.* Good mothering, a happy relationship, depends less upon whether a mother goes out to work or not than upon whether the mother is contented, and enjoys being with her children when she is with them.

If you are a working mum and you derive satisfaction from your change of surroundings, the company of others (as well as the extra income) don't worry too much about your child. Just make sure that you save up enough energy, keep enough in reserve, to enjoy the companionship of your child when you are home. If the child is older, say of school age, explain why you go out to work (to benefit the family) and set aside a time in the week when you can have a little time with each child, just the two of you, together. Children are very tough, very flexible. They'll adapt, providing that they know what is going on.

If you do have to go to work here are some guide-lines which may be useful to you:

If you leave your child with a child-minder make sure she is a suitable person to look after your child. She should be warm, loving, and a person who likes children, and has a home which is adequate for their needs, with plenty of toys for the children to play with. (Note that any person who looks after children not related to her for two hours or more a day, *and is paid for it,* is required to register with the local social services department. No good child-minder should refuse to accept regular visits, advice and support from the social services department.)
Talk to the child-minder. Ask her what your child has done in

the day. Tell her what your child does at home. Don't divide the child's world in to two different parts with no continuity between the two.

When your child is three-years-old take him along to a playgroup. Make sure you stay with him, for the first few days, long enough for him to settle in. Children learn a great deal from playing with, making friends with, other children and the break from mother does them (and mother) a lot of good.

Think carefully before taking a full-time job. A part-time one may be adequate for your needs, both financial and emotional. You don't want to miss out on *all* the fun of being with a young child.

Do take a suitable part-time job (if you can find one that you enjoy) when your children are at school. They may prefer you to be at home, sewing and baking all day, but not if it turns you into a grumpy, miserable mum. You may find that the energy that the job releases in you will give you *more* energy when it comes to relating to the children, not less. You may find that being sociable outside the home, makes you more pleasant and interesting to be with when you're inside. *That's what children really want: a mother who's fun.* Whether she works or not is of less importance to them than we suppose.

Writing

How do you get your own children interested in putting their ideas down on paper? I don't mean formal writing (for that, see section on **Handwriting**) but rather an eagerness to express themselves, put their thoughts into words, make some kind of record of an experience.

What you can do, when your child is about four, is to make a book by folding large sheets of paper in half (rolls of lining paper used in paper-hanging are very useful here). The paper can, if you wish, be stapled, or sewn, together at the edges. What kind of book do you make? It could be a book of cats, or dogs, or flowers, or birds. A book of food is a good idea: the child cuts out (with rounded scissors) pictures of fish fingers and other food from magazine adverts and, with your help, sticks them in the book. You can, if you wish, write fish fingers (lower-case letters, *not* capitals) above the picture. The idea to get across is that you can read books; you can also make them. During the pre-school stage the most vital contribution you can make to your child's acquisition of language is to talk to him (see section on **Reluctance to Speak**) and read him lots of stories and nursery rhymes (see section on **Reading**). Writing follows reading; if your child can't read he won't be able to write.

When your child goes to school and can write (I'm talking here of a child of about, say, eight) how do you encourage this skill? Whatever you do, don't kill his enthusiasm by making him write about everything he does. You need a delicate touch here. No forcing him; a child who wants to write will write; your job is to encourage and to suggest ideas. Don't make it like school; make it fun. Here are some things your child can do. He can:

Use a tape-recorder for interviews, making up his own radio-show, recording the dawn chorus or even just recording his own thoughts.

Buy an old typewriter to use. Some people (like me) are reluctant to set pen or pencil to paper but are happy bashing away at a typewriter. Anyway, it's something different and the results often look neater and 'more professional'.

Make a scrap-book. It can be of 'My Holiday' (stick in old bus tickets, entrance tickets, post-cards, theatre programmes and other mementoes) or a book of football heroes or some hobby which the child is particularly interested in.

Make a tele-strip cartoon. You need a box (in which you cut a 'window' and a couple of kitchen roll holders). The child makes up a strip cartoon, or a picture-story, and devises a script to go with it.

Make up his own 'magazine' or 'newspaper'. Items can be of his own choosing and he can write captions, jokes and stories which he thinks people might like to read.

Keep a diary, jotting down the events of the day.

Make up a book of jokes, rhymes, riddles and poems. All children like jokes. Why not record them in an attractive-looking book and add a few funny anecdotes for good measure?

Encourage your child to write letters, not only 'Thankyou' letters to granny but to radio, to his heroes and to somebody who is an expert in the field in which your child is interested. It's nice for a child to get a reply (they often do) and you don't get a reply if you don't write!

When you take your child out and if he's particularly fascinated by what he sees leave plenty of paper (and jars of felt-tip pens) about the place so that he can write about it if he wants to. Never force it. Many the school child who has said: 'I'd love to go to the zoo if only Miss, or Sir, wouldn't make us write about it when we come back.' Making a book, making lists of things (anything from train numbers to trees, makes of motor-car, Kings and Queens of England) all encourage the child to commit himself to paper rather than think of books (including those he has made up himself) as a chore.

As this goes along the child should be encouraged to go along to the local library to look things up and to take our reference books as well as story books. Most libraries now offer an absolutely first class service to children. Going to the library is a habit, so do encourage the habit and go along with him a few times. This stimulates his curiosity and gives him input, access to new experiences, through books. (Remember: no output without input. He's not going to write about anything until he finds that he's really 'sparked off' by something and, then, he should be keen to make some kind of record for himself.)

Lots of praise for his efforts! Many's the potential writer who has given up the ghost through unkind criticism at too early a stage in his career. If he's making out a list of cars, composing a thriller or just making up a comic-strip of his own, do encourage him. Writing *can* be fun if we don't worry too much about spelling and grammar (we can worry about that when he's really got started). Many children don't write very much because they don't realize that they can write their own books about what interests *them*. It's worth a try and it's better than doing all those dreadful, formal compositions that you and I had to do in school.

Xmas – What it Means to Children

One Christmas when my sister and her family were staying with us her little daughter, aged three, told me that Baby Jesus was in the fridge. Alarmed, I looked in. She pointed up at some small, triangular objects and I realized she was talking about 'baby cheeses'. I like having children around at Christmas – it makes it much more humorous and exciting. Nowadays, we overdo (in my opinion) the commercial aspects of the festival, with an emphasis on eating, buying people presents, sending Christmas cards. For many people, Christmas seems to have reverted almost to being a pagan festival – a time to eat, and drink, a great deal and sit around watching television. It's a pity, since Christmas, for children at least, is a magical, very special time of the year.

Children, even older children, like all the rituals associated with

Christmas: decorating the house, buying a Christmas tree, sending off Christmas cards (some of which, I hope, they've made themselves), buying a turkey, giving and receiving presents. My teenage children still hang up their Christmas stockings. My teenage son isn't sentimental about many things but he's sentimental about Christmas. He wants us to stick to all the traditions associated with this time of the year. You'll find, too, that children in school get very excited as Christmas approaches. They like the carols, the decorations in the school hall, stories about Christmas and the visit, for younger children, of Father Christmas. The fact that there's one Father Christmas in one store and another in the department store just down the road doesn't seem to bother them. They believe it all and, even though we adults are a little more sceptical, some of us have sufficient imagination and sympathy with youngsters to see the festivities through the eyes of a child.

Ceremony and ritual are very important to all human beings. When we do things traditionally we affirm that we live together, spend time together, *belong* together as a group. We can affirm our corporate identity by having an office party, a farewell luncheon, a wedding, a coronation, even a funeral. All these group ceremonies are vital to our sense of being part of a group. Both adults and children like to celebrate, affirm, special occasions and to bear witness, in a traditional way, that this is a special occasion. At home, when I was a boy, an important ceremony was an institution known as Sunday tea. A vast spread of goodies was assembled, everybody sat down as a family. Sandwiches were eaten first, then cakes, then pineapple chunks with evaporated milk. It was a symbolic way of showing that we were a recognizable group – a family of people living together.

Christmas is a celebration of the birth of a baby, Jesus Christ, many years ago. Whether you adhere to the Christian religion or not, whether you go to church or not, I think you'll agree that Christmas is a family time, a time when relatives, or friends, get together and try to enjoy themselves. I say try to because many, many people are lonely and miserable at Christmas; many adults are, during this time, reminded of their own isolation and despair; many grown-ups find little comfort in the Christmas message, Be of Good Cheer. For some people, and I think it's worth mentioning this, Christmas is a very unhappy time.

For children, and especially young children, the Christmas festivities are probably amongst the happiest days of the year. Children are believers. Most young children believe in the wonderful story of the birth of Jesus in Bethlehem. They believe in the three wise men, and in the Virgin Mary. The magic of the Holy Birth is there, for them, underlining all the rituals and the ceremonies of this time. Children, or at least most children up to the age of six, believe in Father Christmas and in the marvellous myth of him coming down the chimneys with the Christmas presents. Some children do, I admit, examine Father Christmas's beard very closely at the local department store and perhaps reject the idea that it's only cotton wool because they *want* to believe. In my local store, last Christmas, I heard poor old Father Christmas say to a child: 'What a lovely looking little girl you are!' 'I'm a boy,' shouted the child, indignantly. He still took his present, and was very keen to tell Father Christmas what he wanted on the Big Day. It's very important for children to adhere to all the myths and the rituals of Christmas time, otherwise they think they're being cheated and missing something. My own children, up to quite recently, would quite fervently hope for snow at Christmas. (This, I might add, was the last thing I wanted.) For them, snow would round the whole thing off and make it a 'proper' Christmas.

No matter what your views on Christmas are I think you should respect the faith of your child, and appreciate the sheer enjoyment that he gets from Christmas. The expense of Christmas may appal you but you don't have to buy costly Christmas cards: you can make your own and deliver as many as possible by hand. (Children will enjoy that just as much if not more, especially if you make some cards with potato cuts or water-colour paints.) *Cut down on the cost but don't miss out on the ceremony and rituals*, is my advice if it's money you're worried about. It's the idea, the tradition, of hanging up a stocking on Christmas Eve that's so important: children will accept that, this year, you may not be able to afford expensive gifts.

A Christmas tree is important (together with presents under the Christmas tree on Christmas morning if that's your family's way of doing things). The size of the tree isn't important: it's the ceremony that's vital, to children. Use the wrapping paper you saved from last year. Brighten the living room with decorations you've made yourselves. It doesn't really matter to children whether you have turkey or a chicken for the Christmas dinner; it does matter that you have paper hats and some crackers: those are the things they remember. Those are some of the things that make Christmas a special time. I don't believe that children, even in these cynical times, assess the value of everything that they are given at Christmas. *What matters to them is the way things are done.* Let them help in as many of the Christmas preparations as possible; try to pick up some of their excitement; don't be cynical and cast a grey shadow over it all. It's ritual and ceremony that binds human beings together and it's a great shame that we live in an age that so undervalues such things as tradition, and customs and believing in something. Children appreciate magic; they retain a sense of wonder. We adults, who deprecate mystery, and have no sense of wonder, miss so much in life. At Christmas, you *don't* have to spend a mint of money. You do have to learn something about magic, about seeing the world through the eyes of a child.

Youth Clubs
See also **Teenagers** *Page* 233

If you want to find out which youth clubs are available in your particular neighbourhood you should contact your area youth officer at the local education offices. He will be glad to tell you of the facilities available. However, it's a surprising fact that only a very small minority of young people actually go to youth clubs provided by the local council, or make use of the facilities provided by the area education authority for evening leisure. What do the majority of youngsters do? Most of them go to discos, bowling alleys, sports centres and cinemas which are commercially run. This is their choice but the snag is obvious: since these institutions are run for profit they charge money and, more and more, there are youngsters who simply cannot afford to go out in the evening and those, rather tragic, unemployed young people who have nothing to do during the day.

Since the local authorities these days are short of money, and facilities for young people are unlikely to expand (some authorities spend £2 per head per annum on the youth service which is a miserly amount considering its importance and the kind of things that could be done) it's clear that, to avoid youngsters being bored, the adults with whom they come into contact – their parents, friends and neighbours – ought to do something on a voluntary basis to help these young people. What can I do? That is the question you may ask and the answer is: quite a lot.

I have known parents who have set up discos for teenagers in the local community hall; other parents who have volunteered to take youngsters camping. One father I know started up a Wednesday evening bike club where youngsters could bring along their motor bikes, repair them under supervision, or just talk. Those meetings were held in a church hall! Any kind of skill that you have may be useful in making contact with teenagers: you may be good with wood, or mending furniture, interested in a sport, or merely able to listen and/or to organize somewhere for two or three adults to get together with a group of teenagers and do something which would be interesting to them or merely to talk about their problems.

These days, teenagers have plenty of problems: and so do parents in communicating with their teenage sons and daughters. I'm surprised that, although we have baby and toddler groups for mothers, we don't have teenager groups: for mothers and fathers to come together over a cup of tea and talk about the kind of problems that they're having with their offspring. These groups would be useful if only to learn that you're never alone if you have a teenager in difficulty. The net result of such groups, I am sure, is that you and I, the parents, would realize that youth clubs, and other state-provided facilities aren't enough. We should be thinking, all of us, of how we can increase the facilities for teenagers in our own neighbourhood.

Could we provide more counselling for teenagers with problems? Could we persuade the local authority to lend us a hall, or a classroom, where we could start up a class, whether it be on judo, dressmaking or country dancing for young people with not enough to do? This is the kind of thinking that's needed. It's rather stupid to spend so much money in punishing teenagers who have gone wrong (and borstals and detention centres do cost an awful lot of money) when you and I and plenty of other adults do so little to prevent youngsters from being bored and getting into mischief simply because there isn't anything else to do.

We live in an age-segregated society but we must all – the young, the teenager, the adult and the senior citizen – learn to mix more, to help each other more. That's the way to lessen the generation gap. So, do get together with friends and see if you can start just *one* club, or meeting place. Don't leave it to the local education authority is my message. They haven't the money, or the people to cope. We don't have much money either but we have plenty of human resources in the community; more than enough to meet teenagers' needs.

Zap – How Not to Lose it in the Presence of Children
See also **Depression** *Page 50*

Here are *Ten Things To Do* if you wish to remain human whilst being a parent:

Stay a Person Yourself The most precious thing that you can give to your child is your time. You'll have to make sacrifices for him but don't sacrifice yourself to him. *There's no output without input.* If you don't have some fun some time, some outside friendships, you won't be able to give your child fun and friendship. Get out of the house and meet other people. Most of them are shy like you so make the effort. A family is supposed to be a base not a prison; children can be a gateway to other friendships, to the world outside.

Don't be a Martyr Your home isn't a hotel with you as chief cook and bottle-washer. Everybody should help. If you expect your children to make a contribution as soon as they're old enough, they'll accept it. If you do everything for them they'll accept that too. A family should be a communal enterprise.

Feel Alive, Rather Than Guilty If you're lucky enough to land a part-time job and your children are with a reliable child-minder, or at school, don't feel that you ought to be at home polishing the silver or, more likely, washing those cracked cups. Your children would rather have you more lively and more outgoing when you're with them than lonely, sorry for yourself and depressed most of the time. The enemy of good mothering and fathering is loneliness and isolation.

Be Yourself Don't try to be a Lovely Mum or the Perfect Dad. For all I know you may have rotten teeth and one ear lower than the other and tell the most appalling jokes. I might mind, but children don't. Your child will love you if you are yourself. You can hardly expect him to love or respect you if you're ceaselessly trying to be somebody else.

Be Flexible About Roles in the Family If dad's good with babies and nappies give him his head. If you want to go to an evening class to learn woodwork do so. Your marriage is a partnership, a shared enterprise. If you don't share the good and the bad you'll miss out on an awful lot.

Don't Get it Wrong The family, despite all its good points, was never meant to provide for all our social needs. Mothering was never meant to be done by isolated women at home; fathering needn't be somebody walking around wearing a badge with *I'm Above All This* on it; children were never meant to be looked after just by their parents, since we simply haven't enough, by ourselves, to give them. *Friends* have to supply, these days, all those supports that were once given to a family by aunts, uncles, cousins and grandparents. The way to make friends is to do things together in the community. Friendship is the antidote to depression.

Set Aside Time to be with Your Child It may be half-an-hour a day or an hour a week but in this time listen to your child, be with him in your mind, not miles away, so that he knows that his Time With Mum (or His Time With Dad) is a sacrosanct institution and that he has your love and attention all to himself. Better half-an-hour a week to have mum all to yourself than (as happens with some children) never.

Grow Old Disgracefully Don't use motherhood, or fatherhood, as an excuse for not living your own life, doing your own thing, and developing your *own* personality. No child wants a cardboard cut-out for a mother or father. Being old is being twenty years older than you are. Fight the whole notion of age (I know some senior citizens who have more zap in their little fingers than some twenty-year-olds have in their whole bodies). When your teenager looks across the breakfast table at you he'll want to see a lively human being – a real person – not somebody who has used the family, and the children, as an excuse for vegetating.

Live Every Day Enjoy your life; it doesn't last long. Our children are only on loan to us and, one day, they'll leave and the whole adventure will be over. What on earth is the point of it all if you and your children don't have some magic moments, together, along the way?

Learn to be Loving All it takes is practice. If you love, you get a lot of love back and it's as good for you as fresh air. There is no better recipe that I know of for a happy life.

My three children, as I write this, are aged nineteen, seventeen and fifteen. In three years time they will all be pursuing their studies, leading their own lives, living away from home. Time is a great thief. It steals our youth, it steals our children, it steals our life away from us. While you have time, I say again, share some of it with your youngsters. It would be a pity to miss it – any of it. Bon voyage.

Also published in Unwin Paperbacks

COMMON SENSE ABOUT BABIES AND CHILDREN
Dr Hugh Jolly

Does your baby really know the difference between a bottle and a breast? Does he suffer if you leave him behind when you go away on holiday? Are fat babies healthy babies? Does your child prefer being awake at night? Dr Hugh Jolly discusses these and many other dilemmas, misfortunes and complaints. He is a firm believer in the importance of a relaxed, commonsense approach to bringing up children and is refreshingly direct in the way he explodes the myths and old wives' tales which still persist. The result is a book which will be helpful and encouraging to all parents.

LIVING WITH A TODDLER
Brenda Crowe

This book is designed to help parents when they often need help and advice most. In it Brenda Crowe, who as National Adviser to the Pre-School Playgroups Association, shared the experiences of literally thousands of children and parents, explains what it is like to be a toddler and what it feels like to look after one. She also offers a wealth of advice about a hundred and one aspects of living with a toddler and gives a fascinating and revealing account of her own and other parents' experience of parenthood, discussing how to cope with the tiredness, loneliness and depression which can wear down even the most capable and cheerful parent.

Also available in Unwin Paperbacks

Common Sense About Babies and Children
   Dr Hugh Jolly   £1.95 □
Growing Up with Good Food
   Catherine Lewis   £2.50 □
Learning Through Play   *Jean Marzollo*
   & Janice Lloyd   £2.95 □
Living with a Toddler   *Brenda Crowe*   £2.50 □
Music with Mum   *Margaret Shephard*   £1.95 □
Parties for Children   *Jean Marzollo*   £2.95 □
Play is a Feeling   *Brenda Crowe*   £2.50 □
The Pre-School Book   *Brenda Thompson*   £1.75 □
Running a Mother and Toddler Club
   Joyce Donoghue   £2.95 □
Superkids: Creative Learning Activities for
   Children 5–15   *Jean Marzollo*   £2.95 □
Supertot: A Parent's Guide to Toddlers
   Jean Marzollo   £2.95 □

All these books are available at your local bookshop or newsagent, or can be ordered direct by post. Just tick the titles you want and fill in the form below.

Name ....

Address ....

....

....

Write to Unwin Cash Sales, PO Box 11, Falmouth, Cornwall TR10 9EN.
Please enclose remittance to the value of the cover price plus:
UK: 55p for the first book plus 22p for the second book, thereafter 14p for each additional book ordered to a maximum charge of £1.75.
BFPO and EIRE: 55p for the first book plus 22p for the second book and 14p for the next 7 books and thereafter 8p per book.
OVERSEAS: £1.00 for the first book plus 25p per copy for each additional book.
Unwin Paperbacks reserve the right to show new retail prices on covers, which may differ from those previously advertised in the text or elsewhere. Postage rates are also subject to revision.